Reality Orientation

PSYCHOLOGICAL APPROACHES TO THE 'CONFUSED' ELDERLY

Una P. Holden BA ABPsS
Formerly Senior Lecturer,
Plymouth Polytechnic,
Plymouth

Robert T. Woods MA MSc ABPsS
Lecturer in Clinical Psychology, Institute of Psychiatry,
London

SECOND EDITION

Churchill Livingstone 🏛

EDINBURGH LONDON MELBOURNE AND NEW YORK 1988

CHURCHILL LIVINGSTONE
Medical Division of Longman Group UK Limited

Distributed in the United States of America by Churchill Livingstone Inc., 1560
Broadway New York, N.Y. 10036, and by associated companies, branches and
representatives throughout the world.

First edition 1982
Second edition 1988

ISBN 0-443-03460-5

British Library Cataloguing in Publication Data
Holden, Una P.
    Reality orientation: psychological
    approaches to the confused elderly. –
    2nd ed.
    1. Senile dementia – Treatment   2. Reality
    therapy
    I. Title   II. Woods, Robert T.
    618.97'6898306   RC524

Library of Congress Cataloging-in-Publication Data
Holden, Una P.
    Reality orientation.
    Bibliography: p.
    Includes index.
    1. Senile dementia – Treatment.   2. Reality therapy.
    I. Woods, Robert T.   II. Title.   [DNLM: 1. Dementia,
    Senile – therapy.   2. Reality Therapy – in old age.
    WT 150 H726r]
    RC524.H64 1988   618.97'6898306   87-18316

Produced by Longman Singapore Publishers (Pte) Ltd.
Printed in Singapore.

Preface to the First Edition

This books owes its existence to MIND – the National Association for Mental Health – who brought us together to lead a workshop on Reality Orientation at a conference in May 1979 in London on 'Positive approaches to mental infirmity in elderly people'. We realised then that there was no single publication on the theory and practice of RO to which we could refer the large number of people from a variety of disciplines who were expressing interest at the conference. The accounts that had been published were in a variety of journals, with often only a superficial description of the methods employed. We resolved then to attempt to meet the need for both a practical guide to RO and for a review of the relevant research.

We have aimed to cover all aspects of RO and related methods. This does mean that different parts of the book are particularly relevant to different groups of readers. Those interested in the research on RO will find this covered in Part I of the book, while those whose interest is more directly practical will find Part II a more useful starting point.

The two parts of the book differ in their approach as well as content. Whereas in Part I constructive criticism of research studies is undertaken, in Part II there are fewer qualifications, fewer references and much more effort to provide 'best guesses' – from the literature and from our experience – for people to be able to use RO in a practical setting. In this – and in the whole endeavour – we are motivated by the knowledge that RO is being used in more and more settings, and that interest is expanding rapidly. We are concerned that there is a danger of RO being used inappropriately, of it being distorted, or of it being established on the wrong basis with resultant disappointment when the programme collapses. We hope that this book may help those setting up, monitoring and carrying out RO to be more aware of all that is involved in it, so that when it is established there is more chance of it having a useful part to play. We have also been concerned to place RO within the context of other psychological treatment approaches that have been developed for use with the confused elderly, and have attempted to show how the various approaches can complement each other.

We owe a huge debt of gratitude to all those over the last few years who in many different ways have contributed to the ideas and research in this book. It would require several pages to name them all individually – colleagues, students, caring staff from all parts of the UK at conferences, workshops and seminars, RO group leaders in the hospitals and old people's homes where we have been privileged to be involved in programmes – we trust they will accept our thanks for their support, stimulating ideas, questions and shared experience as well as for the hard work they have put in! We are particularly grateful to our colleagues who have been kind enough to share their findings with us prior to publication, which we hope will lessen the effects of the inevitable delay between writing and publication of this book. Our typists – Lucille Gray with help from Barbara Stead – deserve many thanks for producing the final manuscript, and we are grateful to Joan Woods for helping to type the early drafts. The Medical Illustration and Photography Department at Leeds University has provided valuable assistance with photography and graphics. Audrey Daniels of Kirklees Social Services kindly gave us permission to print two of the photographs. Finally, we could not have completed this project without the help and support of our families – who have had to live with RO for several years now!

We are happy to acknowledge appreciatively the many people who have given us so much; however we wish to dedicate the book to the elderly people who are its inspiration – to Danny, Annie Mac, Mary, Charlie, Catherine . . . . . ., to all those who have been labelled old and 'confused', but have managed to teach us a great deal.

1982   U.H.
                                                                                         B.W.

Preface to the Second Edition

In preparing this second edition, we have been surprised at how many changes there have been in the course of the past six years. More and more, those working with the elderly are alive to the possibilities of working with them in a positive, constructive way that recognises the person's social, psychological and emotional needs. There are still, of course, places where such thinking has not penetrated. The gap between such homes and wards and those where more positive attitudes prevail is probably growing wider and wider. The book must now speak to a greater range of expertise and experience. Some will have already mastered the basics and be wanting to develop their skills and knowledge to a further, more advanced, level. Others will still be discovering for the first time that the care of people with dementia involves more than feeding, toiletting and dressing.

Our own ideas have also developed, of course. Although there has been less progress in the research literature on certain key topics than we would have liked to have seen, some advances have been made. Our understanding of the concept of dementia has grown, and we have become much more aware of how the words we use to describe people with dementia can influence the reader's perception of them and their disabilities.

In view of these changes, we felt it necessary to restructure the book by bringing forward to a pivotal point our attempt at a practicable, integrated approach to work with people with dementia. This is an approach in which RO has a part, but it is an approach that is more readily applied to the individual's whole range of needs than RO often seems to be. We hope that the new Chapter 5 will provide a new emphasis and focus to the theory and research that precede it and the practical issues that follow. The book was never intended to be just about RO, and our aim is now to make even clearer the sort of psychological approaches we think should be being widely applied.

Where other sources of information have now become widely available, we have been able to omit material of rather specialist interest (e.g. cognitive and behavioural assessment). This has made space for other topics to be covered in greater depth – particularly reminiscence, strategies for institutional change and work in the community. In up-dating existing material, well over a hundred new post-1980 studies, reviews and articles have been included, and the opportunity taken to prune many redundant references.

We are glad to acknowledge the help of Ian Hanley and Winslow Press in providing new photographs for this edition, and we again thank Joan Woods for help with typing, graphics and organisation! Our families have again been most patient and supportive, and we are grateful for their encouragement. We have also been greatly encouraged by letters from many people trying to apply positive approaches in many different places – we are always glad to receive your comments and will try to answer any queries that arise.

Una Holden-Cosgrove
Ironmacannie Mill,
Balmaclellan,
Nr Castle Douglas,
Kirkcudbrightshire,
Scotland

Bob Woods
Department of Psychology,
Institute of Psychiatry,
De Crespigny Park,
London SE5 8AF
England

They're lucky here Lord,
　　They each have a wardrobe and a dressing table,
　and the large dormitory is divided so that
　　　there is some privacy when they go to bed,
　　　there is space to keep clothes, a few photographs,
　　　some books, a box of chocolates:
　　　yes they're lucky here, not like some of the others:
　　　　the first day Mrs Lawrie went to the
　　　　Old Folk's Home they emptied out her handbag
　　　　to make sure there were no valuables in it –
　　　　nobody had ever touched her handbag before;
　　　　Carrie lay in a bedroom with nine others,
　　　　one tatty bedside locker each, and a jam jar
　　　　with flowers in it to share between them,
　　　　a transistor crackled somewhere,
　　　　but nobody was listening,
　　　　they stared at each other,
　　　　stared, and said nothing;
　　　　they let Vi have her canary and kept it
　　　　in the living-room,
　　　　but she couldn't keep books by her bedside,
　　　　and she loved books;
　　　　Bill used to sit with his buttons undone,
　　　　he was beyond pride and caring
　　　　and nobody seemed to mind,
　　　　clothes were something to shamble in and out of,
　　　　morning and evening.

Lord, those who care for the aged do a job I couldn't do,
　　give them the strength and kindness,
　　　patience and cheerfulness
　　　to do it;
　　and may those who organize the care of the elderly,
　　government, local councils, hospital boards,
　　voluntary agencies, trustees —
　　may all of them create conditions in which
　　people can grow old with dignity,
　　enjoy the life that remains to them,
　　and die, cradled in love.

(Reprinted from 'The old folk's home' by Michael Walker, with the permission of the publishers, Arthur James Ltd.)

Contents

PART | ONE

Positive
approaches:
theory and
research

'Old age is for life what the evening is for the day.
So one may call the evening the old age of the day
and old age the evening of life.' *Aristotle*

1

Introduction

Normal ageing
  Intellect
  Memory and learning
  Personality and adjustment
  Conclusions on normal ageing
Dementia
A positive approach

Although the evening of life has arrived for the elderly it does not follow that old age is something to be feared, dreaded and regarded with distaste. Glorious sunsets only occur in the evening which is also the time when the problems and pressures of the day are eased with relaxation and peace. Many elderly people *are* unhappy, but many more are not. A number of factors are involved in determining a person's reaction to advancing years – social, economic, health, personality and so on. Generalisations about 'the elderly' should then be made cautiously.

This book concerns itself primarily with a section of the elderly population often described with such terms as 'confused', 'senile' and 'demented'. These people could be said to be ageing abnormally; they form – as we shall see below – a minority of elderly people. However those working with them day-by-day may lose sight of what constitutes 'normal ageing', of what the evening of life can be. To provide a context for the abnormal, some psychological findings on normal ageing will be briefly discussed. A fuller review is provided by Woods & Britton (1985) and in-depth coverage of the area by Birren & Schaie (1985).

NORMAL AGEING

Intellect

In the past intellectual ability was thought to reach a peak in early adulthood. A decline in functioning from this time on accelerated as the seventh and eighth decades were reached. This view is reflected in standardisation data for commonly used intelligence tests (see Woods and Britton, 1985, p 25). It adds support to the general belief that most elderly people suffer from deterioration of intellect.

This straightforward notion of progressive decline throughout the adult years is now accepted to be totally misleading. It is now recognised that age-related decline has been over-estimated for many reasons. Among the most important are:

Cross-sectional differences

The early studies that showed progressive deterioration were cross-sectional in nature. Results of, say, groups of 20, 30, 40, 50 and 60 year olds would be compared on a particular measure. The problem here is that the groups differ in many other ways apart from age per se. Educational opportunities in 1920 and 1960, for example, were considerably different, and may have restricted the education and intellectual development of today's 60 year olds.

Differences in nutrition, culture, environment and medical care in the early years of life could also significantly disadvantage the older groups. At the time of assessment differences between age groups in physical health, economic status and social contact could be present – all of which could have some impact on intellectual test performance. Intelligence tests often seem to be designed for younger people; the older person may be less motivated and less competitive and so not perform as well as a younger person. The 80 year old in a wheel-chair may fail to see the relevance – to take an extreme example from Wechsler's Adult Intelligence Scale – of what one should do if lost in a forest in the day time!

Ideally (but impractically) longitudinal studies over a person's life-span would be needed to map out intellectual changes with age – although even here practice effects from repeated testing would complicate interpretation of the results obtained. Schaie & Strother (1968) and Schaie & Labouvie-Vief (1974) report a combination of the cross-sectional and longitudinal approaches. Groups of subjects at different ages from 20–70 years were administered the Primary Mental Abilities Test in conventional cross-sectional fashion. These groups were then followed up 7 and 14 years later and the testing repeated. Confirmation of the over-estimate of decline by cross-sectional methods was obtained, but some deterioration in performance did seem to occur as groups reached the age of 60 or so.

Differential relationship of age with various aspects of intelligence

In the Schaie & Strother (1968) research, mentioned above, it was noted that some aspects of intellectual performance showed decline at an earlier age than others. In particular, tests with a large speed component show deterioration most rapidly; tests of verbal knowledge, on the other hand, may well show improvements, at least to the age of 60. These findings have been repeated many times, and have been related by Savage (1973) – among many others – to the notion that intellectual abilities can be subdivided into 'fluid' and 'crystallised'. Fluid intelligence is involved in adapting to novel situations, grasping new ideas, reasoning rapidly and so on. Crystallised intelligence reflects the person's acquired knowledge or accumulated wisdom. Fluid intelligence then is seen as declining more rapidly with age, while crystallised intelligence may well increase.

The whole question of intellectual changes with age remains the subject of much – often technical – controversy (see Botwinick 1977). However, it can be concluded at this stage that decline in intelligence has been over-estimated in the past; that some functions, especially where speed is involved, decline more rapidly than others. The scale of these changes should also be emphasised; there remains considerable overlap between younger and older people on many functions, so that some older people will still perform better than some people 40 or 50 years younger! Finally, the importance of other factors which affect performance on tests apart from intelligence per se should be remembered. For example, the older person may be less prepared to take risks and may be more cautious in responding. The older person is more likely to suffer from ill-health, which may well have an impact on test performance.

Memory and learning

The old adage that 'you can't teach an old dog new tricks' reflects the stereotypical view of the elderly person's memory and learning ability. They are thought of as living in the past, with excellent recall for years gone by, but inability to recall the events of the previous day!

Research evidence, however, gives similar findings to those in the area of intellectual ability. There have been fewer longitudinal studies involving memory skills, however, and so the above mentioned difficulties with cross-sectional studies have to be borne in mind. Craik (1977) reviews the evidence; generally deficits in memory performance are found in older subjects. However, these deficits vary according to the type of memory involved and the experimental conditions. Immediate memory span (that part of memory where, for example, telephone numbers are rehearsed between finding them in the directory and dialling) is very little affected. Recall of new material after a longer period of time has elapsed is generally more impaired. If, however, memory is tested by a recognition method (e.g. 'was this word one that you learned?') then the deficit is less. Similarly if retrieval cues are given (e.g. 'some of the words were flowers') performance is similar to that in younger subjects.

Regarding memory for past events, there is conflicting evidence. For example, Warrington & Sanders (1971) found no evidence that old people remembered past events better than recent events. On tests of memory for past recognition of well-known faces, older people generally performed worse than younger subjects. Botwinick & Storandt (1980) reported that memory for past famous events was generally good with all ages, and suggested that discrepant results have been obtained when the 'past' events did not go as far back as the 60 year period in their study.

The memory loss that has been described is again relatively small. Older people tend to be more variable in their performance, and a large overlap remains with the performances of younger people. Normal elderly people are able to learn and remember new things; the conditions under which learning and recall take place are much more important, however. They are particularly impaired by fast rates of presentation of information and differentially helped by retrieval cues, for instance. A study in Australia showing that a group of 65–85 year olds were able to learn German for the first time as proficiently as 16 year olds (Naylor & Harwood 1975) affirms the capabilities of normal elderly people!

Personality and adjustment

Assessment of personality at any age is fraught with difficulties. With the elderly, conventional personality questionnaires often seem inappropriate, having been designed for college students. As Neugarten (1977) points out this area 'reflects the .... disarray .... in the general field of personality'.

However some points can be salvaged which may at least help question stereotypical views of the elderly person's personality.

Neugarten (1977) states that the best replicated and most consistent finding is that older people tend to be more introverted and inward-looking than younger people. This is an 'average' finding, and does not imply that all elderly people necessarily become introverted. Disengagement theory – first stated by Cumming & Henry (1961) – proposed that the decreased social interaction often noted in old age was not simply inflicted by society on the elderly. It was thought to be a mutual withdrawal, part of a normal ageing process, and necessary for successful adjustment to old age. The opposite view is that the well-adjusted elderly person will be the one who maintains his previous activities or develops new ones, despite the external disengaging forces of retirement, bereavements, loss of mobility, economic hardship and so on. Neither view seems to be universally applicable, however. The evidence suggests that some well-adjusted people remain busy and active, others disengage and are perfectly happy to sit back and relax. Conversely elderly people of both types show poor adjustment. The activity theory probably applies to more elderly people, however (Havighurst et al 1968). Neugarten (1977) stresses that it is life-long personality which is important in relation to how a particular elderly person will find satisfaction in old age, under the same social, financial and medical conditions. Continuity of personality seems to be an emerging theme, interacting with the vicissitudes of old age, but not being essentially changed by advancing years.

Conclusions on normal ageing

In this extremely brief review three major areas of psychological functioning have been considered. It has been suggested that changes do occur, but that these are usually relatively small. The diversity of the elderly must be stressed; their performance and personality show a great deal of variability between different elderly people. Normal ageing can be rich and full; it can be empty and sad. The whole range exists and cannot be constrained into any stereotype or image, whether blissful or miserable.

The importance of other factors – rather than change in the

person themselves – relating to poor performance should be noted. Physical health is particularly important here; Eisdorfer & Wilkie (1977), for example, review the relationship of raised blood pressure to impaired cognitive functioning in elderly people. It could indeed be argued that many apparently age-related changes may be brought about by the increased incidence of ill-health in the elderly. This serves as a reminder also that the passage of time itself does not bring about any changes in functioning. It is other processes – of disease, environment or whatever – also varying in time, that actually lead to changes in behaviour.

Losses of various types are experienced by most people as they age. Sensory losses, reduced physical speed and power, loss of physical health, loss of hair, loss of loved ones, loss of status and so on. The remarkable feature of elderly people from a psychological perspective is their ability to cope in the face of losses and adversity. Most elderly people are able to show good psychological function and adjustment, especially in those areas of life which they see as important and relevant.

DEMENTIA

Dementia is a broad term, encompassing a number of disorders. The Royal College of Physicians (1981) define dementia as 'the global impairment of higher cortical functions including memory, the capacity to solve the problems of day-to-day living, the performance of learned perceptuo-motor skills, the correct use of social skills and the control of emotional reactions, in the absence of gross clouding of consciousness. The condition is often progressive though not necessarily irreversible.' The pattern of disruption of these functions and the impact on daily living and social behaviour vary greatly. Dementia is such a blanket category label that it can never be considered as an adequate description or explanation of a person's condition.

The dementias should be distinguished from delirium. Here the patient is not alert and shows clouding of consciousness. It usually arises from an acute illness – infection, drug intoxication, the effects of surgery and so on. The major treatment approach to delirium is, naturally enough, to treat the under-lying cause. Many doctors use the term 'acute confusional state' in place of delirium. The condition may occur with younger people during a fever or coming round from an anaesthetic: not knowing where they are or what is happening to them; seeing things that aren't there, becoming disturbed and restless, perhaps. In older people, the delirium may persist for a much longer period, often at a less intense level.

Traditionally dementias were divided into senile and pre-senile, according to the age of onset. The dividing line was usually the arbitrary figure of 65 years. Although some differ-ences have been reported between younger and older dementia sufferers, the benefits from continuing with this arbitrary and rigid distinction are few. The major form of dementia in both middle-aged and older patients is Alzheimer's disease. This is associated with particular brain changes – including plaques and neurofibrillary tangles – seen under the microscope at post-mortem. The frequency of plaques and tangles has been found to correlate with deterio-ration in intellectual and behavioural function (Blessed et al 1968; Wilcock & Esiri 1982). It should be noted that small numbers of plaques and tangles are often found in patho-logical studies of the brains of normal older people at post-mortem. Larger numbers seem to be required before any impairment occurs. The pathological research is reviewed in a Scientific Report of the World Health Organisation (1986) and by Perry and Perry (1982). The latter authors also describe research that is indicating deficits in certain chemical substances in the brains of Alzheimer's disease sufferers. This reduction in the amount of certain neurotransmitters has led to hopes of pharmacological therapy, by replacing the missing substances. In practice this has proved difficult to achieve so far. There are some encouraging signs of progress (e.g. Wilcock 1984; Little et al 1985), but as yet there is no proven medical treatment for Alzheimer's disease.

The second major form of dementia that has been ident-ified is multi-infarct (or arteriosclerotic) dementia. This results from a number of small strokes damaging brain tissue. Its progressive decline is usually described as sudden and step-wise, in contrast to the gradual, steady decline of Alzheimer's disease. There may even be a period of improvement if the interval between strokelets is long enough. Multi-infarct dementia occurs more commonly in people with other cardio-vascular problems (e.g. high blood pressure).

At post-mortem, about half of a population of elderly people with dementia will show the characteristic Alzheimer changes, a fifth will have areas of brain damaged by strokelets and a further fifth will have evidence for both conditions. In the remaining tenth, either one of the rarer dementias will be identified, or no cause will be apparent for the person's dementia. Medical assessment of patients with dementia has as its primary aim the exclusion of the potentially treatable causes for the person's condition (see Marsden 1978) and treatable dementias (Cummings 1984). These – with the exception of depression, discussed below – are, regrettably, rarely identified in older people in practice.

Whatever the type of dementia, memory difficulties are usually prominent among the first indications that something is wrong. Typically, new learning ability will be particularly impaired. Well-established habits and memories from the past are usually retained – initially at least. Those affected may forget an appointment, or arrive on the wrong day. They may become lost in unfamiliar surroundings or reach the shops and forget what they had intended to buy. The person loses the ability to grasp complex ideas, and reasoning becomes less abstract. Self-neglect may occur, and as the condition progresses the person may lose the ability to look after such personal needs as washing, dressing, toiletting and even eating.

As a result of there being a number of different conditions – Alzheimer's disease may for instance include several sub-types – the pattern of dysfunction varies from person to person. Some may have particular difficulties in speech, or in tasks like dressing and other practical skills requiring hand–eye co-ordination. The rate of deterioration is also vari-able – although the progressive nature of the disease may be an important feature in distinguishing these conditions from static damage to a specific area of the brain. The rate of deterioration often seems slower when the condition begins in the 80s, rather than when the person is 60. As a group, their life-expectancy is much reduced, but the total time

course is extremely variable. Personality changes do sometimes occur, and the person may lose a sense of what is
socially acceptable. Relatives are very distressed to see
patients begin to swear crudely for the first time in their lives,
for example. Retention of personality traits – pleasant and
unpleasant – is more frequently encountered than this
distressing reversal of personality. Some patients retain an
excellent social facade and are able to engage in small talk
despite severe deterioration.

Sufferers from these conditions are often said to lack
insight into what is happening to them, as it is the very organ
of insight that is dysfunctional. Certainly, very few sufferers
have awareness of their condition in the sense of being able
to name it. In our experience, however, many people do have
some level of awareness, particularly when the condition is
less advanced. It is not unusual for a sufferer to show signs
of anxiety and depression, perhaps in response to the
repeated failures being experienced. Some patients admit loss
of memory, or show awareness of disintegration. One
severely impaired lady, for example, responded 'my brain has
gone' to an enquiry about her health. Through a miasma of
rambling, confused talk that was difficult to comprehend, this
comment had a poignant clarity. The sufferers who do deny
their problems, perhaps to the extent of accusing neighbours
of stealing a purse that they have mislaid, may be seen as
defending themselves from an awesome reality. Despair,
anxiety, self-blame and anger are all reactions seen in unimpaired people in the face of severe stress. It may well be that
by giving more attention to the processes by which the
dementing person is attempting to cope with what is
happening to him, differences in behaviour between different
sufferers could be better understood (e.g. Cohen et al 1984).
The so-called 'happily dementing' person may have found his
or her own way of facing the threat to his or her identity
which dementia poses, in acceptance and resignation to the
disability involved.

Disorders like Alzheimer's disease can at present only be
conclusively diagnosed following the patient's death. The
diagnosis is confirmed by certain changes in the brain,
apparent only on microscopic examination. However, when
the patient is seen over a length of time and the disorder is
fairly advanced, diagnosis during life is reasonably accurate.

It is not always feasible to distinguish multi-infarct dementia from Alzheimer's disease, however. As noted above, in a proportion of cases both disorders are ultimately found to have been present. Careful evaluation and investigations to exclude other possible causes of the presenting picture are important in every case. In the early stages of these disorders some diagnostic problems do arise. Most people would probably have to admit to episodes of forgetfulness. Thankfully, a saucepan boiled dry or a missed appointment do not in themselves mean some form of dementia is present! A history of progressive decline is a more serious indication.

Some older people who are depressed show some memory problems and other cognitive difficulties. This has been described as 'depressive pseudo-dementia' (Post 1965). In many cases these deficits improve to some extent following the depression being appropriately treated. A diagnosis made while the person remains depressed is likely to be unreliable. Certain psychological tests are claimed to discriminate well between groups of patients suffering from depression and dementia (Kendrick et al 1979), particularly when the assessment is repeated after six weeks or so. However, there are still patients who remain diagnostic puzzles over a period of months or even years. Diagnostic tests are usually standardised on groups of people with clear-cut depression and dementia. These are the patients who rarely need to be assessed in this way in practice!

The nature and cause of cognitive impairment in depression remain unclear (Woods and Britton 1985, ch 4). Deficits are likely to be less consistent, more task specific, and may be in part related to depressed people's reluctance to 'guess' when not completely certain of their answer, and their inability to produce sustained motivation and effort in demanding tasks. Depression can then lead to diagnostic errors, unless a 'wait and see' approach is adopted. If depression is present it should be treated; time will tell whether the person also has a progressive cognitive impairment. In studies such as Marsden (1978) and Ron et al (1979) it is depression which leads to many errors in diagnosis at the initial assessment. These mistakes, which became evident in the course of time, illustrate the pitfalls of relying on assessment at a single point in time only.

It often seems to be assumed that depression and

dementing disorders are mutually exclusive; of course they are not. They are both common disorders in older people. Both could occur together simply by chance, even if depression were not a predictable reaction to the experience of the early stages of a dementing disorder. Finally, on the relationship of depression and dementia, in a number of studies of measures such as ventricular enlargement on computed tomography (CT) scans, depressed patients occupy an intermediate position between dementing patients and normal controls (Jacoby & Levy 1980). There is a possibility that these results, rather than arising from changes in all depressed patients, relate to the presence of a sub-group of depressed patients with cortical or other physical dysfunction, reflected also in a higher mortality rate (Jacoby et al 1981).

Most elderly people do not and will not experience a dementing process. In what has become the classic study on the prevalence of dementia, Kay et al (1964) assessed a representative sample of over-65's in Newcastle-upon-Tyne. Five per cent were judged to have severe to moderate mental deterioration; a further five per cent had a mild degree of dementia. The prevalence rises rapidly for elderly people over the age of 80; nearly a quarter of these were found to have some degree of dementia. This is particularly relevant as it is the 'old old' age groups that are continuing to grow in size. The overall number of over-65's in the U.K. is no longer rising. The proportion of very old people is continuing to grow, and these are the people with by far the greatest risk of suffering from a dementing disorder.

Whilst people with dementia form a minority of elderly people, they are a sizeable, visible group. They make great demands upon health and social services. Although many are accommodated in institutions, in the UK something like three-quarters of dementia sufferers will be in the community – living alone, with relatives or friends. Families play a large part in supporting them (Bergmann et al 1978) and the strain on them can be considerable (Gilleard 1984c). Kay et al (1964) indicated that institutional placement is not simply determined by the severity of the disorder. Many severely disabled people with these conditions are supported by families, neighbours and social services.

Psycho-social factors, such as life events, isolation, bereavement, social class and personality have not been shown to have any significance in causing dementias (Gilhooly 1984). It is possible that factors such as diet and exercise which contribute to better cardiovascular function would be preventative factors in relation to multi-infarct dementia also. In some cases a bereavement, change of house or other upheaval brings the dementia to the attention of family members living away from the person, doctors and social workers. Usually close examination reveals, for example, that the spouse who died was doing a great deal to compensate for the person's deficits that were developing before the bereavement. Similarly, the change of house removes a number of environmental props that were helping to sustain the person's failing function.

Dementia is then a blanket term for a number of conditions involving progressive decline in intellect, skills and memory, which affect a large minority of elderly people. Diagnosis needs to be carefully made, to exclude any treatable conditions, and to ensure that depression is appropriately treated. There are currently no medical treatments available for the most common dementias – Alzheimer's disease and multi-infarct dementia. These conditions place great strain on families, hospitals, residential care and community services. Of all the problems experienced by elderly people, it has the most distressing impact for all concerned. Its study has been particularly hampered by the assumption that it is an inevitable part of old age, that nothing can be done to alleviate its impact or modify its course. In recent years this attitude has begun to change and Alzheimer's disease is now attracting considerably more attention. More resources for research and care are becoming available and interest is growing rapidly. This trend must continue, for the sake of the sufferers, their families and indeed for all our futures.

A POSITIVE APPROACH

Attitudes towards the elderly in Western society have often in the past been discriminatory, rejecting and negative. Those attributes that elderly people do have have been discounted in a society where speed, innovation and physical attributes are placed on a pedestal. Wisdom, experience and a sense of perspective are not valued as much as in certain other cultures, where to be an elder is an aspiration – rather than a fear – of the young.

If healthy elderly people have received a raw deal, how much more have mentally and physically disabled elderly suffered? In terms of facilities medical geriatric and psychogeriatric units have often been housed in the oldest buildings, quite unsuitable for the purpose. Such hospitals may be in splendid isolation, many miles from relatives, friends and familiar surroundings. The surroundings may be glorious, but few go out and enjoy them. Visitors – often equally elderly – find that the journey restricts visits severely.

The role of the staff has been seen as custodial rather than restorative or treatment-orientated. Morale, typically, has been low; recruitment of staff difficult. Extra payments for working on geriatric wards in the UK have been considered necessary. Nurses would be deliberately moved from geriatric wards after a certain time. The expectation was that the work must be unpleasant, tiresome and depressing. Anyone expressing a desire to work in this field was viewed with surprise and bewilderment, as if no one in possession of their senses would choose to do so.

In recent years the growth in the old old population that has been and is taking place has grasped the attention of those at every level of health, social and voluntary services. Fresh approaches are being pursued, more resources directed towards the ageing population. Custodial care concepts have been replaced by 'community care' as the sheer number of disabled elderly people being supported by relatives, friends and other social supports outside institutions has been realised. More positive approaches are filtering through some institutions catering for the elderly; there is more readiness to review traditional practices.

Attitudes have by no means changed completely. Often there is resistance to change. New ideas often need more resources that are not forthcoming. The elderly are still perceived generally as an unattractive group with whom to work; problems of recruitment in this field occur in a variety of professions – doctors, psychiatrists, nurses, social workers etc. Our own profession of clinical psychology has shown an enormous increase in the last ten years of the number working at least part of the time with the elderly. Yet this area remains unattractive for most trainees coming into clinical psychology, until they experience the potential scope for positive psychological approaches at first hand.

This book focusses on positive approaches to working with elderly people disabled by a dementia. Positive approaches can be misdirected, of course. A current approach, for example, is to give elderly people a great many tangible gifts at Christmas and other special occasions, when many elderly people would prefer companionship throughout the year, rather than being the recipients of seasonal handouts. The development in the UK of a 'hotel' model for residential care to replace the previous work-house system was another well-intentioned positive attempt to improve the lot of the elderly. It can now be seen however, to have resulted in old people's homes where by and large residents have no active role, where interaction is minimal, and where elderly people sit day after day, as if waiting to die.

The book takes its title from one particular positive approach, Reality Orientation (RO). It is certainly the most intensively researched of the available psychological approaches; it is widely applicable and it does attempt to tackle the sufferer's psychological needs. We have become increasingly aware that RO means different things to different workers, over and above any differences in application due to the special needs of a specific group, or a particular locality. As Hanley (1984) puts it, 'RO can be all things to all people.' Attempts have been made to define RO more rigorously, to pin down the techniques and their effectiveness, as we shall describe in Chapter 3. There have been attempts to compare and contrast RO with other approaches, such as reminiscence, as if the approaches were in competition with each other.

We must make our position plain from the outset. We are not advocating that all those working in this field should carry out a particular set of techniques on all their clients! Rather, we are commending a much more broadly based means of working with these people. It begins with basic attitudes, values and principles concerning the worth, humanity and dignity of those suffering from dementia. Any positive methods not based on such values and attitudes may do more harm than good. They must be the starting point for good practice in this area. Then there are techniques for helping communication, maintaining and developing skills and abilities and for tackling common areas of difficulty. Our experience is that positive approaches can complement, rather than compete with, each other. Our scheme has roots in reminiscence therapy, learning theory, the social psychology of group interaction and communication, individual programme planning and the nursing process, as well as in James Folsom's pioneering work, with his colleagues in the USA, on RO. It is not a cure-all or a magical formula to solve all the problems of old people. We emphasise the importance of seeing each elderly person as an individual and as a 'whole person' with psychological, social and emotional needs in addition to the physical needs which have been the main focus in the past – perhaps because they are in many ways easier to meet.

We hope readers will take from this book an integrated, individualised, value-based means of working and communicating with elderly people with dementia. It is much more than RO – if RO is defined rigidly – but RO is as good a way as any into this area. We commend this approach not simply because of any benefits that may accrue in terms of quality of life for the elderly people concerned, but also because of the increased morale often noted among those using such methods. This may then bring further benefits for the elderly person.

Part II of the book gives practical guidance as to how to put this philosophy and these techniques into practice. The remainder of Part I focusses on specific approaches, giving the background on strategies contributing to our overall scheme. There is still a need for further development; there is always scope for fresh insights, better research studies, more inspired theorising, greater experience. No approach should be static or incapable of further development and revision. The challenges of working positively with people afflicted by what can be such severe and disabling conditions are immense. They need to be tackled with determination, flexibility and persistence.

2

An overview of psychological approaches to the treatment of dementia

INTRODUCTION

Psychological approaches to working with people with dementia have taken many different forms and been described in a variety of ways. Several reviews of the earlier reports have appeared (e.g. Barns et al 1973; Miller 1977b; Woods & Britton 1977; Shaw 1979; Leng 1982). As will become evident, any categorisation of these approaches is inevitably somewhat superficial. There is considerable overlap and much common ground. Our grouping of approaches is rather arbitrary, but should help in drawing together the many disparate studies.

We have tried to exclude approaches not applicable to people with dementia. It must be appreciated that there is a wide variation in the degree of dementia and impairment of function from individual to individual. Some approaches may not be applicable to severely impaired patients, but be useful for those with more moderate difficulties and vice versa. Attempts will be made to identify the population used – unfortunately sufficient details regarding diagnoses are often not included in a study. The work of Copeland and his colleagues (Copeland & Gurland 1985) should be noted. This indicates differences in diagnosis between the UK and the USA of what they describe as 'organic brain syndromes'. It appears that a number of patients have this diagnosis in the USA who would not be so diagnosed in the UK. Finally the methodology of many of the studies does not meet strict criteria for evaluation of therapeutic approaches. This review then is intended to be indicative of the range and type of approach and suggestive of the kind of results obtained from them.

STIMULATION AND ACTIVITY PROGRAMMES

Sensory deprivation

Cameron (1941) demonstrated elegantly that the often observed increase in confusion and wandering at night in elderly people was related not to the effects of fatigue but simply to the effects of reduced sensory input, by showing that such confusion occurred in a darkened room during daytime. Elderly people may have reduced sensory input by virtue of normal deterioration in sensory acuity. Sight can show loss, as can sensitivity of hearing and touch. Some of the environments in which elderly people live – in institutional care or isolated in the community – can be monotonous and lacking in sensory stimulation. There are instances of voluntary deprivation when a person will choose withdrawal and reject stimulation, refuse to respond to the environment or react to it. In some cases this may be a means of coping with a large, unfamiliar institution.

These considerations suggest that, firstly, sensory deprivation can increase confusion in elderly people, and secondly, that many elderly people are deprived of sensory stimulation. Inglis (1962) drew a parallel with experiments on sensory deprivation in younger people. Briefly these experiments (reviewed by Corso 1967) removed all avenues of sensory stimulation. Some of the methods used included total immersion in a tank of water, bandaging, special helmets and incarceration in a polio life-support. It should be noted that sensory deprivation results as much from the provision of sensory monotony as from the removal of stimulation.

The point to be stressed is that it is *change* in sensory input that is stimulating. In general, a period of such sensory deprivation on young, normal, volunteer subjects produced behaviour similar to that observed in psychotic patients. Such responses included difficulties in thought and concentration, perceptual distortions, thought disorder, hallucinations and deterioration in reasoning, logic and word finding.

Inglis (1962) argued that elderly patients with memory deficits would be much more vulnerable to the effects of sensory deprivation, because when sensory input is curtailed the person must fall back on his recent memory in order to maintain orientation and clarity of thought. With an impairment of recent memory confusion will occur very quickly indeed as the person has nothing to provide support in the absence of continued input from the environment. So sensory deprivation is seen as interacting with and exacerbating (but not necessarily causing) the memory disorder and underlying cerebral pathology. The weakness of the comparison is that sensory deprivation in elderly patients is presumably long standing, chronic, and partial, whereas for the young volunteers it was acute and probably more extensive. Hodge (1984) points out that in Cameron's classic experiment social input was also removed. Studies which have sought to increase the person's level of stimulation have usually included both sensory and social inputs. They could potentially provide supportive, practical evidence for the importance of sensory and social deprivation in increasing impairment in people with dementia.

Stimulation programmes

Early studies showed some positive changes compared with control groups.

Cosin et al (1958) found changes in behaviour following the increased stimulation of full occupational therapy, social and domestic activities. Purposive, appropriate types of behaviour increased in their experimental group of elderly patients with dementia. Gains tended to be made in the early part of the programme and were lost when, after four weeks of treatment, the increased level of stimulation was halted for two weeks.

In Australia, Bower (1967) used a similar programme of stimulation with 25 female patients having dementia, working specifically from the theory outlined above that the effects of organic change and sensory deprivation interact to produce the behavioural deficits of dementia. Structured stimulation was programmed for four and a half hours a day five days a week over a six month period. Significant improvements were noted on independently carried out psychiatric, occupational therapy and nursing assessments. A control group which could only be rated by the psychiatrist showed a significant deterioration. However, the rating of changes by staff directly involved in the stimulation programme introduced the possibility of some improvement being attributable to staff expectation of change, rather than to objective observation. Also, the control group was different in important ways from the experimental group and so the results, whilst encouraging, are not conclusive.

The study of Loew & Silverstone (1971) included a more directly comparable control group. 14 much older (mean 87.5 years) male patients were exposed to physical, social and

psychological stimulation. The diagnostic details, unfortunately, are vague, but apparently the patients were deteriorated physically and/or mentally. Quantitative and qualitative
increases in general energy level following stimulation over
a six month period were found. The experimental group
showed a tendency towards improved cognitive functioning.
A 10 month follow-up suggested that these changes had been
maintained. The patients in the experimental group were
rated as being more 'critical, demanding and challenging'. It
is arguable whether this should be treated as a negative
finding as to some extent these attitudes may be seen as
healthy for an elderly person in this situation, compared with
the previous apathy and inactivity.

These studies do suggest that activity and stimulation may
be beneficial. No direct link, however, has been established
with the sensory deprivation theory. Many of the reported
changes might be seen as the results of staff encouraging and
reinforcing more active patterns of behaviour rather than
simply additional sensory stimulation leading directly to
changes in behaviour. For example Loew & Silverstone's
(1971) programme included toilet re-training, encouragement
of self-dressing, having meals together, keeping a daily
calendar and joining off-ward events. There was even a sheltered workshop available. Undoubtedly, all this is stimulating,
but it is surely simplistic to view this varied, wide-ranging
programme only in such terms. A more tightly controlled
experimental situation would be required to test the sensory
deprivation hypothesis further and to evaluate to what extent
alleviation of sensory and/or social deprivation per se is
sufficient to produce changes.

Much more specific forms of stimulation were used by
Norberg et al (1986). They evaluated the effects of music,
touch and objects expected to stimulate the person's senses
of taste, touch and smell (e.g. fur, hay, bread, camphor). Two
severely impaired patients with dementia, who showed little,
if any, verbal communication were carefully observed whilst
receiving the various forms of stimulation. The results indicated a definite positive response to music, but no differences in reaction to different objects or to touch were
detected. This study is particularly important in its focus on
patients who would normally be excluded from evaluative

studies, and its development of means by which contact with uncommunicative patients can be monitored.

Physical exercise

Many of the above studies have deliberately or incidentally included a fair amount of basic physical exercise (e.g. Loew & Silverstone 1971). In this section further research will be described in which this component of activity and stimulation programmes has been isolated.

Bassey (1985) has reviewed and examined the literature on the effects of exercise on physical health and well-being in older people. Concern has been expressed as to whether aged muscles and weakened stamina could stand the strain of exercise. Bassey concludes they can and that there is sufficient evidence to show that inactivity is the major weakening factor. Improvements may be slower and smaller, but contribute greatly to independent living and to circulation. She states that exercise may be of *more* value to the aged than to the young.

Although Bassey's review was concerned primarily with the person's physical state, the findings do imply that other changes are likely. Other studies have concentrated on the cognitive improvements possibly associated with exercise. Powell (1974) examined the effects of an hour of mild exercise five times a week over a 12 week period on elderly psychiatric hospital patients (mean age 69.3 years). Average length of stay in hospital was 24.3 years, so clearly many had chronic disorders. The 30 patients involved were in three groups – no treatment, exercise therapy, and a 'social therapy' group to control for the effects of increased attention. The 'social therapy' group had no physical activity, but did take part in arts and crafts work, games and so forth, for the same length of time and with the same amount of staff involvement as the exercise group. Changes in cognitive functioning, as measured by the Wechsler Memory Scale and the Progressive Matrices tests – favouring the exercise group – were found. Corresponding improvements in the patients' behaviour as rated by the nursing staff were not apparent – indeed there was a slight non-significant trend for the exercise group to deteriorate compared with the other groups on these measures. Powell offers the interpretation that this may arise from increased self-sufficiency, following on from cognitive improvement, awakening antagonism towards hospitalisation and its enforced routine, which again may be seen as an improvement over apathy. The lack of improvement in the 'social therapy' group is seen as related to the possibility of 'shutting off' these therapeutic activities through lack of interest, whereas the physical exercise is much more difficult to avoid covertly.

Further support for the effectiveness of physical therapy, on cognitive functioning at least, is provided by Diesfeldt & Diesfeldt-Groenendijk (1977). Their 40 patients were an older group (mean age 82 years) and all were thought to have a dementia, with an average duration of hospitalisation of 19 months. Two cognitive assessments were made with a one month interval. Half the patients took part in a 40 minute mild exercise session shortly before the retest, the other half did not. Patients who took part in the exercise session did better on a memory task than the control group, both on recall and recognition measures. General behavioural changes were not examined in this study.

Physical activity in these two studies has been highly structured – light bending and stretching exercises whilst sitting in a chair, throwing a ball, knocking down skittles, brisk walking, rhythmical movements etc., all demanding task attention. The fact that the most active group of psychogeriatric patients – the so-called 'wanderers' who often appear to be walking around the ward or home from morning to night – do not treat themselves by their continual activity (Cornbleth 1977) suggests that it is the structured aspect of the exercise that is important. There is, therefore, some evidence that physical exercise, by itself, can produce changes of a physical nature as well as in cognitive functioning, but further studies are needed to elucidate the nature of the changes and how they are brought about. Physical exercise may be important in that it is one of the simplest forms of activity for this population.

CHANGES IN THE ENVIRONMENT

Introduction

This group of approaches is based on the underlying idea that the elderly person will respond to his or her environment, which can be manipulated to produce and maintain positive changes in the person's functioning.

Clearly there is an overlap with the previous section, where a stimulating environment was the therapeutic tool, and the next section where behavioural methods largely based on environmental manipulation (together with a reinforcement system) will be discussed. RO also has effects on the person's overall environment through 24 hour RO. In this section those studies not subsumed under the other approaches will be discussed. It is conceivable that all these approaches owe whatever effectiveness they possess to processes they have in common. A priority for future research must be the finer analysis of the mechanisms of change.

Physical changes in the environment

This includes attempts to bring about changes by structural alteration or by rearrangement in some way of the physical environment.

The classic report is that of Sommer & Ross (1958) concerning a ward for geriatric patients whose mean age was 74 years and where the predominant diagnosis was 'arteriosclerosis'. They reported that, despite cheerful renovation and up-grading, the ward showed little sign of any human interaction! Chairs, for instance, were arranged mainly around the walls (see Fig. 2.1a) and unsociably side by side, making interaction very difficult. Sommer & Ross sum up the position in this way:

'It seemed we had made strangers of our patients. They became observers; silent individuals sitting eternally in a waiting room for a train that never comes'.

Social interaction was recorded to establish a baseline. Then chairs were arranged in small groups around coffee tables (see Fig. 2.1b), so that the patients sat facing one another to allow conversation to flow more freely if desired. The tables were useful resting places for magazines, flowers and other materials. Social interaction almost doubled after this re-arrangement.

However, the implementation of such an apparently simple change was not without problems. The patients themselves continually moved the chairs back to the walls and the staff found it hard to adjust to a less tidy and organised arrangement which impeded cleaning and ease of movement.

This endeavour has probably been duplicated many many times over the past few years and Peterson et al (1977) have published a study replicating Sommer & Ross's work. They showed that talking increased with the arrangement of a few chairs around a table, but if the group was enlarged somewhat there was no improvement in comparison with the around-the walls arrangment. Once again these authors

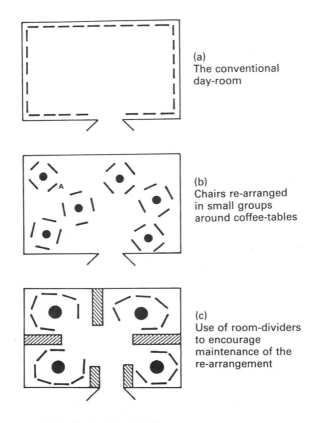

(a)
The conventional day-room

(b)
Chairs re-arranged in small groups around coffee-tables

(c)
Use of room-dividers to encourage maintenance of the re-arrangement

Fig. 2.1 Day-room seating arrangements

found the patients persistently returning the chairs to the walls! In our experience if patients do not do this the domestic staff will in order to facilitate their work. Sommer & Ross suggest that people usually prefer to have their backs to something solid. This may be to increase security or to satisfy curiosity and ensure that all visitors and ward activities remain within their scrutiny! For example, the chair marked A on Figure 2.1b offers a much more restricted view of what is going on in the room than any of the chairs in the traditional arrangement. A sense of territory and the sanctity of the status quo in the institution may also be important factors in accounting for the patient's resistance to change. For example, Lipman (1968) has documented the extraordinary discomfort old people's homes residents will accept rather than move from 'their' particular seat. It may be necessary to place obstruction – partitions, pieces of furniture and so on – behind the chairs in the new arrangement for it to become permanent (see Fig. 2.1c). Other workers have attempted to redesign sitting areas in such a way that furniture is difficult to move and yet arranged so that good interaction is promoted (Wattis & Church 1986, p 160–2).

Similarly Davies and Snaith (1980) successfully increased social interaction at mealtimes in a geriatric ward in the UK. Instead of patients sitting around the walls, with individual trays attached to their chairs, a more normal social situation was created. Patients now sat around tables in groups of six. Table-cloths, water jugs and so on were provided, and, to make conversation easier, efforts were made to reduce the high level of background noise. There was an immediate increase in social interaction; patients began to help each other and converse more.

On a wider scale there has been some interest in the effects of the design of residential homes on the pattern of activity, interactions and functioning of the residents. Cluff & Campbell (1975) have related in an old people's home the layout of the corridors on which the residents' rooms are placed to residents' satisfaction, social relationships, frequency of activity etc. For instance residents placed in a room at the end of a corridor spend more time in their own rooms. Harris et al (1977) arrived at a similar conclusion regarding the tendency of lengthy corridors to discourage residents' mobility in an observational study of eight purpose-built homes of widely varying design. They further reported that if residents were grouped in areas easily accessible to staff then the latter behaved in such a way as to encourage dependency.

A major aim of this particular study was to examine the extent to which residents who were 'confused' related and interacted with residents who were 'rational'. All the homes included had a mixture of 'confused' and 'rational' residents: there has been some controversy as to whether this mixing is the most appropriate way to meet the needs of the two groups. The case for integration includes the idea that the confused residents will benefit from the stimulation of being with rational people who are able to help their confused companions. Against integration is the notion that the rational ones will ostracise and exclude confused residents and that far from helping them may in fact refuse to have anything to do with them. In the UK both mixed and segregated homes have been built in different areas. Harris et al's careful observational research showed clearly that in fact mixed homes are not integrated in practice. Confused residents are segregated – in different sitting areas in a different wing or floor, with little if any interaction occurring between the two groups. This effective segregation seemed to occur despite the different designs of building. However, Harris et al feel that the design of a home that would make segregation and unnecessary dependence on staff more difficult than integration and independence would have more chance of success in combating staff and resident attitudes that appear often to be in the opposite direction. These design ideas are amplified by Lipman & Slater (1977) and include the notion of a small home built with a vertical (rather than the conventional horizontal 'corridor' arrangement) grouping of 'family units' in which about eight rational and confused residents would be mixed, with residents having a flatlet that could be used as more than a bedroom and in which they could prepare some meals if they so wished. Staff areas would be designed to be well away from these 'family units' to encourage independence, although some small communal facilities for use by any resident, closer to staff access, would be provided. These ideas have yet to be put to the test and as Lipman & Slater admit, changes in staff attitude are needed together with changes in design if their aims of integration and independence are to be achieved. The physical and attitudinal changes needed for 'family units' to be established within an old people's home or hospital will be discussed in the section on group living below.

Finally Matthews & Kemp (1979) report a study in which the day room of a psychogeriatric ward, housing 'severely mentally infirm' patients, in a large mental hospital was divided into four areas each decorated and furnished in different period 'styles' – Victorian/Edwardian; 1920s/1930s; 1950s; and also a normal modern hospital upgraded style. Direct observations of patients' behaviour were carried out before and after the change took place. Overall there were improvements in activity levels – both purposive and non-purposive – and a reduction in passivity. However, social interaction did not improve. As regards the particular rooms the oldest type was less used whereas the 1950s and modern rooms were quite popular. This was a surprising result in view of the hypothesis that older people would react better to surroundings reminiscent of their youth when they were perhaps happy and more active. The authors note that the rooms less used were also farthest from the toilet and this, in view of proneness to incontinence, is probably a significant observation. The nursing staff also commented that these rooms were probably too 'posh' to be other than admired and the objects on display fit only to be polished and carefully replaced. The chairs too may have been less comfortable. This part of the study suggests important variables which need to be adequately controlled and matched in future projects of this nature. The overall changes in activity levels noted earlier clearly cannot be be attributed to any specific environmental changes and may be a response to non-specific aspects of the investigation. An important finding that may be of general significance however, was a dramatic reduction in the number of accidents; there was now much more solid furniture around to be clung on to and carpets had replaced linoleum obviating the risk of slippery floors.

There is then some evidence for physical environment having an influence on the behaviour of people with dementia and although efforts to improve function by changing the physical environment can only be said to have shown limited success, in other sections it will be seen that these physical changes are often an important part of other approaches.

Prosthetic environments

For a variety of physical disabilities aids, or prostheses are available to help in the restoration of a competent performance, e.g. dentures, glasses, hearing aids. Lindsley (1964) advanced the notion of creating a prosthetic environment for geriatric patients in which their disabilities are compensated for by special features of that environment. Miller (1977a, p 133) expands on this theme, relating it specifically to confused and demented patients.

The elderly person is not exactly retrained – although some prostheses may require the person to learn how to use them before they can be effective. Thus for a patient who has difficulty in finding the toilet, and because of this is incontinent, a coloured line leading to the toilet marked on the floor could be part of the prosthetic environment (Pollock & Liberman 1974). This would presuppose that the patient could learn the new piece of information – the blue line leads to the toilet.

Other examples of prosthetic aids for this population are the special implements devised by occupational therapists and others to assist those with poor eating and dressing skills – nonslip mats for plates, thick handles for utensils to assist grip, Velcro fastening to replace buttons etc. Signs and memory aids which will be discussed later are also prosthetic. Jones & Adam (1979) have suggested that microprocessor technology could lead to the use of much more complex memory aids. A cassette recorder for instance, could provide the person with information and also store information for later use. In order for such a system to prove valuable to those living in the community a great deal of development will be necessary. Some applications of new technology have emerged. For instance, some wards now have a system which alerts staff when a patient wanders off the ward. This operates on the same principle as alarms used in shops and libraries to indicate when goods and books are being taken without being checked out. The system allows the ward door to be unlocked, so that patients not at risk of getting lost outside are free to come and go as they please. The system works well in practice with patients who wander through the ward door without any particular intention of 'escaping' from the ward. They are easily guided back again onto the ward (Stokes 1986a). However, patients who are very determined to leave may be much more difficult to persuade to return. This system then runs the danger of precipitating a number of unhelpful confrontations when patients of this type are on the ward.

Lindsley makes a number of suggestions as to how input to the elderly can be more effective – the use of more than one sense (e.g. both a gong and a flashing light to indicate lunchtime) and how to facilitate their responses (larger switches, and less susceptible to being triggered off inadvertently).

Fine (1972) in a discussion of 'geriatric ergonomics' describes how the physical environment can effect mobility and micturition – two essentials for the survival of the elderly person. Urinary incontinence may result from losing the 'race between bladder and legs' and in this context high hospital beds and excessive distances to the ward toilet are undoubtedly unhelpful. As was shown above, more stable furniture on a ward can assist mobility. The vast empty space on many wards must seem like an eternity of space to a frail old person faced with the prospect of finding her way to the toilet. Observations have shown difficulty in negotiating even the new 'highly polished' non-slip vinyl flooring. To old eyes it appears dangerous and it is walked upon as though it was a sheet of ice – the assurances of the designers are not enough to promote confidence! Willmott (1986) has demonstrated empirically that such flooring reduces the length of stride and speed of walking of elderly patients, in comparison with a carpetted surface. There have been few other attempts to evelute prosthetic or ergonomic approaches, except in relation to sign-posts and memory aids, reviewed in Chapter 3. The ideas are promising and well worth further development and research.

Changing the pattern of care

In order to bring about changes in function of elderly people with dementia it is necessary not only to modify the physical environment, but also to concentrate on improving the social and interpersonal atmosphere of the ward, and the expectations of staff and patients.

In a nursing home in the USA, where presumably some proportion of the residents are suffering from dementia (no details supplied in the study), Langer & Rodin (1976) showed that a very brief, simple manipulation of expectations could be effective. One group of residents had stressed to them that they had a great deal of control and choice over their lives in the home; another group were merely told that the staff wished them to be happy. The first group improved significantly over the latter control group, on measures of alertness, active participation and general sense of well being.

Gustafson (1976) reports an evaluation of a change of regime emphasising choice and encouraging self-responsibility for patients with dementia in a Swedish hospital (see also Melin & Gotestam 1981). Twenty-one elderly patients, most having dementia and a high level of behavioural disability, were divided into an experimental and a control group. The changes were introduced sequentially, allowing a multiple baseline design for the experimental group. Changes in social interaction, eating skills and level of activity were monitored by direct observation of time-sampled behaviour.

The first change was to afternoon coffee. Previously this had been brought to the patients on a tray, sugar and cream had already been added, and a piece of cake provided. It was made unnecessary for them to move from the chair in which they were sitting. The experimental group now went to another room where coffee, cups, and all the necessary ingredients were placed on two tables. Staff were not present, and they were left to fend for themselves. They were left to choose what they wanted and where they were to sit. In short, a single environmental manipulation allowed more independence and choice and created a social situation. Meal times were also changed for this group. The previous routine based on time, when patients would be fed if they were too slow was eliminated, and free choice and unlimited time were offered instead.

The final change was to provide activity material on the ward – games, books, jig-saws etc. For one week this was left to patients' initiative to use and was available to both exper-

imental and control groups. Then for one week the experimental group was encouraged by staff to use the material,
then for another week the patients were again left to their
own devices.

The results of the study are clear-cut and dramatic. Social
interaction during afternoon coffee increased greatly in the
experimental group and eating skills improved following the
meal-time changes. Their level of activity increased when
compared to the control group in the final week of the study
after they had been encouraged to use the materials. The
results provide strong support for the use of such an
approach, encouraging independence and choice, particularly
where the existing milieu may have led to under-functioning
and patients not using all their skills and abilities to the full.

This approach is, of course, dependent on staff attitudes.
It can be difficult for staff to accept patients taking responsibility for themselves and being more independent. So often,
the old pattern of care re-emerges. Davies (1982) reports how
a year after the successful intervention discussed in 'Physical
Changes to the Environment' above, 'only token symbols of
the "changes" remained'. This happens even though the new
regime may involve less apparent burden for the staff (e.g. in
not feeding patients unnecessarily). The lesson to be learned
is that staff attitudes can be extremely resistant to change, and
that sources of reinforcement may be complex and subtle.
They may for example involve a desire to care for someone
physically (Godlove et al 1980) which becomes difficult to
satisfy with this sort of change of regime. Practical aspects of
staff attitudes will be discussed in Chapter 10, but suffice to
say here that in many ways they are the key to implementing
and maintaining this, and other approaches. Where attitudes
are positive and appropriate, changes to the regime are more
likely to retain their initial effects.

Sheltered workshops

Extensively used with chronic psychiatric patients, there are
few reports of people with dementia being included in a sheltered workshop setting. Nathanson & Reingold (1969) have
demonstrated their feasibility with patients having moderate
to severe chronic brain syndrome. These patients were able
to maintain their participation in the workshop for periods of

well over three months. MacDonald & Settin (1978) showed that participation in a workshop was related to improvement in life satisfaction and social interest for nursing home residents (no diagnostic details given) compared with no treatment controls and a basic RO group. No changes in ward behaviour as rated by the nursing staff were apparent, however. Workshop sessions were held three times a week for 50 minutes over a five week period. The activity was making gifts for a children's home. The last session involved going to the children's home and actually giving them the gifts. The activity was purposeful with a clear end result. This is probably preferable to an activity which is repetitive but seems to have little intrinsic purpose or value. However, with severely deteriorated patients the problem will be to find an activity simple enough for the patient to be able to manage. The sheltered workshop is worthy of further exploration and may be of particular value with 'mild' to 'moderately' impaired patients attending a day centre.

Group living

The group living concept combines changes to the regime with some fundamental changes to the physical environment. It is currently attracting much interest in the UK and is being implemented in many old people's homes. Evaluation of its effects has been mainly anecdotal; Booth & Phillips (1987) review most of the relevant empirical research.

Although not involved in the first group living homes, Marston & Gupta (1977) and Gupta (1979) have done much to develop the concept in theory and in practice. They point out that a group of 40 or 50 – quite common in the lounge of many homes – is so large as to inhibit personal interaction. Marston & Gupta suggest that groups are at their most effective when there are eight to 12 members. One might speculate that people with dementia in particular would be adversely effected by larger groups, in view of their greater difficulty in remembering who people are and in forming relationships. For a group to work it requires a shared interest, activity or purpose – manifestly lacking in many homes. The rationale for having groups at all is the often reported loneliness and apathy experienced in many homes. If effective groups can be established then resident-to-resident interaction will increase. Together with this aim, choice and involvement of individuals in their own self-care were identified as objectives in raising 'quality of life' for residents.

A home with 40 residents would then be split into four or five groups. Each would have its own lounge/diner, with tea-making facilities, TV etc. Each group shares the range of self-care activities. They can get up in the morning at any time and help themselves to a light breakfast. At lunch and evening meal the group members set the table, serve themselves and afterwards wash up. They make their own drinks and have a choice of food, and are even consulted regarding menus! They are encouraged to participate in the choice of furniture and decorations for their rooms. They may make their own beds and clean their rooms. It has proved possible to adapt older homes at very little cost to this system which certainly does not need to be confined to purpose-built homes. Residents with dementia are integrated into the groups and are helped by their fitter peers, whilst carrying out what tasks they can. Rejection of the less able seems to occur less frequently in smaller groups.

Implementation of this approach requires consultation with residents, relatives and staff. Training in the new methods is needed for the latter and considerable support for all concerned in the first few weeks (described as 'utter confusion' in one home!) as the transition takes place and all concerned adjust to the new pattern.

The results – anecdotally – seem promising and exciting. Residents who were thought to be confused now play leading roles in the life of some homes. The dormant abilities of some residents have been revealed. They became more vocal and active, with activity centred around the domestic tasks rather than craft work etc. Staff now have more time to spend with residents and know them much more closely, and 'the number of so-called very confused people has been dramatically reduced'. Incontinence is also less. Relatives, volunteers and neighbours come into the home more and are entertained to tea by the groups who are now in a position to offer hospitality.

That this type of approach is also feasible in hospital settings is shown by an experimental placing of geriatric patients in a group living bungalow ward while their traditional ward was being upgraded. An anecdotal report on this was made by Adams et al (1979). Marked changes in activity and interaction were apparent with the change in environment, which allowed the patients to do more for themselves. Incontinence and confusion, once again, seemed to improve and a number of patients improved enough to be discharged home.

One study has documented the effects of introducing group living in a home where a number of residents suffered from dementia. Rothwell et al (1983) report a marked increase in purposeful activity, from observations made in the home before and after the implementation of group living. A proportion of the residents completed brief tests of verbal orientation and life satisfaction. Only the latter showed significant change, with residents reporting greater contentment under the new regime. Booth & Phillips (1987) report the results of a large-scale study comparing dependency levels over a two-year period in 292 residents living in group homes with those of matched residents in traditional homes. Essentially, there seemed to be little difference in outcome between the two types of homes, in terms of number of residents becoming more or less dependent over the two year period. If anything, group living homes seemed to lead to more improvement and less deterioration on a rating of mental state, which focussed on orientation and wandering. However, differences were very small.

This study has several drawbacks. The two year comparison meant only the 50% surviving were considered; the dependency rating scales were probably not very sensitive to change, with the majority of residents showing no change, and certainly not covering some of the quality of life aspects important in any evaluation of group living. What does emerge is that group homes are more likely to have a positive approach to the residents' capabilities, but that a number of traditional homes were adopting similar policies without the group living format. The physical changes in themselves did not always provide a good indication of what went on within the home!

A controlled evaluation of group living would be of immense value. Ideally it should take as a comparison a large group situation where choice and independence in self-care were systematically encouraged. The problems group living has to contend with are firstly, elderly people who are 'loners' and do not wish to integrate into a group, who may even feel threatened by such unaccustomed intimacy. Some arrangements would have to be incorporated to allow such people to be apart as they wished. Secondly, there is the inevitable problem of staff attitudes. Marston & Gupta (1977) report that senior staff felt threatened by the proposed change and Adams et al (1979) also report that some staff felt unable to adjust to the idea of independent patients. Residential care in the UK is largely based on a model with all services being provided for residents, perhaps as a reaction to the old workhouse system and its abuses. The model accepting that care is *provided* is so well-established that a new model to encourage independence is quite contrary to the old rule and as such is bound to encounter resistance. If group living can gain empirical support for its effects on confusion it will be in a strong position to overcome this resistance, and to replace a model that has encouraged apathy, withdrawal, loneliness and a neglect of psychological needs in far too many residential settings for the elderly.

BEHAVIOURAL APPROACHES

Introduction

Behaviour modification has been extremely important in a number of areas of therapeutic endeavour in recent years – mental handicap, chronic schizophrenia, various problems of children etc. It is a rapidly expanding and developing field based on an empirically derived body of knowledge and related to psychological models of how behaviour is learned and maintained – such as operant conditioning. In essence, behaviour is broken down into specific, clearly defined components – this makes programme targets easier to establish. The conditions under which the behaviour will occur are ascertained (the discriminative stimuli) and the consequences of the behaviour are examined. If the result is something the person wants or desires then the behaviour has been positively reinforced and is more likely to occur again. If following the behaviour something unpleasant is removed then this is described as negative reinforcement. Again the likelihood of the particular behaviour recurring is increased. On the other hand if something pleasant is removed, or something unpleasant added, then the behaviour is punished. For further details of the behavioural approach see Patterson (1982).

Since pioneering work by Lindsley (1964) and Cautela (1966, 1969), a number of authors have advocated using behaviour modification with the elderly e.g. Hoyer et al (1975), Harris S L et al (1977), Baltes & Barton (1977) Hussian (1981, 1984), Wisocki (1984). They have all written encouragingly, if speculatively, about the possibilities of a behavioural approach to the elderly and their problems. Although biological processes do occur in ageing and dementia, the elderly person's actual performance is always a result of interaction with the environment. If any learning is possible for the dementing person then the behavioural approach will facilitate the learning process. It will indicate the environmental conditions needed for new behaviour to be learned, or for existing behaviour to be maintained – which is just as important. The environmental changes here are very finely regulated and individualised. They relate to the antecedent conditions and consequences which the environment – in its broadest sense – provides for the behaviour in question. Barrowclough & Fleming (1986) have produced a simple manual which helps staff to examine these aspects so that retained skills and interests can be used to develop the positive aspects of the person's behaviour.

Although Woods & Britton (1985) have argued that many of the other approaches reviewed in this chapter can be usefully conceptualised in behavioural terms, there is still disappointingly little research on the use of behaviour modification per se with patients clearly diagnosed as having dementia. Before reviewing relevant literature, it is important to clarify the learning potential of the dementing person if the approach is to be seen as at all viable with this population.

Can elderly people with dementia learn?

Studies have already been described showing the responses of elderly people to environmental conditions and so demonstrating that all learning ability has not been lost. The characteristic of dementing conditions – a deficit in learning new material – is easily observed for example by providing a patient with a fictitious name and address and asking for a recall in five minutes. Such tests reveal the existence of a learning deficit and are not designed to provide evidence of any retained ability. What is of interest is to examine what conditions are most favourable for learning to take place.

Miller (1975) showed that younger patients with dementia did badly in comparison with normal controls in learning lists of words when the amount of learning was assessed by recall or recognition. However, if recall was aided by giving the patient the initial letters of the word to be recalled then near-normal retention was apparent. Morris et al (1983) have obtained similar results with older people with dementia. Under these cued-recall conditions it seems that less impairment of learning is evident. These findings have immediate practical application in the giving of clues and prompts. They demonstrate a method by which people with dementia can be helped to achieve success in responding correctly. It should not be assumed that they help the person achieve 'normal' memory. There is a great deal of evidence that such techniques help normal people achieve good scores on memory tests when their memory trace is in fact quite weak (e.g. Woods & Piercy 1974; Mayes & Meudell 1981). Little et al (1986) have shown that patients with a moderate degree of dementia may retain information over a one or two month period. After at most 5 repetitions of a pair of words, patients showed significant retention of the association even after this lengthy delay. This was demonstrated by better performance on repeated pairs than on new pairs of words.

Elderly patients who have suffered more localised damage to their brains following cerebrovascular accidents are also capable of some learning. Halberstam & Zaretsky (1969) successfully increased particular verbal responses simply by the experimenter saying 'very good' when the response was given. Halberstam et al (1971) focussed on avoidance learning. In a laboratory situation subjects learned to make a motor response when a sound or light was switched on to indicate that a mild electric shock would follow. Again brain-damaged subjects showed clear learning of the required responses, although they were slower in making the response. An overlearning procedure, in which a large number of additional conditioning sessions were given, proved of benefit in improving the speed and quality of the responses.

Patients with dementia-related memory disorder were required to pull a lever to obtain a reward in a laboratory task of operant conditioning carried out by Ankus & Quarrington (1972). Forty-eight patients (aged 55–86 years) were included in the trial, and it appeared that the appropriateness of the particular reinforcer used for particular patients was of importance. Female patients preferred monetary rewards, and the male patients fluids – beer etc. Apparently this could be related to the opportunities females had to spend money in the setting involved. When the appropriate reinforcer was used relatively normal learning took place of the relationship between lever pulling and reward operative at any particular time, particularly if only gradual increases in the ratio of pulls to reward were made.

It would seem that people with dementia do have some learning potential on which behaviour modification may build. Particular attention will have to be given to creating the best possible conditions for learning to take place.

Applied studies of behaviour modification

Disappointingly few studies have been directed at the problems posed by dementia. In many of the studies that have taken place in old age institutions it is extremely difficult to ascertain the nature of the patients involved. In the following sections, on particular areas of application of behaviour modification, some attempts will be made to delineate the kinds of subjects taking part.

Eating

Several workers have reported one or more single-case studies. Geiger & Johnson (1974) increased the proportion of meals that six 'geriatric patients' ate correctly, in the sense that they consumed at least a specified portion of the meal. Prompting and reinforcement were used to bring about the changes. When these were withdrawn the amount eaten dropped again until they were reintroduced. Baltes & Zerbe (1976a, b) report two cases where nursing home residents who were fed by care staff were helped by a careful training procedure, including graduated prompts and social reinforcement, to be much more independent in their eating. One of the subjects was 79 years old and had suffered a stroke, but the other subject was not reported to be cognitively impaired in any way. None of the eight subjects reviewed here were reported to have a dementing disorder, although the techniques used would be useful with many patients with difficulties in eating.

Self-care

Although this is an area often impaired in people with dementia, few studies have applied behavioural techniques to the improvement of self-care skills. Rinke et al (1978) used prompting and reinforcement to improve self-bathing in six nursing home residents. They were aged from 67 to 90 years, and all had a diagnosis of 'chronic brain syndrome'. Each of five components of bathing (undressing, soaping, rinsing, drying and dressing) were in turn the focus for intervention. This multiple-baseline design allowed for the specific effects of the behavioural intervention strategies on the person's self-care to be monitored. As a further control, two of the subjects received no intervention. These control subjects showed little change throughout. The other four residents responded well, with each component of the overall task reaching near maximum levels when it was prompted and appropriate reinforcement given. The respective contributions of reinforcement and prompting were not established, but there were suggestions from the data that either might have been sufficient alone in some cases to bring about or maintain improvement. Prompting included physical prompts, e.g. handing the resident a towel, and verbal instructions. Among the rewards offered were praise, a choice of 'grooming aids' (powder, lotion etc.), visual feed-back on a wall chart and a choice of things to eat. A certain number of appropriate responses were required to earn the tangible rewards.

In a family setting, Pinkston & Linsk (1984) report teaching family members to use differential attention to reinforce the self-care of a 70-year-old lady with dementia. They praised her when she brushed her teeth, combed her hair, had a bath or remained dressed for several hours. They ignored inappropriate behaviour. In this case, prompts had proved ineffective and had been seen as nagging, resulting in a number of negative interactions between the patient and her family. The intervention led rapidly to a near maximum level of self-care function.

Mobility

Here again several case reports are available. Libb & Clements (1969) were successful in increasing exercise rate (on an exercise bicycle!) in three out of four subjects. They received tokens as reinforcers which were exchanged at the end of the session for something more tangible. These patients were not described in detail, other than 'regressed' with a diagnosis of chronic brain syndrome. Sachs (1975) includes two case reports of residents with mobility restrictions following a hip fracture some time previously. One had a chronic brain syndrome with Parkinson's disease. The walking of both improved when walking was systematically and specifically reinforced. Two further residents – one aged 92 years with a mild memory defect – who were confined to wheel-chairs for no clear physical reason were shown to increase their frequency of independent walking when, and only when, this was reinforced and prompted (MacDonald & Butler 1974). Burgio et al (1986) successfully applied a prompt and praise procedure to increase independence in walking in eight nursing home residents (four reported to have a dementia). For six of the residents the improvement was evident as soon as the intervention began; the other two residents improved within a few days of baseline observations – before the intervention! Not only did most residents walk further, but most progressed to more independent means of mobility, e.g. needing less staff assistance, using less prosthetic aids, not using a wheelchair etc. An important component of the intervention (and of the baseline observation procedure) appeared to be the opportunity it provided to the resident to walk. The authors suggest that immobility was related, at least in part, to 'environmental contingencies that either discouraged walking or failed to prompt and reinforce the behaviour'. Efforts were made to teach the nursing home staff to adopt the intervention procedure, and gains were generally maintained at a four month follow-up. Although still only a few studies have been performed, a fair degree of improvement has been noted and there is an indication that some cognitively impaired residents were included.

Social and verbal interaction

Lack of conversation is a frequent observation in institutions for the elderly (see Woods & Britton 1985, ch 9). Several studies have used behavioural methods in an attempt to increase the amount of social interaction. For example, Gray & Stevenson (1980) gave positive feedback for accurate statements to patients during weekly group sessions. Social interactions between patients increased significantly in three groups, each of around six members, all of whom appeared to have been disorientated.

A group activity was also the focus for intervention by Linsk et al (1975). Here 15 or so residents were involved who were 'a cross-section of the alert and confused residents', including some people probably with dementia. Evidence is presented that the group's verbal behaviour increased during treatment phases; it was much less in the baseline and return to baseline phases of the reversal design employed. Related changes in the group leader's behaviour were noted. Increases in the number of questions asked (prompts to talk) and the amount of the leader's listening behaviour (a reinforcement for talking) were recorded. Arranging favourable conditions for talking (games, questions etc) can be of great importance in eliciting this behaviour in socially withdrawn elderly people, thus providing appropriate behaviour to be reinforced.

This assumes that the elderly patients involved, if reinforced for social interaction and placed in a situation which prompts and is conducive to such interaction, do have the necessary skills to interact successfully. However an alternative model might emphasise that admission to a residential facility, as Berger & Rose (1977) argue, is a dramatic change to the patient's social environment. This necessitates an adjustment to a range of new situations and may require the development of new skills previously not in the patient's

repertoire. Berger & Rose taught such residents social interaction skills with limited success, using behavioural methods
of social skills training used widely with younger patients. The
residents involved were selected to exclude disorientation. A
more recent study by Lopez et al (1980) also excluded those
with severe organic impairment, but nevertheless simple
cognitive testing indicated a 'moderate level of confusion'.
Structured Learning Therapy (SLT) (Goldstein 1973) was the
interpersonal skills training package used to teach 56 elderly
in-patients the skill of 'starting a conversation'. Positive results
were obtained, with some evidence of generalization from
the learning situation to new situations especially when 'overlearning' – repeated practice – was used. In a further study
Hoyer et al (1980) sought to identify patient characteristics
related to the skills of 'expressing a complaint', using SLT with
a similar group of patients. Mental status – i.e. current information, orientation etc. – was the best predictor of outcome.
This suggests that more demented patients would benefit least
from this approach, although the fact that the mean length
of hospitalisation in both studies was around 20 years
suggests that poor performance on Mental Status may have
been related to other factors (apathy, withdrawal etc.) than
memory disorder related to dementia.

In some ways it seems rather unreasonable to necessitate
elderly patients learning the new skills needed to interact in
current residential care facilities. Perhaps more important as
a priority is establishing conditions in residential care where
normal social behaviour is encouraged and elicited, and the
social skills that most elderly have before admission could
then be maintained and enjoyed by all concerned. Some
patients may still have difficulties in social skills, but to concentrate on training adjustment to unsatisfactory conditions is
misguided. It is preferable to attempt to change the environment itself. A potentially more appropriate application of
social skills training is described by Praderas & MacDonald
(1986). They taught four moderately cognitively impaired
nursing home residents telephone conversational skills –
expressing common courtesies, asking questions etc. Results
were generally positive, with marked improvements in skill in
two residents when assessed in a role-played telephone
conversation. Unfortunately none of these residents had any

contacts in the community they could telephone (two had been in institutions for many years), but the aim of helping residents to be skilful enough to maintain their community links is laudable. Green et al (1986) report a single-case where a wife was able to learn to use contingent reinforcement (touch, praise, smiles) to increase her husband's spontaneous and appropriate verbal behaviour. He had had a stroke three months previously and seldom conversed unprompted. The intervention was maintained at a six month follow-up; its success was a great encouragement to the wife, who had been distressed by the apparent permanence of her husband's disabilities.

Participation in activities

Lack of activity is another often-described feature of institutions (see Woods & Britton 1985, ch. 9), and goes hand in hand with low levels of social interaction. Quilitch (1974) used token reinforcement to increase the numbers of elderly persons undertaking purposeful activity, but did not test whether it was simply the provision of the activity, (a Bingo game) that led to the increased activity. On this occasion tokens were exchanged for refreshment at the end of the Bingo session. The increase in activity occurred despite many residents being 'disabled, regressed and incontinent'.

Two studies by McClannahan & Risley (1974, 1975) increased participation in activities in a 100-bedded nursing home, where half the residents were diagnosed as having 'arteriosclerosis and other heart and vascular diseases'. The first study employed a somewhat artificial activity – residents went to a designated area, had a brief conversation with the experimenter and received a little spending money. The number of residents taking part was shown to be influenced by whether or not the activity was previously announced and whether or not spending money was given. Thus the least number of residents took part when there was no announcement and no money and most when there were three types of announcement and money. The second study involved puzzles and games being available on some days for an hour a day. Results indicated that when encouragement to use the equipment was given an average of three-quarters of the residents were engaged in activities; on days when no equip-- ment was available only 20 per cent were active in some way or other; and when equipment was available, but no prompting given, only a slightly higher proportion were active (25 per cent) than when the equipment was not there. Prompting and encouragement then have a big role in the usefulness of recreational equipment. Similarly Jenkins et al (1977) in the UK increased the number of residents engaged in activity by providing material for 45 minutes a day in two old people's homes. Again considerable prompting was used, and also continued praise and encouragement throughout the session. Of particular importance here is that one home was specifically for the 'elderly mentally infirm' where all had a diagnosis of dementia. Further studies by this research team have explored other activities (e.g. Powell et al 1979, on indoor gardening) and how – given the considerable encour- agement required to obtain participation from residents – these programmes can prove feasible in homes where staff resources are limited.

Burton (1980) reported an increase in the purposeful activity of patients with dementia during occupational therapy sessions. This was achieved through staff consistently prompting patients to use materials and reinforcing them when they did so. It was also noted that patients slept less during the OT sessions following the introduction of this approach! McCormack & Whitehead (1981) report similar increases in engagement (and reduced sleeping) on a geriatric ward when individual or group activities were provided and encouraged.

An intervention aiming to increase both participation in an activity and social interaction was attempted by Blackman et al (1976). They increased attendance at a social area of a home for the aged, by providing reinforcements and prompts to attend. Social interaction was not specifically prompted or reinforced, other than by the social setting and by enjoyment of the interaction. The increased social interaction was entirely between residents. Staff-resident interaction levels were not altered. Two-thirds of the residents were described as 'confused and disoriented' by nursing staff and so probably included a fair number with dementia. Carstensen & Erickson (1986) sound a cautionary note. They similarly increased attendance and social interaction by serving refreshments, but showed that most of the dramatic increase was accounted for by 'ineffective vocalisations' i.e. nonsensical and unreciprocated speech. In future studies it is essential that both quantity *and* quality of interaction and activity are considered.

Continence

In our experience incontinence is one of the most difficult and disturbing problems facing those caring for the aged. It need hardly be said that the problem is deeply disturbing for the elderly patient. Woods & Britton (1975) found that over a third of elderly patients in a large psychiatric hospital were incontinent of urine by day more than once a week. Over half of these patients were in fact incontinent several times daily.

Whilst early reports of behavioural interventions involving elderly patients with chronic psychiatric conditions were encouraging, studies involving patients with dementia were initially much less successful. For example, Grosicki (1968) reports negative findings from a controlled study, where the experimental group were rewarded for being dry and for using the toilet. Unexpectedly, incontinence reduced in the control group who were on a different ward where the 'usual procedures' were followed, but not in the experimental group. Similarly, Pollock & Liberman report no significant reduction in incontinence in six male patients diagnosed as having dementia, following social and material reinforcement for being dry. Hodge (1984) reviews this latter study in depth, and shows how the very short period of learning allowed, the assumption that the person's neuropsychological problems would not be a barrier and inadequate behavioural analysis may have contributed to these negative findings. In essence, it is argued that incontinence is more complex and with more variations in cause than these early programmes envisaged.

The same considerations apply to the attempt by Collins and Plaska (1975) to reduce nocturnal incontinence, using the 'bell and pad' method. This method is generally fairly successful in treating enuretic children. It involves an alarm being sounded as soon as the person begins to urinate in the bed. Nineteen elderly residents of a nursing home (two-thirds judged to be seriously impaired in awareness of their surroundings and others) were paired with control subjects.

Both were awoken and toiletted whenever the experimental subject set off the alarm as he began to urinate in bed. Thus any effect of the bell and pad could not be related to the increased amount of nocturnal toiletting but rather to the pairing of desire to urinate and getting up and going to the toilet. Results over an eight week treatment period were by no means dramatic, but there was a significant, although small, reduction in bed wetting in the experimental group. Conditioning seemed most useful when the buzzer was activated immediately the resident began to urinate, without delay. There was some evidence that the buzzer did halt the urination and encourage urinary control. The authors suggest using the bell and pad together with operant techniques (e.g. rewarding dry beds, rewarding using the toilet etc.) over a longer period in order to increase the method's effectiveness.

More recent studies have included some with more positive findings. Hussian (1981) attempted a programme of regular toiletting with twelve 'regressed institutionalised geriatric patients'. Prompts and reinforcement for toiletting and praise for being dry led to a dramatic reduction in incontinence in only a fortnight! Prompting alone was sufficient in maintaining the behavioural change. The rapid toilet-training method developed by Foxx & Azrin (1973) for use with people with a mental handicap was used successfully with two elderly patients with dementia by Sanavio (1981). For over two years, both had been incontinent of urine and/or faeces day and night, and never used the toilet independently. One patient began within four days to use the toilet without prompting, with a corresponding reduction in the number of episodes of incontinence. This improvement was maintained eight weeks later, and Sanavio was able to demonstrate its relationship to the intervention method, using a reversal design. The second patient's faecal incontinence virtually disappeared, and again independent toiletting was reinstated.

This level of independence may not be attainable for all patients – for those with physical disability and mobility problems remaining dry may be the more realistic goal. Schnelle et al (1983) report a programme used to teach 21 immobile patients with dementia to ask for help from staff when they needed to urinate. The programme included prompting, social reinforcement for asking to be taken to the toilet and for being dry, and social disapproval for being wet. The results indicated that incontinence decreased and appropriate toiletting requests increased compared with controls. The results were so rapid (from the first day) that the authors attribute the improvement to better staff–patient management, rather than to patients re-learning skills that had been lost. A necessity in this instance was for staff to actually respond to patients' requests for help!

Less positive results have emerged from two studies involving psychogeriatric patients with a severe degree of dementia, reported by Rona et al (1984, 1986). In the first study, following baseline assessments of the level of incontinence on three wards (involving two-hourly checks), each ward was fitted with signs, distinctively painted toilet doors, and floor-markings leading the way to the toilet. On one ward baseline measures were continued for a further three weeks, in case the regular checks were helpful in themselves; one ward had no further intervention; and the third ward had a toilet-training programme based on each patient's individual peak times for voiding. Verbal and tangible reinforcement were provided for appropriate responses. The results in terms of the number of episodes of incontinence favoured the ward where training had taken place. Although the improvement there was only slight, it became significant when compared with the large increase in wetting episodes on the other two wards. The authors point out that the differences may have been due in part to differences between the three wards, and so in their second study they compared a training group and a control group drawn from the same wards. Here the results were less positive. Improvements were only noted for patients who were incontinent less than once a day. A follow-up assessment three months after the training was completed showed that patients who had been more frequently wet did not improve with the training procedure. It is not clear what toiletting procedures were carried out during the follow-up period for patients who had received training. Being on the same ward as control subjects brings problems of its own, not least a possible carry-over effect of the treatment of one group on the other.

Clearly, a behavioural approach to incontinence in people with dementia has so far failed to prove effective in a range of studies from a variety of settings. Results are at best mixed, in some instances negative. In view of the importance of incontinence we will discuss some factors that may contribute to these poor results and offer some hope for the future.

Firstly, incontinence is the most difficult, practically, of the target problems so far reviewed. All the previous interventions could possibly be confined to an hour or two a day, and intensive work carried out then. By its very nature incontinence has to be modified throughout the day and throughout the night and so limited intervention is more difficult. This in turn means much greater commitment and cooperation from care staff on the ward, as Turner (1980), in a useful review of the behavioural approach to incontinence in the elderly, indicates.

Secondly, correct toiletting requires a number of skills – dressing, mobility, ability to find the toilet, ability to recognise it, to control urination until the toilet is reached etc. This chain of behaviours can break down at any point and so an individual analysis of problems will be required in order to identify the problem in each case. Thus the poor results of patients with dementia do not indicate that the incontinence is necessarily 'organic' and therefore untreatable. For example in Woods & Brittons' project (1975), already mentioned, eight elderly female patients with dementia who were regularly incontinent were studied intensively and comprehensive data on their toiletting collected. Five of the eight had problems in finding and getting to the toilet at the appropriate time and seemed to have little difficulty in using it correctly once there. Thus with these patients a strictly 'organic' incontinence seemed unlikely in that the micturition response still functioned normally.

Thirdly, goals of treatment need consideration. An ideal goal might be complete continence and independent toiletting. With patients suffering from a severe degree of cognitive impairment a more attainable goal might be remaining dry with regular prompting. If the individual's micturition pattern guides the toileting programme it could be more efficient and rewarding for all concerned.

Certainly, as in King's (1980) highly successful, multi-modal approach to the treatment of incontinence there is a need in this area for both medical and psychological intervention to maximise the chances of success with such a complex problem. Smith & Smith (1986) provide a detailed discussion of these issues, together with other important aspects, e.g.: Should fluids be restricted in the evening? Is 'habit training' effective? They conclude that behaviour modification has much to offer in maintaining continence in people with dementia, but that there is room for improvement in the quality of behavioural methods being applied.

Behaviour problems

A variety of behaviour leading to difficulties for the patients and/or staff has been tackled; most reports are of single-cases. For example, an increase in safe smoking behaviour was reported in a 74-year-old patient with a diagnosis of Korsakoff's syndrome with dementia whose carelessness with cigarettes posed a considerable fire risk (Seidel & Hodgkinson 1979); a decrease in complaints of feeling hungry (which occurred even after a full meal) was reported in a 58-year-old man with dementia (Burton & Spall 1981). Sachs (1975) attempted to improve oral hygiene in three nursing home residents who had sustained 'brain damage'. Results were mixed with one resident not responding at all to intervention.

One of the most difficult problem behaviours for staff (and other patients) to live with is a patient persistently shouting and screaming. Some success in reducing (but not necessarily eliminating) screaming and shouting has been reported in single cases by Baltes & Lascomb (1975) and Birchmore & Clague (1983). In the latter study the patient was a 70-year-old lady with dementia, who was also blind. The plan was to reinforce her when quiet, but finding an effective reward proved difficult. Touch, in the form of rubbing the patient's back, proved most helpful in this case. Hussian (1981) reduced a patient's self-stimulatory stereotyped vocalisations, providing reinforcement for 10 second periods without noise. The impact of the intervention was increased by employing 'artificial discriminative cues', i.e. brightly-coloured, large cardboard shapes, which were specifically paired with reinforcement in brief training sessions. These perhaps serve to highlight the difference between behaviour judged appropriate and inappropriate.

Garland (1985), reporting findings from a series of eleven 'noise-makers', points out the variety of factors to be considered in a behavioural analysis, and the range of treatment options available. Apparent causes included delirium, communication difficulties, self-stimulation, in the context of sensory or social deprivation, echoing noise made by others, and seeking attention from carers, some of whom responded to noise-making but ignored the person when quiet. A further factor that should always be considered is pain: when the person is unable to communicate the experience of pain verbally, shouting or screaming may be a way of expressing discomfort. Garland notes that in the eleven cases examined, most seemed to be affected by several of these factors. Four patients died within 3 months of referral, reflecting perhaps physical health problems. Three of these patients showed no response to psychological interventions, whilst the remaining seven all showed some response. In four of these cases there was a marked reduction, maintained at a six-month follow-up. Garland reports that among the most useful therapeutic strategies identified were the use of distracting auditory stimulation (e.g. playing relevant music through headphones), carers differentially reinforcing appropriate behaviour and ignoring noise, and brief periods of removal to a quiet area when noise occurred. In each case it was important to develop an individual package of interventions. Stokes (1986b) provides a guide to examining the various possibilities resulting in a person screaming or shouting, coupled with practical suggestions on management.

A related problem arises from inappropriate verbalisations. For example, Pinkston & Linsk (1984) describe the case of a 73-year-old man with Alzheimer's disease, living at home with his wife. The patient expressed a number of 'worried statements' each day, e.g. repeatedly asking 'Do I have money in the bank?'. By training the wife to reinforce positive statements with praise and attention and ignore worried statements, worried statements were reduced markedly, the patient spoke more positively, and the wife's subjective level of burden in caring for her husband at home was also reduced. Similar methods reduced the frequency of accusations in a further single case (Green et al 1986). Tarrier & Larner (1983) report an intervention with a group of four immobile stroke patients, who repeatedly asked to be taken to the toilet (although not needing to urinate). The patients seemed to have found an effective way of capturing staff attention, although the staff were becoming frustrated by the frequent false alarms. The intervention consisted again of differential attention to appropriate behaviour: staff spent time with the patients at other times than toiletting. The frequency of false alarms was reduced, and patients called for help less often. In this instance the staff did not perceive the objectively measured changes.

Finally, Hussian (1981) has reported the use of the 'artificial discriminative stimuli' mentioned above in relation to several other sorts of problems, with apparent success. Thus wandering was reduced in three patients with dementia. Here one form of cue was paired with reward and another with an unpleasant stimulus (a loud hand-clap). The two types of cues were then placed in appropriate places – the latter at danger points, those with positive associations in the patient's room. Another target in one case was the reduction of inappropriate sexual behaviour. The patient, who frequently masturbated in public, was taught to masturbate only in private places. A further two patients repeatedly manipulated any objects in reach in a stereotyped manner. They were reinforced for a similar but appropriate activity (clay modelling), again in the presence of an artificial cue. It remains unclear how these cues work; fading the cues by reducing the size seemed effective in maintaining improvement in some cases; some patients required booster sessions after a few months to re-train the association between cues and consequences. It is debatable whether they should be preferred to cues with overlearned associations (e.g. a red sign saying DANGER). Their size and colour may aid concentration and attention to the relevant aspects of the learning situation. As yet they unfortunately seem to have not been used by many workers other than Hussian.

Individual planning

In the early 1970s a series of publications emanating from a research team at the Philadelphia Geriatric Centre highlighted the subject of individualised treatment of excess disabilities of mentally impaired elderly people. Excess disabilities (EDs) are those functional incapacities that are greater than expected in view of the patient's level of impairment; in other words the discrepancy between the potential and actual level of function. In this study such excess deficits were isolated by a consensus of opinion from a multi-disciplinary team following extensive assessment of the patient. Two groups of matched female patients were involved (mean age 82 years), living in identical accommodation; one group received individualised therapy for the EDs and the other did not. Treatment continued for a period of one year, when the baseline assessments were repeated and external raters evaluated progress in each excess disability, blind to whether the patient had received treatment or not (Brody et al 1971). The results indicated that the treatment of EDs had been successful, with the experimental groups showing more improvement; changes in areas not directly treated were not found. Both groups showed a deterioration in general health over the year. EDs in the areas of family relationships and activities responded most to treatment.

At follow-up nine months later (Brody et al 1974) EDs in the experimental group had deteriorated, and it seemed that continued treatment input was required to maintain improvement. It should be noted that the institution involved has relatively good resources and a reputation for sophisticated care; however, it is clear that in some areas this was insufficient to produce and maintain maximum functioning without an additional individualised treatment programme.

The treatment programmes derived from multi-disciplinary assessments covered a wide range – activities of daily living, behavioural, interpersonal, environmental and social disabilities, occupational and recreational activities, physical, emotional and psychiatric problems were all covered. Specific goals of treatment were set, with the components of the therapeutic plan clearly set out, together with the responsibilities of each team member for carrying them out. Treatment plans apparently included modification of environmental factors such as furnishings, decorations, staff attitudes etc. where necessary (Brody et al 1973). Others involved consultation with medical specialists e.g. for visual problems. Two case illustrations are provided by Brody et al (1973), but unfortunately it is still extremely difficult to ascertain the exact form of the treatment methods used. This study is an early example of an individualised approach, with clearly specified, graded treatment goals and explicit treatment plans, which help to ensure a consistent approach across disciplines. This is an approach which will be described in more detail in Chapter 5. A couple of recent studies are available to give some indication of its practical usefulness. Patterson (1982) describes an extensive behavioural treatment and rehabilitation programme for elderly psychiatric patients, about a third of whom appear to have some degree of dementia, although diagnostic details are not given. It is evident that patients with a severe degree of dementia would have been excluded. A wide range of treatment options were available including training in social skills, hygiene, dressing, verbal orientation etc. Each patient had an individualised programme from these various training modules, together with any individualised intervention that was required. Results were generally encouraging, although for ethical and practical reasons a straightforward controlled comparison was not attempted. Each treatment module was shown to achieve its purpose, and overall there were increased community placements and reduced relapse rates. However, poorer performance on a simple cognitive test predicted slower rates of learning skills in the various modules and a greater chance of relapse, so it is likely that results were less positive for people with dementia.

Miller (1985) reports a comparison of geriatric wards in the UK, some of which used individualised care-planning (based on nursing process models) whilst others used a system of task allocation, where nurses were responsible for particular tasks, e.g. toileting, bathing, feeding etc., for a large number of patients.

Observations on the different types of wards suggested that on the task allocation wards 'nursing practices were pushing patients into dependency', whereas 'when a nurse had to . . . write out a care plan for every patient, she was . . . more likely to take the patient's real needs and self-care skills into account.' Empirical support for these observations comes from assessment of the functional abilities of patients on the three wards of each type included in the study. Patients admitted to the six wards had similar dependency levels, but patients who had been in hospital a month or more were significantly more dependent on the task allocation wards. On both types of wards, patients' scores on a test of verbal orientation fell into the impaired range, but patients scored higher on the individualised care wards. Miller also shows that dependency levels fell on one ward when a nursing process approach, emphasising individualised care, was introduced.

Obviously, research of this kind is fraught with difficulties. Did the wards differ in other ways? Were the patients or staffing or resources different? Miller recognises these problems; wards were matched carefully, and the absence of differences in short-stay patients adds credence to the results. What cannot be answered from this study is whether it is the whole individualised approach, or rather certain attributes of it, or the people implementing it that leads to these results. *Something* about this individualised approach, on wards in three different hospitals, seems to have led to lowered dependency levels. In our view, it is within the context of an individual-centred approach that psychological approaches to older people with dementia will have their greatest impact. This is borne out in work with people with dementia in the community, where individualised assessment and care-planning is emerging as feasible and valuable in a number of community support schemes (e.g. Challis & Davies 1985, 1986).

REMINISCENCE

In recent years there has been a surge of interest in using reminiscence with older people. Coleman (1986) provides a comprehensive account of theoretical and therapeutic aspects. One important factor has been the influential work of Butler (1963), developing the concept of 'life review', as a task to be accomplished in the last phase of life.

The person is seen as actively attempting to make sense of his or her life, its value, its purpose, the accomplishments, the disappointments, the joys and the sorrows. Acceptance is the goal of a successful life-review, despair the consequence of a life seen as useless and worthless. Encouraging

the person to reminisce was seen as a valuable therapeutic activity which helped the person get to grips with and put into perspective a lifetime of experiences. Reminiscence began to be seen as a positive activity, rather than as a negative attribute of old people, forever saying 'When I was young . . . . .'!
At least two other factors have also been important. Firstly, the increasing availability of aids to reminiscence. In life-review work, often old photographs and other memorabilia would be used to stimulate the person's recall of experiences from different phases of their life. In the UK, Help the Aged (1981) have produced 'Recall', a set of six tape-slide sequences depicting events and experiences spanning the years 1900 to the present, in a manner intended to be relevant to the current generations of older people. This pack and other photographic material, such as the 'Nostalgia' packs (edited by Holden 1984b), have, by their wide availability, stimulated many people working with older people to attempt reminiscence work with their clients, usually resulting in mutual enjoyment.

Secondly, many people working with older people with dementing conditions have discovered that talking about events in the person's past often helps communication and interaction, and that the more they understand the person's past life and experiences the more they can make sense of the person's current conversation and behaviour. As we shall see in Chapter 7, these findings form part of a practical approach to communicating with people with dementia, and often are included as an aspect of RO.

These different factors have all led to 'reminiscence therapy' being widely used, but there is still considerable confusion as to the aims, target population and techniques of the 'therapy'. As Merriam (1980) points out, the life-review process, where memories are analysed and evaluated, is only one form of reminiscence. Other types include *informative* reminiscence, 'telling a story' about past events and experiences and *simple* reminiscence, recalling the past. There is debate as to whether the person's memories should be brought up to date (as would usually occur in RO), or whether re-living the past is sufficient in itself. Reminiscence has been used both with patients who are depressed and those with dementia; it should be recognised that the aims and techniques may need to be different in each case. Norris (1986) provides an excellent description of the practical application of reminiscence techniques.

Coleman (1986) reports findings from a ten year study of the use of reminiscence by elderly people which have important implications for its therapeutic use. He identified four groups for whom reminiscence had different implications. Group I enjoyed reminiscing and maintained high morale throughout. Group II reminisced compulsively, but as their past had been full of troubles, this increased their depression and anxiety. The third group did not reminisce at all, as they found the present and future more stimulating. Like Group I, this group enjoyed high morale. The final group found the past a depressing topic, not because of past difficulties, but because of the contrast with a less fulfilling present. There is clearly a need to be aware of these individual differences, to learn as much about the individual as possible and to anticipate individual differences in response to reminiscence-based activities.

Life review, like bereavement, could well be a very private matter. Pressing those who dislike reminiscing to talk about the past could do more harm than good. The person will become either bored or even depressed. Careful enquiry relating to the person's attitudes and needs is required before rushing in! Empirical research on reminiscence with people with dementia is scarce. Thornton & Brotchie (1987) provide a detailed review. Few published studies are available, despite several positive anecdotal evaluations (e.g. Lesser et al 1981; Norris & Abu El Eileh 1982). Kiernat (1979) describes a life-review activity group. Twenty-three residents in a nursing home – all 'confused' – met twice a week for an hour in three groups for 10 weeks. Materials were brought in to stimulate discussion of the past, with attempts being made to use items to stimulate all the senses; obtaining these materials required a fair amount of preparation. Life-events were discussed in chronological order, up to the present time. It is not clear whether this refers to one session or to the whole period. Evaluation of the results is difficult, but it seems that residents who attended sessions most frequently showed the greatest improvement in their behaviour.

More recently, Baines et al (1987) have evaluated reminiscence in relation to RO in a study that will be discussed more fully in Chapter 3. Staff involved in a reminiscence group acquired much more individual knowledge of the residents in the group than they did of residents in a control group who received no additional treatment. Residents were rated as deriving a great deal of enjoyment from the groups both by staff taking part in the groups and staff who saw the residents only outside the groups. Attendance at the reminiscence groups was consistently high. The elderly people in the study were living in a residential home for the elderly, and all had a moderate to severe degree of cognitive impairment. Some effects on cognitive and behavioural function following reminiscence sessions were apparent in a group of five residents who had previously responded well to a month of RO sessions. They showed a reduction in scores on a problem behaviour rating scale, as well as an increase in verbal orientation. A group who had a month of reminiscence sessions before going onto RO sessions showed far fewer positive changes in relation to the untreated controls.

Baines et al's evaluation of a number of aspects of their treatment approaches is commendable. Enjoyment of sessions and greater staff knowledge of the residents may be just as important aims as improved cognition and behavioural function. They may indeed be more appropriate goals in working with people with dementing conditions. Further studies could usefully look at what happens in the group session. Does interaction between residents increase? Does reminiscence capture their attention and interest and stimulate response more than other activities? What styles of group leadership are most helpful in increasing residents' participation in discussion? How much analysis of events is required – is simple recall enough? Are particular prompts – music, pictures, objects – particularly helpful for different people? Then there are a number of other techniques to be examined. One-to-one work with more impaired people; life-history books for each patient, telling the person's life story in words and pictures, illustrated with appropriate personalised photographs from family albums and local history collections (e.g. Jones & Clark 1984); reminiscence outings, visiting places of interest and relevance from the person's past; reminiscence theatre, enacting events and experiences from the person's life (e.g. Langley & Corder 1978).

Reminiscence opens up many horizons in work with older people with dementia. There is a pressing need, not for research which tells us whether or not it's a 'good thing', but rather how best it can be carried out with different people, in different settings, for particular purposes.

REALITY ORIENTATION

Origins

Reality Orientation can be traced back to 1958 when an 'aide-centred activity programme for elderly patients' was set up at a Veterans Administration Hospital in Topeka, Kansas, USA, where Dr James Folsom was then working. Almost certainly RO existed before then, but at this time a structure and a name began to be applied. The programme went with Dr Folsom to the VA Hospital at Tuscaloosa, Alabama via Mount Pleasant, Iowa, and was further developed and refined. By the mid-1960s published descriptions began to appear (e.g. Taulbee & Folsom 1966) and the methods were beginning to crystallize. In 1969, the American Psychiatric Association published a short booklet, outlining the methods of RO together with the comments of a psychologist and a physician, entitled 'Reality Orientation: a technique to rehabilitate elderly and brain-damaged patients with a moderate to severe degree of disorientation' (edited by Louise Stephens). An RO training programme has been in existence at Tuscaloosa for ten years or more, and nurses and others working with the elderly from all over the USA and from other countries have participated in short training courses there. In 1978 the training team there published a practical guide to RO (Drummond et al 1978).

RO is of course now used in many countries. The first published account of its use in the UK was by Brook et al (1975). This was the first controlled study reported, and was carried out at Warley Hospital in Brentwood, Essex. It is likely that the methods were being used elsewhere in the UK before this. The growth of interest in the UK has been rapid; some adaptations and developments of the methods have been attempted. Workshops and courses on RO attract a great deal of interest and in a variety of settings throughout the country RO is being implemented in one form or another. It has been applied to other populations, e.g. younger people with head injuries (Corrigan et al 1985) and patients with chronic psychiatric problems (e.g. Wallis et al 1983). Several practical manuals are available, detailing techniques used in different implementations of RO (e.g. Cornbleth & Cornbleth 1977; Hanley 1982; Rimmer 1982). Countless descriptive articles have appeared in recent years (e.g. Hahn 1980; Holden 1979a,b; Hanley et al 1981b).

Varieties of RO

Three major components of RO are usually identified. The first is 24 hour RO (sometimes called 'informal RO' or the 'Basic approach'). This is a continual process whereby staff present current information to the person in every interaction, reminding the patient of time, place, and person and providing a commentary on events. Confused and rambling speech is not reinforced. The environment is structured with signs and cues to help the person remain aware of the surroundings. RO classes, or intensive sessions, are a supplement to 24 hour RO but in some centres have been used in isolation. These sessions are also variously called 'Intensive RO', 'Formal RO', 'RO Groups'. Sessions are held daily for half an hour to an hour with three to six patients depending on the level of impairment.

Group leaders do not require particular professional expertise, and qualities such as enthusiasm, a positive, flexible and creative approach are more important. Specific training in the procedures is needed however. Sessions may be divided into different levels according to the degree of deterioration. Often basic, standard and advanced levels are described. In Basic group sessions ('classes') the emphasis in on presentation and repetition of current information and orientation material related to simple information on day, weather, names and months. The Standard group uses sensory stimulation and past/present discussion to develop interpersonal relationships and learning. In the Advanced group there is less emphasis needed on basic orientation so activities are wider ranging. In some hospitals in the USA, 'graduation' ceremonies have been arranged when patients have benefited as much as possible from RO or are being promoted to an

Advanced group. A diploma is presented to a group member by a senior staff member. In the UK the emphasis has been more on a social setting than a classroom, with, for example, the use of simulated pubs. Possibly the creation of a social environment helps the patient to feel less pressured, more comfortable and less likely to withdraw than in a potentially threatening classroom situation. However, this factor may well be closely related to cultural aspects. In the USA graduation has greater social implications and connotations of increased self-esteem which are not operable in UK or in other countries which have their own situations associated with social pleasure, esteem and relaxation.

The final traditional component of RO is the use of prescribed attitudes (Attitude Therapy) to be used by all care staff with a particular patient. These include kind firmness, active friendliness, passive friendliness, matter of fact and no demand, which are chosen according to the patient's personality and needs. Their use is thought to facilitate staff consistency in approach to each patient. However, their actual use has been little documented and with some patients different attitudes may be required by different situations, thus complicating their use considerably.

Application of RO and relationship to other approaches

Obviously much more will be said about the effectiveness of RO in Chapter 3 and about the actual methods involved in Part II. In this chapter we have sought to describe other approaches so that RO can be seen in a wider context.

At this point we should stress that RO is specifically designed for people who are disorientated and have severe problems in memory and learning. It is appropriate for use with people suffering from the range of dementing conditions, although not limited to them. It is a flexible approach. Different levels of groups are described and it is appropriate for different degrees of impairment. It is based on interaction between staff and patient, both in the 24 hour RO and RO sessions, and provides, of course, many opportunities for prompting and social reinforcement of desired behaviour (often correct verbal orientation). It also involves environmental changes through the use of memory aids, signs etc.

Above all it is a communication approach that enables care staff to make contact with people with dementia, giving the staff member some principles to apply to a situation that is often fraught with difficulties and where crossed wires are more common than true communication.

RO involves staff and institutional attitudes; it involves positive attitudes which indicate that talking and explaining things to a person with dementia is worthwhile even if it seems to be forgotten immediately. It also involves a respect for the elderly person. Communication implies listening as well as talking, and listening applies to what is unspoken as well as what is verbalised. Without this respect no communication takes place and RO becomes a pointless exercise.

RO can operate in some ways as a prosthetic environment. In the group or outside the person is enabled to succeed. Clues and prompts are given, he or she is shown where to find the answer to the question. The person is asked questions that he or she is still able to answer. The effects of any memory problems are minimised rather than emphasised, as it is so easy to do. Perhaps by succeeding in this way the person will in fact function better as he or she gains confidence; certainly it will be a refreshing enjoyable change from the repeated failures which characterise the process of dementia.

There is much common ground with reminiscence. A major difference is that it is easier to envisage RO being applied in a continuous fashion, not only in specific sessions. When past events are used in RO they are always brought up-to-date so that the person is able to integrate past and present. The similarity with activity and stimulation approaches will become clearer when the methods are described in more detail, but certainly in RO sessions it is activity and stimulation that are often as apparent as the continuous orientation to current surroundings. Given the success (limited but clearly apparent) of these other approaches we would emphasise that they are not mutually exclusive, and we favour the strategy of using the most effective parts of each in any overall programme for a particular group of patients.

3

The effectiveness of RO

This chapter will consider what many would believe to be the fundamental issue about RO: does it work? The evidence that is available will be reviewed and discussed and related questions will be examined – such as under what conditions and with which elderly people it may be most effective – before identifying as yet unanswered questions that future research might profitably investigate. Most of the research that has been carried out on RO will be reviewed here; some of the implications of this research for theories about how RO might work will be extracted and discussed in the next chapter.

The evaluation of the efficacy of any treatment method is fraught with difficulties. Debates continue about the effectiveness of many well-established therapeutic methods with other client groups. In some ways the task is more difficult with elderly populations; patients fluctuate a great deal more, have more risk of becoming physically ill and even dying, perhaps quite independently of the treatment procedures being used. Other difficulties will become clear as the literature is reviewed but these general considerations do emphasise that a definitive, unqualified answer is almost impossible. Hopefully the present review will clarify some of the issues involved in answering 'does RO work?'

Finally, by way of introduction the importance of this question should be considered. It could be argued (as Hanley 1984 has done) that RO represents an approach to the patients that is to be valued on humanitarian grounds in that it gives emphasis to interactions based on respect, concern and recognition of individual identities. In this light RO may be a 'good' thing whether or not it changes the patients. What may be important is that staff and others concerned treat patients in a genuinely caring fashion. The question of 'does RO work?' remains. However, the emphasis is shifted from changes in the elderly person to changes in the caring person.

DOES RO WORK?

The final point above indicates the need for amplification of this apparently straightforward inquiry. Additionally it should be asked on whom it works, and also what is meant by 'work' in this context. Thus the issue must be raised of exactly how to tell if RO is working or not and what criteria might be applied. Taulbee & Folsom (1966), pioneers of RO, noticed that with some of their patients 'their look of hopelessness changed to hopefulness' when they began RO. If changes are occurring then it is necessary to define along what dimensions these changes are taking place, whether it be facial expression, memory for current events, self-care skills or whatever. As far as staff are concerned the changes might be in attitudes to their patients, changes in the way interactions are made with patients and so on.

A further complication with elderly people in particular arises over our concepts of change. Suppose measures of some attribute of the patient are made and then one month after they have begun RO that attribute is re-assessed. If it is exactly the same as before this could be thought of as indicating no change; but suppose that if that person had not had RO he or she would have deteriorated – as over a period of time patients with a dementia are usually considered to do – then absence of change may still indicate a positive effect of treatment. Thus even a deterioration could still be consistent with a positive effect of treatment, as long as the deterioration is less than it would have been without treatment!

So changes are being sought – in patients or staff – that are more positive than they would have been without RO. 'Positive' can be difficult to define more precisely; it is straightforward enough if memory is being assessed – improved memory is a positive change. However 'amount of complaining' is another matter; some might see it as a good thing if the person becomes more complaining and asserts himself or herself more; others might see it as an unnecessary nuisance. Value judgements may then come into play here; generally changes in the direction of more independence on the part of the patient and more recognition of the elderly person as an adult individual by the staff are viewed as positive, but there will of course be grey areas, open to debate and interpretation.

DOES RO CHANGE THOSE EMPLOYING IT?

The effects on care-staff of using RO have been relatively little explored. Effects on relatives using it have not been examined in any systematic way. Taulbee & Folsom (1966) described how RO could involve nursing assistants, who spend much more time in contact with the patients than any of the other professionals, becoming members of the rehabilitation team. Through RO they become more than agents of physical care, they become in effect therapists; clearly in some instances this could lead to greater job satisfaction and morale. Holden & Sinebruchow (1978) actually had as an objective of their study of RO the development of 'an approach which would attract the interest of nursing staff' and reported, anecdotally, that providing the nursing staff with their own therapeutic approach had given them a sense of achievement. In contrast, Woods (1979) reported that care-attendants in his study of RO reported a preference for leading a social conversation group rather than an RO group. The extra resources of imagination, creativity and planning needed to prevent RO sessions from being boringly repetitive were seen as being important here. It may be that staff in different settings and of different back-grounds react differently to carrying out RO – and may well use quite distinct methods. The whole question of staff-attitudes will be discussed in more practical detail in Chapter 10. In one study staff attitudes to elderly people were assessed before and after an intensive five day training programme in the RO approach. Smith & Barker (1972) report a marked increase in positive attitudes to the elderly in a group of 94 trainees, which was maintained after a six month interval. A variety of occupational groups were included, but generally did not differ in their amount of attitudinal change. This is an encouraging result – especially as attitudes are often extremely difficult to modify so quickly. It should be noted, however, that it is in response to training in RO and that the trainees were not necessarily involved in RO over the succeeding six month period. What we are considering here is more an attitude change in response to *involvement* in RO over a period of time. Bailey et al (1986) attempted to assess such a change in staff involved in implementing 24 hour RO on a ward in a geriatric hospital. Using the same measure as

Smith & Barker (the Oberleder scale), no change in attitudes to elderly people was evident over a five month period.

There are a number of difficulties in assessing attitude change in this way. Neither before or after the study were the scores of the staff in the range which would imply a negative attitude to the elderly. The questions may well not relate to the particular group of elderly people with whom the staff are working. It would be quite possible for someone to have positive attitudes towards the 'elderly' and negative attitudes towards the actual patients on the ward, with all their disabilities, demands and needs. Finally, as the authors point out, such questionnaires may readily be answered in the positive, socially desirable direction, and may show little relationship to actual practice (see also Adelson et al 1982; Saxby & Jeffrey 1983).

In an interesting and detailed study Baines et al (1987) used an information questionnaire and semi-structured interviews to explore staff reactions to leading RO and reminiscence sessions. They showed that both types of group led to staff having much more personal knowledge of the residents involved – an important step towards individualised care. After 4 weeks of group sessions, staff were able to answer correctly an average of 25 items about each resident, compared with 5 items initially. After a further 4 weeks of group meetings, staff scores had increased to an average of 29 items per resident. The effect was specific to knowledge about residents within the groups. There was no change in scores relating to information about patients who had not been involved. The interview data suggested staff reappraised their view of the ability of residents with dementia to respond to a small group. They found the sessions more beneficial than they had anticipated in improving their communication with and their knowledge of the residents. Job satisfaction was also reported to be increased. Staff morale, sense of achievement and job satisfaction have been reported to be improved in several studies (e.g. Merchant & Saxby 1981) and would merit more systematic attention in future research.

Although it is of course highly desirable to see changes in these aspects, part of their value has to be in increasing the elderly person's quality of life, by improving the quality of staff–patient interaction. In fact there is remarkably little evidence to show that staff carrying out RO actually behave differently from their previous practice. Only three studies have attempted to examine empirically whether the RO programme was being implemented as planned.

Clearly if long-term beneficial effects in attitude and morale are to be attributed to involvement in RO there must be some indication that RO is actually in operation. Change in a person's behaviour is often a precursor to attitude change.

An increase in the proportion of time the care-worker acts in a manner consistent with RO may well be seen as a desirable aim, if the RO approach to the person is seen as incorporating humanitarian values. Particularly with 24 hour RO, it can be difficult to ensure RO is being carried out appropriately. If the frequency of staff–patient interactions is very low the amount of 24 hour RO that is possible must also be low. Woods & Britton (1985, Ch. 9) show that many institutions are indeed characterised by low levels of staff–patient interaction. Even in the group setting, patently un-reality orientated statements are made by staff from time to time. If they occcur there, they are almost certain to occur in the broader environment of the ward.

One study has examined the quality of RO carried out in RO sessions before and after specific training in RO techniques ((Woods et al 1980). Training consisted of a talk illustrated with slides; discussion, a handout summarising the major points, some demonstration and role-play of RO techniques. RO group sessions were recorded on audio-tape and then analysed to assess changes in RO behaviour. A critical issue here was to define precisely the nature of RO behaviour – in this case of course only verbal behaviour could be considered. This proved to be a difficult task. Different workers view RO in slightly different ways, and it is probably fair to say that it is a dynamic, developing concept. However an operational definition was finally arrived at (Table 3.1) and each staff statement on the tapes carefully categorized accordingly. Table 3.2 shows the findings with a significant increase in the proportion of RO behaviour occurring after training. The proportion of negative RO statements showed little change; training seemed to help these staff be more

Table 3.1 Operational definitions of verbal RO

These are guidelines for placing remarks made by leaders in RO sessions into the following three categories:

1. *RO* – remarks and comments in line with the methods of RO and so aiding the RO process.

2. *Negative RO* – remarks and comments clearly in direct contradiction to the methods of RO giving person incorrect information, encouraging incorrect response etc.

3. *Neutral* – these are things said that do not fall into either of the above categories; they neither aid nor hinder RO; they neither orientate nor disorientate the person.

For making this decision the following general definition of verbal RO is used:

staff verbal behaviour that orientates residents to reality

orient – to acquaint with the existing situation

reality – that which has actual existence and is not merely an idea or imaginary

Thus statements giving the person correct, current information are clearly RO.

However, when displaced reality is being discussed for RO to be coded the displacement must be made clear in the statement e.g. 'You *used* to work as a tailor, Mrs Smith'.

When a question is asked it is coded RO if:

a. it gives the person information also, e.g. 'Have you seen the rain outside, Mr Jones?'

b. it is about a point of fact and the staff member has the information available to check the person's response

c. it relates to feelings or opinions *and* provides some information e.g. 'Did you like your dinner of *fish and chips* today, Mr Brown?'

Other comments are coded as RO if they reinforce the person's previous reality-orientated behaviour e.g. praise, repetition, encouragement, agreement may all be RO responses.

Table 3.2 Mean proportions of staff statements consistent with RO, inconsistent with RO and neutral in RO sessions carried out by five staff members before and after training

	Before training	After training
RO statements	77.4%	89.4%*
Neutral statements	21.1%	9.4%*
Negative RO statements	1.5%	1.2%

* Before-after difference significant at 5% level (correlated t-test, 1 tailed).

efficient RO leaders, with less remarks being 'wasted' (from an RO viewpoint) following training.

Some of the post-training recordings were made some one to two months after training so this effect is probably not merely transitory although its duration is of course uncertain. In the same study it proved impossible to carry out a similar exercise outside the RO group room and to evaluate the effects of training on the amount of 24 hour RO carried out. A high proportion of the staff-resident interaction occurred in relation to bathing, dressing, toileting etc., and not in the 'public' areas of the Home where interactions might be observed relatively unobtrusively. However, Hanley (1984) has been able to attempt such an investigation, and reports considerable difficulty in implementing 24 hour RO in a hospital setting. He devised a system in order to assess both the quantity and *quality* of 24 hour RO being carried out, before and after the implementation of 24 hour RO.

He found no change in the number of interactions staff had with patients (approximately nine interactions per patient in an eight hour period), and even more disappointingly no change in the *quality* of the interactions, measured by the mean number of the following six features of 24 hour RO present per interaction.

Quality features of 24 hour RO (as used by Hanley 1984)
Staff member: engages patient verbally
              names patient
              names self
              refers to time or place
              explains procedure
              refers to orientation aid

Most discouraging of all was that when staff rated their own interactions with patients they indicated that they thought they were carrying out many of these procedures, when the direct observation of interactions indicated clearly that they were not. For example all 15 nursing staff involved said that most of the time they called the patient by name, whereas in fact this only occurred in 48 per cent of the interactions. All staff said that most of the time they explained procedures to the patients, but this only occurred in 14 per cent of the interactions and finally 13 of the 15 nurses stated that they named themselves and the same number said they referred to aids at least once in a while. Neither of these interactions occurred in *any* interactions observed. Hanley's work raised serious doubts as to the extent to which 24 hour RO is actually implemented. More recently Reeve & Ivison (1985) have obtained more positive results. In 24 hour RO they have focussed on the staff member's reaction to the patient, rather than on staff-initiated interaction. Their results, again from direct observation, showed an increase in staff behaviour consistent with RO following training. There were further improvements as the project continued.

As has been demonstrated in other settings (e.g. Milne 1985) it is not sufficient to train staff in a particular procedure and then simply to expect that staff behaviour will change in relation to their patients. Nor is it sufficient to ask staff whether they are putting the procedure into practice. Ways of ensuring the training has had an effect, and of developing more effective training are of great importance.

RO is not implemented in a vacuum. In different institutions 24 hour RO will already be applied to differing degrees, there will be different types of staff, different attitudes, different institutional goals. The effects of different institutions on the implementation of 24 hour RO is of great practical importance, but is difficult to evaluate satisfactorily. The extent to which the institution values staff-patient interaction, patient independence, is patient- rather than staff-centred, and is rehabilitative rather than custodial, will all have an impact on 24 hour RO.

Work on evaluating changes in staff is relatively underdeveloped. Some positive changes in staff attitude have been reported, although aspects such as staff morale and job satisfaction have yet to be evaluated in detail. Some increase in behaviour consistent with RO in RO sessions and in 24 hour RO has now been found following training. Little is known of the long-term effects on staff carrying out RO, whether positive attitudes are maintained, or whether the RO itself is maintained, without additional training and support. These areas are worth exploring, together with the effects on relatives of being asked to carry out RO – whether they can use it, what factors make it difficult for them to carry it out and how their attitudes to their elderly relative change through using RO.

DOES RO CHANGE THE PATIENT?

Anecdotal reports and uncontrolled studies

A great deal of the early work on evaluation of RO consisted of anecdotal material, case reports, uncontrolled studies and so on. Although carefully controlled data is needed to answer the question the anecdotal material gives some indication of the dimensions along which change may take place and the possibilities that might exist.

The picture emerging from the early studies at the Veteran's Administration Hospitals at Topeka, Mount Pleasant and Tuscaloosa is of patients becoming livelier, more socially active, more cooperative, showing improvements in self-care and generally having more dignity and pride in themselves and their accomplishments (Taulbee & Folsom 1966; Folsom 1967, 1968). The implication is that patients were discharged who would otherwise have remained in hospital (Stephens 1969). Interestingly, some of the early case studies featured patients who had been in hospital for many years with chronic psychiatric problems, rather than patients admitted from the community suffering from a dementia.

A number of studies have been reported using a 'before and after' design, looking at changes in patients following RO, but lacking any control group to allow for changes that might have occurred if the RO had not been implemented. For instance, Cornbleth & Cornbleth (1979) reported general behavioural improvements related to the introduction of RO sessions, over a 3 month period in 22 male patients suffering from dementia. With the exception of a study by Barnes (1974) the results have generally been encouraging. Barnes reported no improvements in residents' verbal orientation after six weeks of RO sessions; there was a clear decline in performance as soon as the RO sessions stopped. However, staff at the nursing home felt there were positive changes, not detected by the assessment measures used. This is an oft-repeated theme in the RO outcome literature – something is happening, but we just don't seem to be able to measure it!

There are particular problems in carrying out evaluation studies with an elderly population in a hospital or home setting where many factors are outside the researcher's control. In Barnes' study, for instance, half the subjects were lost through death, ill health, non-attendance at sessions and so on, and some patients' medication was changed, for physical reasons. This can lead to studies using small numbers of patients, with very short intervention periods. Well-designed controlled studies, using appropriate assessment measures, are needed as there is a danger of continuing with programmes that are ineffective because they *appear* to be useful. There is the danger of wasting staff time and raising false expectations. Also the procedures used may never be refined nor matched with the particular patients for whom they are most likely to be beneficial. Anecdotal reports and uncontrolled studies are helpful in programme development and in the identification of likely areas of change, but there must be more stringently controlled trials to take our knowledge further.

Controlled trials of RO

The first controlled trial of RO was carried out by Brook et al (1975) at Warley Hospital, England. Eighteen patients were assigned either to daily RO sessions or to control groups. The control patients went to a specially equipped RO room for half-an-hour a day but simply sat in a circle and, unlike the RO group, received no encouragement from the therapists to use the RO materials; their questions were answered as briefly as possible. Ratings of the patients' self-care, orientation, socialisation etc. were made fortnightly by nursing staff who were not aware to which group particular patients belonged and so could not have been inadvertently biased in favour of RO. Results were presented for three levels of initial functioning, high, medium and low, so that any differential effects of RO at different levels of patient functioning might be seen. The results are shown in Figure 3.1; all groups seemed to improve in the first two weeks. After this the control groups deteriorated while the RO groups either maintained progress or continued to improve. The most deteriorated patients showed the least improvement in RO.

This first controlled study clearly favours RO with this group of elderly psychiatric patients (all but one having a diagnosis of dementia) whose mean length of stay in hospital was just under two years. Note that changes in observed behaviour

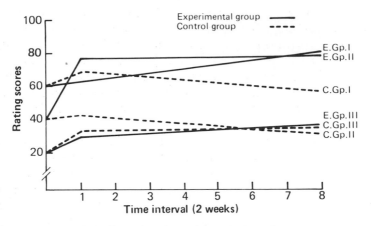

Fig. 3.1 Ratings of intellectual and social functioning of patients in RO (experimental) and control groups by nursing staff unaware of group membership over the 16-week experimental period. Reproduced, with permission, from Brook et al 1975, British Journal of Psychiatry 127: 42–45

were found, and these were backed up by anecdotal reports (Degun 1976) of improvements in incontinence and table-manners, reductions in withdrawn social behaviour and so on. Two patients at least were discharged, where continued hospital care might have been the expectation. Again patients initially more demented showed less improvements generally. Although only one or two patients were thought to regress after the end of the study period, no systematic follow-up seems to have been carried out. These changes were found using RO sessions in isolation from 24 hour RO, but add weight to the possible effectiveness of the total programme. It can be argued that if improvements are possible with just three hours or so therapy a week, the potential of 24 hour RO could be very great indeed. The study does not of course prove that RO produced the reported changes. The RO group received additional attention from interested, enthusiastic staff, whereas the control group had the experience of being taken somewhere novel and potentially interesting, but then being virtually ignored! Being exposed to RO techniques was not then the only important difference in the way the groups were treated.

Since 1975 a number of other controlled trials have been reported. These are summarised in Table 3.3. In order to draw conclusions from these studies it is important to notice the many differences between them – in target population, in setting where the project was carried out, in intensity of RO used, in the experimental period, in the methods of assessment used etc. Some of these important variables are listed in Table 3.3. The cross-national diagnostic differences mentioned in Chapter 2 are again of relevance here in interpreting results obtained.

In a state mental hospital, Harris & Ivory (1976) evaluated the effects of 24 hour RO and RO sessions introduced on one ward, using a similar ward where traditional treatment was given as a comparison group. A number of significant changes in verbal orientation were found over the five month treatment period, and improvements in the psychiatric aides general ratings of the RO patients' orientation, 'crazy talk' and social interaction were also evident. Attempts to assess behavioural change in other areas – dressing, self-care etc., were largely unsuccessful, apparently due to pre-treatment group differences, which the authors attribute to different expectations of the staff on the two wards. On face-washing and bathing – where comparisons were made – no improvements were noted. Harris & Ivory point out some of the methodological difficulties with their study; the RO ward received much more external attention than the control ward, it acquired the status of a 'special' ward and thus staff morale there was probably higher. By carrying out RO the staff gave the patients much more attention than they normally received. The aides who carried out RO also carried out the various assessments and so may have been expecting improvements more than their control counterparts, although as the two assessment periods were separated by five months this probably had little effect. There is, however, reinforcement for the hypothesis that RO – through attention, innovation or of itself – is related to more change than is no treatment, in this case with rather young, long-stay patients (presumably with chronic psychiatric conditions).

Similar results with much older patients were obtained by Citrin & Dixon (1977). After 2 months of the total RO programme, patients showed improvements on a test of verbal orientation compared with untreated controls. However, on the Geriatric Rating Scale, covering more

Table 3.3 Controlled studies of RO

Authors	Location	Setting	Mean age	Mean length of stay	24-hour RO	No. of RO sessions per week	Number and sex of subjects	Control groups	Duration	Assessment methods
Brook, Degun & Mather 1975	Warley Essex UK	Psychiatric hospital. Dementia (1 head injury)	73.3	1.9 years	No	Daily	18 10F 8M 9 RO 9 Control	Group taken daily to RO room No active therapy	16 weeks	Behaviour Rating Scale
Harris & Ivory 1976	Florida USA	State Hospital CBS, OBS, others	66.6	24.6 years	Yes	Daily	29 RO 28 Control all F	NT	5 months	Florida State Hospital Behaviour Rating Scale (i) Ward behaviour (ii) Verbal orientation (iii) Aides' impressions
Citrin & Dixon 1977	Nebraska USA	Nursing home Moderately disorientated	84	—	Yes	Daily	12 RO 13 Control	NT	2 months	RO information sheet Geriatric rating scale (GRS)

Study	Location	Setting	Age	Length of stay	Control	No. sessions	Numbers		Duration	Measures
MacDonald & Settin 1978	New York USA	Nursing home	64.4	—	No	3	10 RO 10 SW 10 NT 21F 9M	SW NT	5 weeks	Life Satisfaction Index NOSIE (nurses' rating) Behavioural Mapping Index
Voelkel 1978	Ohio USA	Nursing home Moderate/ severely mentally impaired	80+	2.67 years	No	3	10 RO 10 RS 19F 1M	RS	6 weeks	Mental status Questionnaire. PSMS Physical self-maintenance scale
Holden & Sinebruchow 1978	Leeds UK	Geriatric Hospital CVA, dementia, others	77	1.43 years	Yes	5–6	46 13M 33F 30 RO 16 NT	NT	3 months	Stockton Geriatric Rating Scale Clifton Assessment Schedule
Woods 1979	Newcastle-upon-Tyne UK	EMI Homes Dementia	76.6	Less than 3 years	No	5	14 12F 2M 5 RO 4NT 5 SA	SA NT	5 months	Wechsler Memory Scale, Concentration test, Information and Orientation test, Gibson Spiral Maze, Crichton Geriatric rating scale

Table 3.3 (Cont'd)

Authors	Location	Setting	Mean age	Mean length of stay	24-hour RO	No. of RO sessions per week	Number and sex of subjects	Control groups	Duration	Assessment methods
Holden & Sinebruchow 1979	Leeds UK	Geriatric hospital CVA, dementia others	80.3	0.9 years	Yes	5–6	16 6M 10F	NT	3 months	Crichton Geriatric Rating Scale Holden Communication Scale
Hogstel 1979	Texas USA	Nursing homes Confused, senile or disorientated	82.2	—	No	5	20 RO 20NT	NT	3 weeks	18 item orientation questionnaire
Johnson, McLaren & McPherson 1981	Dundee UK	Psychiatric hospital Dementia	80.1	—	No	5–10	75 RO 23 NT	NT	1 month	26 item orientation questionnaire
Zepelin, Wolfe & Kleinplatz 1981	Detroit USA	Nursing homes Dementia, CVA	82.4	—	Yes	5	36 32F 4M 22 RO 14 NT	NT	1 year	24 item orientation test 7 Activities of Daily Living Scales 3 Appropriateness of Behaviour scales

Hanley McGuire & Boyd 1981	Edinburgh UK	Psychogeriatric hospital Old peoples' Home Dementia	79 81	—	No	4	57 53F 4M 28 RO 29 NT	NT	3 months	Geriatric Rating Scale Koskela Test (includes verbal orientation) Orientation Test
Merchant & Saxby 1981	Plymouth UK	Geriatric hospital 'mildly to moderately confused'	83	3 years	No	Daily	10 4M 6F	NT	8 weeks	Clifton Assessment Procedure Crichton Geriatric Rating Scale Holden Communication Scale Slater and Lipman Confusion Scales
Goldstein, Turner, Holzman, Kanagy, Elmore & Barry 1982	Pittsburgh USA	VA Medical Centre Dementia, Neurological disorders	59.1	1.46 years	No	5	14M	NT	3 weeks	18 item orientation test Activity level rating
Wallis, Baldwin & Higginbotham 1983	Yorkshire UK	Psychiatric hospital Dementia (20) Schizophrenia (14) Affective (4)	69.8	organics: 3.7 years Functionals: 19.7 years	No	5	38 25M 13F 18 RO 20 OT	OT	3 months	Crichton Geriatric Rating Scale Orientation test

Table 3.3 (Cont'd)

Authors	Location	Setting	Mean age	Mean length of stay	24-hour RO	No. of RO sessions per week	Number and sex of subjects	Control groups	Duration	Assessment methods
Reeve & Ivison 1985	Sydney Australia	Psychogeriatric ward Dementia	Over 65	—	Yes	3	19	ST	3 months	Crichton Geriatric Rating Scale Holden Communication Scale CAPE Orientation test Mini-Mental Status Test Ward orientation Scale
Baines, Saxby & Ehlert 1987	Plymouth UK	Old people's home moderate/severe cognitive impairment	81.5	3.3 years	No	5	15 14F 1M	REM NT	4 months	CAPE cognitive tests CAPE Behaviour rating scale Holden Communication Scale Problem behaviour rating scale Life satisfaction index

OT = Occupational Therapy
NT = No Treatment Control
OBS = Organic Brain Syndrome
CBS = Chronic Brain Syndrome
REM = Reminiscence
CVA = Cerebrovascular Accident
SW = Sheltered Workshop
RS = Resocialisation
EMI = Elderly Mentally Infirm
SA = Social Attention

general aspects of behaviour, the authors conclude that 'it is questionable whether RO had any effects on the behavioural functioning of the residents involved'. Some doubt must apply to this statement as the RO group showed a significantly better level of behaviour after treatment than the controls, where before treatment there had been no significant difference between the groups. This seems to be overruled by the authors as the RO group were (non-significantly) better before treatment. Perhaps a statistical analysis allowing for this could have led to more conclusive results. So there were definite cognitive improvements, but more general changes remained doubtful. The problem of the RO group receiving greater attention than the control group – present in all three reports – can be overcome by the controls receiving an alternative therapy offering a comparable amount of staff input. If it is seen as relevant and as likely to succeed as RO then staff expectancy effects may also be brought into line. In attempting to control for quantity of staff attention inevitably RO sessions are the prime focus, as it is much more practical to have alternative therapies for a fixed time period than to have a continuous therapy parallel with 24 hour RO. MacDonald & Settin (1978) and Voelkel (1978) compared three times weekly RO classes with other therapies – a sheltered workshop and resocialisation groups respectively. In neither study were behavioural changes shown in the nursing home populations used. Voelkel's resocialisation group improved more on an information and orientation test than the RO group – but the RO group before treatment were generally at a lower level, so the resocialisation group, Voelkel suggests, may have had more capacity for re-learning and responding to their group. MacDonald & Settin's assessment of changes was more wide-ranging than any previous study and included an index of life-satisfaction (LSI) in self-report form. On this scale, and on nurses' ratings of the resident's social interest, the sheltered workshop group improved; the RO group in fact tended to deteriorate on the LSI, whereas untreated controls showed little change.

These two studies, both tending to favour alternative approaches challenge the efficacy of RO. Were they however a fair test of RO? Scarbrough et al (1978) certainly argued that MacDonald & Settin's interpretation of RO was erroneous.

Voelkel's description of her resocialisation group resembles closely activities other workers have used in RO. MacDonald & Settin's sheltered workshop group would certainly be beyond the capabilities of many patients included in other RO programmes. They comment that their RO residents mentioned to staff 'that the sessions seem boring and useless'. Similarly Voelkel states that most of her RO participants read the RO board without any difficulties and several were irritated at having to read the information, the approach thus appearing child-like. It seems clear that in both studies the RO technique may not have been pitched at the appropriate level for the residents concerned and the alternative therapies may have been much more rewarding and satisfying for the residents. There is an indication here that RO must be adjusted appropriately for the residents involved, and that techniques appropriate for severely disorientated patients may need to be withdrawn with patients who are more in touch with reality. This highlights the difficulties of defining exactly what RO is or is not.

Woods (1979) also controlled for the effects of staff attention. Residents with a severe degree of memory disorder either attended RO sessions or a conversation group each held on five days a week for 30 minutes, over a five month period. A similar group of residents in another Home received no additional treatment but were assessed at the same intervals as those in the experimental groups. The care attendants in the conversation (or 'social therapy') group were instructed to encourage the residents to talk about anything at all and to praise them for participating. RO materials were not used in this group (although it was held in the RO room) and residents were not corrected if they began to ramble. In addition to the often-used information/orientation test and a behaviour rating scale, other cognitive measures were used including the Wechsler Memory Scale (the WMS assesses a number of different aspects of memory and learning) and a concentration test. The results of the various cognitive assessments were clearly in favour of the RO group. Significant differences were found on the concentration test, information/orientation test and on the Wechsler Memory Scale (Figs. 3.2, 3.3 and 3.4). On the concentration test the 'social therapy' group seemed to fare worse than even the untreated

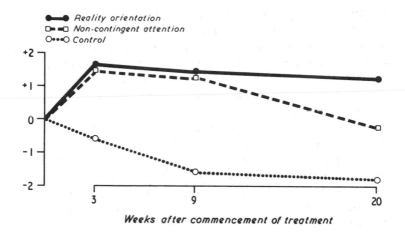

Fig. 3.2 Mean changes in total score on composite concentration test over time in Woods' (1979) study. Non-contingent attention group significantly less improved than RO throughout, and relative to untreated control group at 3 and 9 weeks.

group. Further unpublished analysis of results from this study suggests that the WMS improvement was not simply related to its information/orientation and concentration components. Although these are two of the three factors consistently found

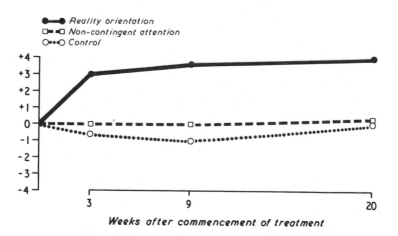

Fig. 3.3 Mean change in total score on composite information and orientation test over time in Woods' (1979) study. RO significantly more improved throughout than combined control groups (which do not differ).

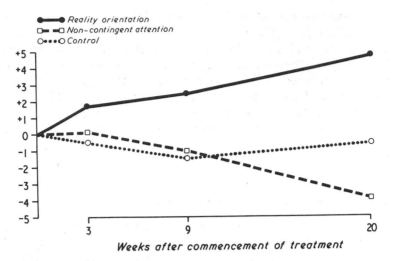

● Reality orientation
□ Non-contingent attention
○ Control

Weeks after commencement of treatment

Fig. 3.4 Mean change in total score on Wechsler Memory Scale over time in Woods' (1979) study. RO significantly more improved at 9 and 20 weeks than control groups combined, which do not differ throughout.

in factor analysis of the WMS (Kear Colwell 1973) in fact it is on the other factor (Kear Colwell's Factor I), which is interpreted as a measure of new learning, that the RO group improved significantly more than the two control groups after nine weeks of treatment. (Mann Whitney U test, $U = 4$, $n_1 = 5$, $n_2 = 9$; $p < 0.025$, 1 tailed). Thus more general cognitive improvements seemed to be occurring here. Despite these encouraging findings in the cognitive sphere no behavioural changes could be demonstrated on the Crichton Geriatric Rating Scale, modified to facilitate comparisons with Brook et al's (1975) results. Possible reasons for this will be discussed later, but certainly the RO sessions were successful in changing the cognitive area of functioning on which they directly focussed. That the conversation group was a viable alternative therapy as far as care staff were concerned was demonstrated by their previously mentioned preference for this group over the RO group, which they found more taxing to lead.

The study reported by Hogstel (1979) is one of the few not to show changes in verbal orientation following RO sessions, when comparisons are made with untreated controls. In contrast, Johnson et al (1981) report significant changes in orientation in a similar study. It is difficult to explain such discrepant findings. Although the duration of treatment was very short in the Hogstel study (3 weeks), other studies have shown changes at this point (e.g. Woods 1979) and Johnson et al only had a 4 week treatment period. They did, however, include many more patients in their trial, and also used a rather longer orientation questionnaire that might perhaps be better able to be sensitive to the small changes involved.

Does general behavioural change occur?

Two large-scale, carefully conducted studies, both published in 1981, highlight this issue. At that time only one study had reported generalised behavioural changes (Brook et al 1975), whereas three other studies had been unable to find convincing evidence of behavioural change. The results from these two studies are remarkably similar. Hanley et al (1981) carried out RO sessions in both long-stay psychogeriatric wards and an old people's home, 4 times a week over a 3 month period. Some small but significant changes in verbal orientation were found, but no differences were evident on a behaviour rating scale. Zepelin et al (1981) carried out the longest reported trial, incorporating both 24 hour RO and RO sessions, over a one year period. The comparison group came from another nursing home. Again, statistically significant changes in verbal orientation could be identified (more so in the first 6 months than the second half of the year). On the various measures of behavioural functioning used, the only significant differences favoured the untreated control group, who were rated as becoming more socially responsive, and as gaining more bladder and bowel control over the year, with changes in the second half of the year on dressing skills and mobility.

The question of whether changes occur in the person's performance of self-care and other tasks and in the person's social behaviour is very important. Changes in verbal orientation are interesting and potentially have some usefulness but there is no doubt that it is improvements in self-care, in finding the toilet, in dressing and in social interaction and so on that workers and relatives would prefer to see, and one might hypothesise that these general changes would do more to increase the person's dignity and self-respect.

It might be argued that behavioural changes are not found in some studies as 24 hour RO is not utilized and so the potential for reinforcing appropriate behaviour outside the actual RO room is not utilized. This is untenable however as the one study that did show general changes in functioning used only the RO room and several studies using 24 hour RO found no changes. Of course, as commented previously, the intensity of the 24 hour RO received might be questioned as it is difficult to establish to what extent it actually occurs and perhaps future work might relate degrees of behavioural change to actual intensity of 24 hour RO. It might be argued that RO cannot be expected to bring about general changes in functioning, as its focus on reorientation is so distinctly cognitive. However, the 24 hour approach is intended to be used during activities of daily living (e.g. Drummond et al 1978) and there continue to be anecdotal reports of changes in, for example, increased participation, greater interest and recognition, even in studies where no objective changes favouring RO have been demonstrated (Zepelin et al 1981).

Possibly, as Woods (1979) suggested concerning the results of his study, the measures of behaviour used are too insensitive, but in the various investigations a variety of measures have been used. The emphasis on group changes may obscure changes in the individual's behaviour and Woods (1979) for example pointed out that the variation in behaviour rating scores increased greatly over the course of his study, indicating that individuals were changing in different ways. In a later section the limited amount of research looking at individuals in-depth rather than at groups of patients will be reviewed. Rating scales can be problematic however and different raters may use the same scale in quite different ways, and it may be that more attention is needed to training raters in the consistent use of the scale or in developing other more reliable methods of assessing behaviour.

In Zepelin et al's study, two of five behavioural measures had to be abandoned because of poor inter-rater agreement. Zepelin et al also point out the difficulties of different raters in the homes at different times making ratings which are then compared with each other – this is particularly so where the control group come from a different ward or home.

There are now several further studies which have succeeded in showing behavioural change on a variety of rating scales. Holden & Sinebruchow (1979) used the Holden Communication Scale (see Ch. 6 and Appendix 2), covering particularly conversation, awareness, knowledge and communication, in addition to the Crichton Geriatric Rating Scale (as used by Woods 1979). In a previous study, Holden and Sinebruchow (1978) had been unable to demonstrate any differences between RO groups and no-treatment controls over a 12 week period using the Stockton Geriatric Rating Scale and the Clifton Assessment Schedule but found differences in outcome nonetheless (see Fig. 3.5) which led them to conclude that these particular assessment techniques were unsatisfactory in this context. It should be noted here that discharge as an outcome should be treated with some caution as it is greatly influenced by the patient's social circumstances and hospital policy.

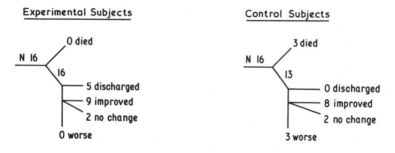

Fig. 3.5 Tree table. Outcome of controlled study based on CAS and Stockton ratings, plus discharge records. Holden & Sinebruchow 1978. Reproduced, with permission, from Age and Ageing 7: 83–90

The setting for the second study was once more a geriatric ward and diagnoses included dementia, depression, Parkinson's disease, strokes etc. The patient were split into two groups who received formal RO sessions alternately for one month each over a three month period. Following their month as an RO group the group would remain together on the ward whilst the other group went to a special room, fitted out in the style of a pub. The nursing staff had considerable experience of RO and certainly to some extent used it on the ward as in 24 hour RO.

The results of the study are shown in Figures 3.6 and 3.7. On the Holden Communication Scale Group I improved markedly in its first RO session period and continued to improve during the control period – perhaps underlining the ward nurses' continuation of the RO. Group 2 really began to improve after the cross-over; some of their gains were lost when they became controls again. The scale may be sensitive to the effects of illness (a viral infection) which affected many patients on the ward at points 3 and 6. The results of the Crichton Scale are similar, again documenting behavioural changes commencing during the group's first period of formal RO sessions and to some extent being maintained and improved on during subsequent control periods. Group 1 showed a significant improvement on this scale between the beginning and end of the study and on both scales the rate of change was significantly different between the two groups in the first two weeks of formal RO sessions.

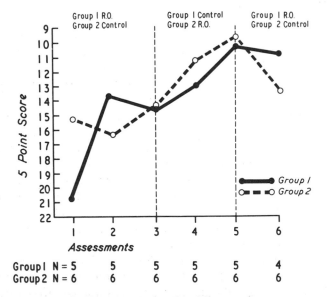

Fig. 3.6 Holden Communication Scale. The difference between improvement rates of Group I and Group II up to assessment 2 were significant (P<0.05)..Holden & Sinebruchow 1979.

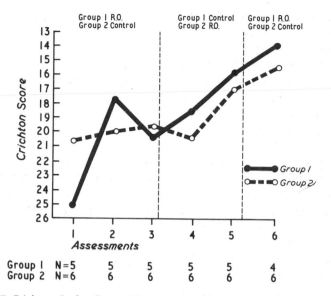

Fig. 3.7 Crichton Scale. Group I improvement between assessment 1 and 6 was significant (P<0.05). The difference between improvement rate of Group I and Group II up to assessment 2 was significant (P<0.05). Holden & Sinebruchow 1979.

There are some drawbacks to the study: the raters were not completely 'blind' to group membership; the control condition may well not have been a pure 'no-treatment' condition after the first month; diagnostic criteria in geriatric wards may differ from other settings and the relationship of the results to diagnosis is unclear. Also in a geriatric ward, with patients with mixed diagnoses, Merchant & Saxby (1981) report improvements in orientation, awareness of others, communication, conversational ability and in socially acceptable behaviour following 8 weeks of RO sessions, compared with control subjects drawn from the same ward. As in Holden & Sinebruchow's studies the emphasis was on a social atmosphere, and Merchant & Saxby emphasise the enjoyment their patients gained from the RO sessions.

In a psychogeriatric ward, Reeve & Ivison (1985) found improvements on the Holden Communication Scale and the Crichton Scale as well as in verbal orientation after 4 weeks of RO sessions. This improvement remained statistically significant for those patients who continued to attend RO sessions for a further 8 weeks. Control patients, again from the same ward, attended discussion groups for an equivalent amount of time.

Baines et al (1987) conducted a study in a large residential home for the elderly. One group of residents attending RO sessions showed a significant improvement on the Clifton Behaviour Rating Scale compared with untreated controls, and residents attending reminiscence sessions. However, when there was a cross-over of treatment and the group orig- inally receiving reminiscence sessions took part in RO sessions, they did not show corresponding behavioural improvements. In fact the group that received RO first continued to improve on verbal orientation during the phase of the study when the residents were attending reminiscence sessions. Thus in this study the positive changes seemed to relate more to a particular group of residents rather than to the specific form of treatment – although the authors attribute their findings to the sequence of the treatments with RO followed by reminiscence being superior to reminiscence preceding RO.

A further study in a psychiatric hospital contrasted RO sessions with 'diversional occupational therapy' sessions (Wallis et al 1983). Here the patients had a mixture of diag- noses, with nearly a third having a diagnosis of schizophrenia, and having been hospitalised for an average of 20 years. Although there were improvements in verbal orientation associated with RO, no differences between groups on the Crichton Scale were noted for either patients with dementia or with schizophrenia.

Negative findings regarding change in ward activities are reported by Goldstein et al (1982). Verbal orientation scores did improve during RO compared with no treatment controls. The authors note that individual responses to the treatment were quite varied, and show that for at least one patient an increase in purposeful activity did occur.

We have to conclude that changes in general behaviour are much more elusive then improvements in verbal orientation, but have now been demonstrated sufficiently often for them to be acknowledged as a possible consequence of implemen- tation of RO. There are a number of factors involved in the apparent discrepancies between studies.

One factor may be the degree to which the RO session is a formal classroom teaching session rather than a social setting where learning is encouraged and where it is possible to capitalise on previously learned social responses. Another may be the subject population and the degree to which the institution has in the past 'encouraged' dependent behaviour. Thus for example if the particular group has been under-functioning in self-care then RO may tip the balance, whereas if the institution is already encouraging independence there may be less scope for improvement. Initial levels of dependence are important here; for example Woods' (1979) residents functioned initially on the Crichton Rating Scale much better than Holden & Sinebruchow's (1979) patients on the same scale. The extent to which staff carry over into 24 hour RO reinforcement of appropriate functioning is probably also important, and again may be related to differences in attitudes and practices between institutions. Some wards or homes may be more receptive than others to RO. For some it may fit well into the ongoing development of the ward, in other places other interventions may have more chance of bringing about positive changes (Haugen 1985). There may well be a complex interaction between the level of development of the institution and the type of intervention that will be most appropriate. This could be a particular problem where the comparison group are drawn from another home or ward.

Woods (1979) and Woods & Britton (1977) have suggested that direct training of a particular skill might be needed if more general changes are to occur. Hanley et al (1981) have applied this approach to ward orientation i.e. the patient finding his/her way from one place to another on the ward. Patients received either no treatment, RO classroom or RO classroom plus some sessions of ward orientation training. This latter procedure involved the staff member taking the patient individually round the ward, asking him or her to locate different areas and giving clues and directions when the person was unable to do so. This latter group did much better than the RO classes alone or no-treatment on a behavioural test of ward orientation. The groups did not differ on amount of verbal orientation assessed in the usual way (see Fig. 3.8). This type of training it might be argued, should be

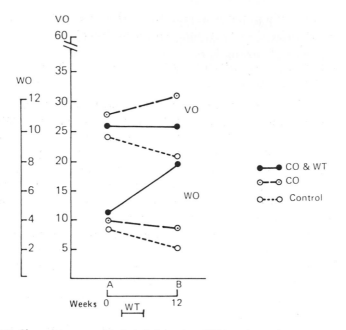

Fig. 3.8 Change in mean Verbal Orientation (VO) and Ward Orientation (WO) after RO sessions (CO) and Ward Training (WT). Reproduced, with permission, from Hanley et al 1981, British Journal of Psychiatry.

part of 24 hour RO, and Reeve & Ivison (1985) were able to demonstrate similar improvements in ward orientation following the introduction of signposting on a ward, together with a form of 24 hour RO. This involved staff responding to residents' initiatives according to RO principles, but not seeking to increase the number of interactions. Improvements in ward orientation may then be feasible if the RO programme specifically includes procedures and modifications to the environment that are likely to be directly helpful. It is quite probable that more general behavioural changes occur when RO stimulates staff and patients to likewise focus on other aspects of self-care and social activity.

Other research findings

Several studies have additionally looked specifically at various factors relevant to RO. These results are presented here to delineate further issues surrounding the effectiveness of RO other than the central facets discussed above.

1. The relative contributions of 24-hour RO and RO classroom sessions

As mentioned above, the form of 24 hour RO and environmental modification used by Reeve & Ivison (1985) was sufficient to bring about changes in ward orientation in patients not attending RO sessions, together with some cognitive and behavioural change. However, patients who did attend RO sessions throughout the experimental period showed a wider range of cognitive and behavioural improvements. This study is particularly important in this context, in that staff were observed to be actually carrying out the 24 hour RO as intended. A further study from this research group (Reeve 1986, personal communication) has been completed, confirming that this form of 24 hour RO is superior to no treatment on both cognitive and behavioural measures, even without RO sessions.

In Zepelin et al's study only 9 of the 22 residents in the RO group consistently attended RO sessions. Although a direct comparison is not made, it seems that most of the positive cognitive changes were attributable to the residents attending RO sessions.

RO sessions probably have an additional impact as far as verbal orientation is concerned, at least in the short term. The differential impact of RO sessions and 24 hour RO on general behaviour is much less clear; ward orientation requires 24 hour RO, but improvements in social functioning may arise from either in some circumstances.

2. The use of memory aids in the environment

One aspect of 24 hour RO is the provision of visual aids in the environment giving items of information. Hanley (1981) has additionally shown that with respect to ward orientation, large signposts identifying different ward locations were not sufficient to improve patients' orientation. But behavioural change was evident when the signposts were used as part of the ward orientation training procedures outlined above. Similarly, Bergert & Jacobsson (1976), in a Swedish study, concluded that environmental cues were useful in re-orientating the person to time and place but that the person had to be taught to use the cues provided; they suggested that when the cues were not present, orientation decreased again. Reeve & Ivison (1985) incorporated colour-coding of doors according to function, verbal and non-verbal signs, sign-posting and large RO boards in their 24 hour RO proce-dure, but did not evaluate their effectiveness in isolation from the staff interactions with residents. There is a need for 24 hour RO to include the active use of these memory aids, with staff drawing the attention of patients to them, as they may well not make use of them on their own initiative.

3. Intensity of RO sessions

As can be seen from Table 3.3 the frequency of RO sessions used in various studies had ranged from once per week to seven times per week. The ideal frequency must depend to some extent on the subject population used, with, presumably, the frequency of sessions being related to the degree of dis-orientation. Positive changes have emerged from studies using only 3 sessions a week (Reeve & Ivison, although this was backed up by 24 hour RO). A puzzling finding emerged from Wallis et al's study where sessions were offered 5 days a week. The patients who attended RO most frequently during the first 2 weeks improved least on both cognitive and behav-ioural measures. The authors suggest that early in the course of treatment daily half-hour sessions were too much for some patients. Much may depend on what stimulation and activity they have been accustomed to previously – patients in this study were those who were unable or unwilling to attend the occupational or industrial therapies already available.

In virtually every study, sessions have been given once only on any particular day. Johnson et al (1981) raised the possi-bility of whether additional RO sessions each day would be of benefit, particularly in situations where 24 hour RO could not be implemented. They compared a group of patients receiving RO sessions once a day with a group receiving twice a day sessions, but found the same range of improvements on verbal orientation with both procedures and no apparent benefit from doubling the number of RO sessions each day.

4. Group v. individual sessions

In certain circumstances a person cannot be included in group RO, perhaps because of severe deafness, restlessness or double incontinence. In these situations individual RO sessions are often recommended. Johnson et al (1981) compared the efficacy of group RO sessions with 10 minute individual RO sessions, and have shown that it is equally as effective as group RO, in improving verbal orientation, but it does not appear to be more effective. Where a person cannot be included in a group for some reason, these extremely brief individual sessions have then been shown to be of use.

5. Maintenance of effects of RO

How long-lasting are the effects of RO? Does it have to be continuously applied in perpetuity or is a brief intensive period or RO sufficient to produce lasting change? Barnes (1974) showed a significant deterioration in verbal orientation only one week after RO classes ceased and reported some corresponding anecdotal deterioration in behaviour. Holden & Sinebruchow (1979) followed up their patients six months after RO sessions finished. They reported significant behavioural deterioration on both the Crichton Geriatric Rating Scale and the Holden Communication Scale. Although cognitive improvements were maintained one month following the end of treatment in Wallis et al's study, the general impression appears to suggest an absence of maintenance, certainly in the longer term and in some instances within a month (e.g. one group in Baines et al (1987) showed a clear cognitive loss to baseline level following 1 month without RO sessions). It has been suggested that less frequent RO sessions may be helpful in maintaining change. Reeve & Ivison included one group who had in successive months 3, 2 and 1 RO sessions per week. They remained significantly better than their matched controls, but did not differ from patients who had only the initial month with 12 RO sessions in total. Again the supportive 24 hour RO environment may be important here, in perhaps aiding maintenance. Given that most gains from RO sessions appear to occur fairly early in the course of treatment, the use of reduced frequency RO sessions for maintenance purposes deserves further exploration.

6. Components of reality orientation

To some extent research on different aspects of RO has been covered in the comparison of the effects of 24 hour RO and RO sessions above. However there is generally a dearth of research breaking RO down into its components and evaluating their relative effectiveness. Johnson et al's previously mentioned comparisons of group and individual RO removed many of the social factors operative in RO sessions, and shows these may not be necessary for cognitive improvement to occur in some populations at least. Riegler (1980) has carried out a fascinating study comparing the effects of RO sessions with and without music on a small number of nursing home residents, and found a clear superiority for the music group in terms of improvement on a basic orientation and information test. The use of music included 'singing and playing rhythm instruments to accompany songs and jingles dealing with names, members, day, date and year'. Other activities included listening to and discussing music concerning particular times and places. It may be the music helped group members participate more, relax more and enjoy the sessions more, making them less serious, classroom-like and formal. Riegler points out some difficulties with her study – relatively infrequent group sessions (only twice per week) in particular.

Hart & Fleming (1985) report a modified procedure for RO sessions, using shaping and reinforcement to encourage verbal orientation, and using role play to increase conversational skills. This procedure was compared wih traditional RO sessions, based around repetition of information from a RO board. The results indicated an improvement on verbal orientation by patients receiving the modified RO. Both groups had been attending traditional RO sessions for the previous 18 months. Disappointingly, no difference was observed in social interaction on the ward between the groups, using a time sampling technique.

Finally, there is the suggestion from the work of Baines et al (1987) that reminiscence sessions should be preceded by RO sessions. The RO sessions did in fact include some reminiscence activity, but comparisons with the present day were always made, and historical accuracy emphasised. The generality of this finding remains to be established. It is becoming increasingly important to look at different aspects of the total RO treatment package, as in this way it is possible to rationally and empirically develop and refine the methods used.

7. Patients benefiting most from RO

As Table 3.3 shows, RO has been applied in a wide range of settings, nursing homes, residential homes, geriatric hospitals, psychiatric hospitals etc., and with patients with a wide range of diagnoses. There are no clear emergent trends from the various studies as to particular settings or diagnostic groups where it is most useful. Care needs to be taken that the form of RO is adapted for the particular population according to degree of disorientation, or the problems outlined by MacDonald & Settin (1978) and Voelkel (1978) of boredom with basic RO groups in higher functioning patients may be encountered. Certainly other therapies should be considered where patients are at a level to participate in them, with RO perhaps being at its most useful where the patient is too confused for other types of therapy. However these issues need more empirical investigation before hard and fast rules are established. Where a diagnosis has indicated the presence of a dementia, Brook et al's (1975) results suggest that the lowest functioning group would show least change. Contrary results are provided by Johnson et al (1981) who found changes in verbal orientation of comparable size at each of three levels of functioning in a long-stay psychogeriatric population. Hanley et al (1981) similarly report that degree of dementia did not appear to be a significant determinant of change, and Wallis et al (1983) found that initial scores did not correlate with degree of improvement. There is little conclusive evidence to indicate the severity level of patients who are most likely to benefit from RO.

8. Use of RO in day-centres and day-hospitals

Increasingly day-hospitals and day-centres are becoming important in the assessment, treatment and support of elderly people with dementia, allowing them to remain in their own homes longer and providing much-needed relief for relations and friends. There has been little study as yet of groups of day-patients receiving RO.

One of us (R. Woods) has used RO in a day-hospital setting, where patients attended at most twice a week, and so sessions were thereby limited to twice a week also. Data for six female patients (all with a dementia) before and after RO are available. Results on a memory and information test showed that four patients made improvements after RO sessions commenced, a fifth scored at the level she had been at seven months previously and the last patient showed a transitory halt and improvement in what had been a downhill trend, before deteriorating very rapidly indeed. The rapid deterioration seemed to coincide with physical ill-health. One of the improved patients returned to a level recorded for her three years previously, having also been showing evidence of a gradual deterioration in memory. The most improved patient had a mixed diagnosis of dementia and depression, but had been receiving antidepressant medication for some time before RO started. Behaviour ratings showed relatively little change; there was a clear improvement for the patient who had also been depressed and the patient who ultimately deteriorated rapidly showed an improvement in her behavioural functioning concomitant with her improvement in cognitive ability.

It is of interest that the most severely impaired patient in this series did show improvement and so RO in a day setting may not be appropriate *only* for patients with a memory loss of a mild to moderate degree, who formed the majority of this sample.

Greene et al (1983) have reported the results of a study of RO sessions in a Glasgow day-hospital. This followed some moderately successful individual interventions (reviewed in the next section). Groups of four to six patients met twice a day on the two days per week that they attended. Patients had a mild to moderate degree of dementia. All were living with a relative who could monitor any changes in their behaviour in their own home or had a relative who lived close by. The relatives completed ratings scales on the patient's mood and behaviour at home, and also on their own degree of stress and their own mood. The 13 patients involved were also cognitively and behaviourally assessed at the hospital. Assessments were carried out at the beginning and end of a three week baseline period, after six weeks of RO sessions and finally after a further six weeks where RO sessions were not held.

Results (see Fig. 3.9) showed a dramatic significant improvement in verbal orientation, following RO. The gain was lost at the six week follow-up assessment. Changes in relatives' ratings of the patient's behaviour and in their degree of stress were not significant, but relatives' mood did improve significantly with RO, and deteriorated again at follow-up. This was despite the relatives being unaware of the procedure being followed in the project. These findings then hold some encouragement for the use of RO in day-settings in that not only was cognitive change found, but also a beneficial effect on the supporting relative.

The individual case

The many studies reviewed so far have, without exception, been looking at group changes, group differences, group effects. Even when changes have proved to be significant the size of the improvement has often been small over the group as a whole. Group studies have their place, but if the extent to which RO works and its attendant limitations are to be really understood individual cases need to be examined, preferably where objective measures have been taken over a period of time. In the behavioural literature particularly single-case design experiments are used a great deal and can be extremely powerful in comparing and contrasting different aspects and phases of a treatment approach.

The first published case studies of this type were carried out by Greene et al (1979). These studies as well as illustrating the responses of three individuals to RO also serve to show its utility in a day-hospital setting, where the studies were carried out, and to demonstrate the effects of simply providing information about time, place and person alone without the other activities and socialisation that usually accompanies RO.

Three cases are reported, all females showing severe to

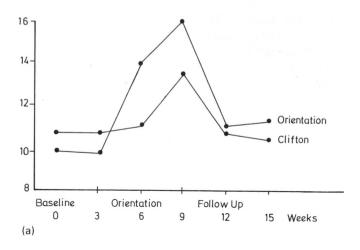

(a)

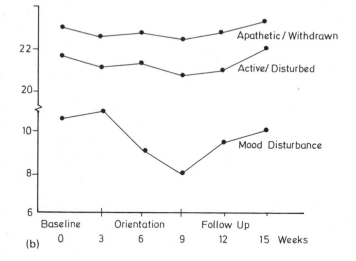

(b)

Fig. 3.9 (a) Patients' Mean Scores on Verbal Orientation Tests (b) Mean Scores on Sub-scales of the Patients' Behaviour and Mood Disturbance Scale (rated by relative) (c) Mean Scores of Relatives on Self-rating of Mood (note that RO sessions only took place during the 'orientation' phase)

Reproduced from Greene *et al* (1983), with the permission of the authors and *Age and Ageing*

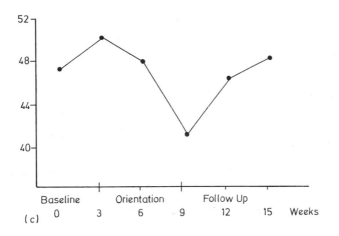

(c)

moderate impairment in all areas of cognition and having a diagnosis of dementia. RO sessions were highly structured in that they consisted of a standard list of questions of general and personal orientation given in conversational manner over a 30 minute period. Each patient was seen individually twice on each attendance at the day-hospital. In baseline phases correct answers were not supplied when there was no response or it was incorrect. In RO phases correct answers were given where necessary. In both phases the patient was told when correct answers had been given. Patient 1 was seen four times a week. Week 1 was a baseline phase, weeks 2–3 and 6–7 were RO phases and in weeks 4–5 a return to baseline conditions took place. Finally the patient was seen once a week in weeks 8–12 under the baseline conditions. Improvements in orientation score were apparent in the RO periods. These were lost in the return to baseline phase and gradually returned to initial levels five weeks after the end of the RO sessions. General changes in the patient's behaviour during RO phases were suggested by anecdotal reports; for example her husband temporarily stopped demanding her admission.

The second case study attempted to systematise the more general effects by including ratings made by the unit OT of the patient's performance and social functioning in OT sessions. The patient was 52 years old and had pre-senile dementia. She was seen on three days per week, and a similar design was followed as with Patient 1, except that in the final phase of once-a-week sessions RO was included. The results showed a clear improvement in orientation in RO phases. This was maintained in the return to baseline phase, and orientation remained at a high level during once-a-week RO sessions. The OT ratings were made without knowledge of the experimental phase, and showed that ratings of performance of activities parallelled the changes in orientation. The patient's social rating increased steadily in all phases. The authors speculate that this may be related to general stimulation effects whereas the changes in performance scores seem more likely to be related to changes in orientation.

The third patient was an older (72 years), more severely demented lady, seen three days a week. Results for this patient were similar with respect to orientation, with a decline in performance however at the return to baseline phase. Changes in OT ratings were not quite as marked, but did show some improvement. Generalisation to items not taught in the RO sessions was tested to ensure that the improvements noted were not simply from parrot-fashion learning. These items, which included differently worded questions, photographs of people included in the orientation test and new items, showed the same pattern of improvement in RO phases.

Greene et al (1979) introduce the concept of a gradient of generalisation; the more a behaviour depends on orientation the more change will be apparent in it following RO. This is a hypothesis well worth pursuing further. Woods (1983) explored further the issue of generalisation from items of orientation that are taught in RO sessions to ones that are not.

The patient was a 68 year old lady who had been an inpatient in a psychiatric hospital for three months with a diagnosis, supported by neurological investigation, of Korsakoff's psychosis. Twice daily structured RO sessions (with specified information *only* being taught) were conducted by nursing staff. If the patient did not know an answer a clue was given, followed by the correct answer if the patient could not make use of the prompt. The experimental design make use of a multiple baseline (Table 3.4) in which all information items

Table 3.4 Multiple baseline design of case-study

Experimental phase	Treatment conditions
Baseline	No RO sessions
Phase I	List I taught
Phase II	List II taught
Phase III	List III taught
Phase IV	All unlearned items taught using a diary as memory aid

were assessed regularly. The RO sessions covered only a proportion of these items at any time. Assessment sessions took place at the beginning, middle and end of each phase, each of which was 9–12 days long, except phase IV which lasted one month. The results are shown in Figure 3.10.

Generally items showed most improvement during the phase of treatment when they were specifically taught. Two exceptions should be noted. The patient's performance on list I items did improve markedly in phase I but continued to improve during phase II, before falling off during phase III, after three weeks of other items being taught. The records that nurses kept of RO sessions suggested that the assessment at the end of phase I gave an understimate of her near-

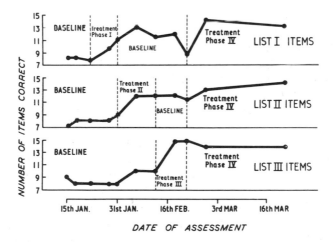

Fig. 3.10 Learning of verbal orientation and basic information in a single-case experimental study – see text for details of multiple base-line design and the phases of intervention

perfect knowledge of list I items at that time; the 'improvement' in phase II was in fact probably maintenance of
improvement already made. The other exception is the slight
improvement of list III items in phase II; these gains were
made on items in list III that had similar content to certain
items in list II. An overall 60 item personalized memory and
information test showed gradual improvement over the
experimental period (see Fig. 3.11). The final phase, in which
all lists reached near-maximum levels, was an attempt to help
her learn to use her diary and to reorientate herself from that,
and improvements seem to be well maintained in this phase.

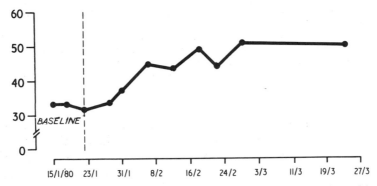

Fig. 3.11 Scores on a 60 item information and orientation test achieved by
subject in the single-case experimental study shown in Fig. 3.9

This specificity of learning has also been demonstrated by
Patterson (1982) with four clients receiving 'Personal Information' Training, a procedure similar to that described here,
and in a group study by Goldstein et al (1982). The evidence
is accumulating that to be learned, the information has to be
taught!

Hanley & Lusty (1984) have taken further the use of a
diary to aid orientation. In a single-case study they taught
an 84-year-old patient with dementia to use a diary and watch
to answer orientation questions, reaching perfect performance on a 30 item personalised test after 2 weeks of training
(see Fig. 3.12). During this training the patient kept a third of
her 'appointments' (e.g. having her hair done, collecting the
daily paper etc.), whereas previously she had only kept one
out of 36. The improvements were soon lost once training was

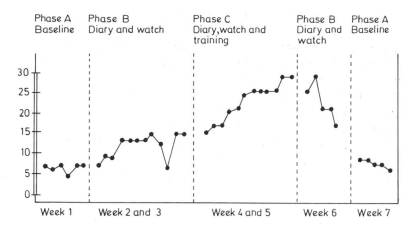

Fig. 3.12 Patient's scores on a personalised orientation test during
(A) baseline phases (B) when provided with a diary and a watch and
(C) when trained to use the diary and watch. Reproduced, with
permission, from Hanley & Lusty 1984, Behaviour Research aand Therapy

discontinued, but the training period was very brief (two
weeks) and took only a few minutes each day, and so could
have been continued indefinitely if necessary. This study did
not require the patient to *remember* any items of information
– she was able to refer to her diary and her watch to find out
the answers, a skill this patient was clearly able to demonstrate, with specific, focussed training and encouragement.

Hanley (1986) reports a further case-study where once more
a memory aid (a notebook) was used. Here, an 83-year-old
lady with dementia was taught to use the notebook in
conjunction with the RO board in order to improve her
orientation, her knowledge of personal information and her
awareness of her husband's death. The patient had become
confused at times about whether or not he was alive, and she
had asked staff during a lucid phase to remind her that he was
dead. In correcting her on this sensitive item, staff took care
to give her time to talk about her feelings, and to give her the
attention and care she needed in doing this. Regular visits to
the cemetry were arranged as a tangible reminder. The results
were clear cut; when this approach was taken she was aware
of the facts about her husband's death on 11 out of 15 days;
beforehand she had no awareness of his death on any of 5

occasions. Similarly, her orientation and personal information scores improved.

Again the patient was not required to remember infor-mation – she only had to use the RO board and the notebook in order to find all the answers required. However, before specific training in doing this was given she showed little improvement. Interestingly, whilst she did rely on the RO board for answers to orientation questions, she soon re-learned the items of personal information, and rarely had to consult her notebook.

A number of single-case studies have been reported in relation to ward orientation training. Hanley (1981) reports eight cases. The results overall indicate a good response to active ward orientation training, where the patient is requested to show the staff member to the next location on a set route. If correct, the patient was verbally reinforced; if not, appropriate prompts and cues were given to enable the patient to find the correct location. There tended to be little carry-over to locations not specifically taught, and following the cessation of training the improvements were gradually lost. Putting sign-posts up on the ward had little additional effect, until further training, incorporating the use of the sign-posts, was given. For some patients, the improvements seemed to be much better maintained once they had been trained to use the sign-posts that had been placed on the ward. Gilleard et al (1981) report similar findings with a further six patients. Although they are more optimistic regarding the effects of sign-posting alone, they confirmed the superiority of combining sign-posting with specific training. Their test was particularly difficult as it was carried out after the signs had been removed, so this was not just the effect of learning to use the signs.

Finally, Lam & Woods (1986) report a single case where an 80-year-old female patient with dementia with marked diffi-culties in finding her way around the ward, was trained to find a number of important locations – her room, the toilet, the lounge etc. Instead of learning a set route around the ward, as in previous studies, the sequence of locations was chosen at random on each day. The training involved giving pre-determined cues if a location could not be found, the cues

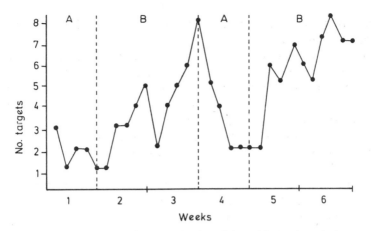

Fig. 3.13 Number of target locations on ward found by patient during (A) Baseline and (B) Training phases. Reproduced, with permission, from Lam and Woods, International Journal of Geriatric Psychiatry, 1986

making use of landmarks and signs on the ward. Figure 3.13 shows the clear improvement in the patient's ability to find the target locations, which is rapidly lost when the training is temporarily stopped, and regained when the training recommenced.

These studies emphasise that re-learning can take place, and that the changes seen are directly related to the training given in verbal or ward orientation. They do not necessarily provide a model for how to carry out RO, but they do illustrate the potential of these techniques when they are harnessed to the needs of an individual case. A delightful example of this is provided by Hanley (1986) who shows how an 86-year-old lady with severe dementia was helped to become continent once again by a ward orientation programme geared to helping her find her way to the toilet.

Generalisation may seem to be lacking, the specificity of learning may seem a problem, the loss of performance when training stops may seem to make training pointless. Perhaps we should, however, look for ways of providing continued support and encouragement for people with dementia to be able to know items of information, and to be able to find the places, that are of importance to them!

CONCLUSIONS

We have seen some evidence then that RO changes patients; in particular verbal orientation has most often been shown to be improved. The question of generalisation to other areas of functioning remains contentious; changes in behaviour have been reported much less frequently. The role of 24 hour RO in encouraging generalisation of changes is beginning to be explored, and Hanley et al's (1981) study of ward orientation training is most encouraging in this respect. More attention as to how staff actually implement (or fail to implement) 24 hour RO is going to be needed in future. Many questions remain to be answered and many of the studies reviewed here are inadequate in one way or another (partly because of the methodological difficulties outlined previously).

Institutional differences are almost certainly of importance in our consideration of at times conflicting results. Woods & Britton (1977) identified the need for researchers to give more details of their institutional settings and Woods & Britton (1985) demonstrate the power of institutions to overwhelm psychological approaches.

By 'institutions' more than just simply large mental hospitals are included. Shepherd & Richardson (1979) have shown that even in small day-centres (for younger people) different institutional attitudes may apply and the same is likely to be so for any facility, large or small, residential or day-care only.

Little progress has been made in this direction as yet. In the long run it may be at an institutional level that RO makes its most important and far-reaching changes. In order for staff to change in ways consistent with RO the whole ethos of the institution may have to change, and in this light RO may be seen as one philosophy for a dramatic change from purely custodial care, to a care that firmly places the emphasis on the needs and potential of the individual. This is a theme to which we will return in Chapter 5.

How does RO work?

In the previous chapter, some positive changes related to RO have been reported. How could any beneficial effects arise in people suffering from dementing conditions? What possible mechanisms could lead to change when we believe that there is generalised damage to the brain in these disorders? Several possibilities that have been suggested will be outlined, together with the suporting evidence. It should be borne in mind that in such a varied group of conditions, different processes may be responsible for improvement in different individuals, and, of course, several mechanisms may be operating simultaneously.

'REACTIVATION OF NEURAL PATHWAYS'

In her introduction to Folsom's work on RO Stephens (1969) states: 'The process can reawaken unused neural pathways and stimulate the patients to develop new ways of functioning to compensate for organic brain damage that has resulted either from injury or progressive senility, or from deterioration through misuse'.

The issues arising from this statement are:

a. Can parts of the brain suffer from disuse? Muscles need to be exercised in order to remain efficient; do neural pathways require regular use for the same reasons?

b. If certain pathways in the brain are blocked, damaged or even dead can other connections be made in order to maintain function by using other routes or a by-pass system?

c. Can brain cells regenerate?

These are very profound and complex problems which have intrigued scientists for at least the past 150 years. The most controversial issue – which relates particularly to a and b above – is the extent to which particular functions are under the control of specific localised parts of the brain. The work of Paul Broca and Carl Wernicke in relating particular speech deficits to specific areas of the dominant hemisphere would seem to support a localisation viewpoint. However, as Hughlings Jackson has indicated, localisation of a deficit is different from localisation of a function. In the light of recent evidence, whilst there is probably considerable localisation of certain major functions, total localisation appears illogical and theories now recognise that many psychological processes depend on several brain areas and their inter-connections being intact.

To what extent is recovery from brain damage possible?

Zangwill in his introduction to the classic work by Luria on 'Restoration of function after brain injury' (1963), states: 'In man, unfortunately, recovery from the effects of brain injury is apt to be a good deal less complete [than in animals] and residual defects are distressingly common'. However, despite quite extensive damage persons sustaining head injury and other brain damage can obtain restoration of function – to some degree and sometimes to an incredible degree. Paralysis, motor and sensory function can all return to near-normal. Even disorders of speech, understanding, recognition, or practical skills can improve dramatically. Four mechanisms for this restoration of function will be considered (see also Miller 1980; Rothi & Horner 1983). Most of the research has considered only brain damage occurring suddenly at one point in time, rather than the gradual, progressive deterioration of most dementing disorders.

Superficial or temporary injury

The injury could be superficial, like any external scratches and bruises, and the systems are only suffering from shock rather than permanent damage. In 1914 Von Monakow defined his concept of 'Functional Diachisis' – recovery is seen as being due to the re-establishment of temporarily impaired neural systems. He inferred a temporary state of shock, or disinhibition. The difference between initial and residual symptoms is then due to a specific lesion temporarily disrupting the neural tissues some distance from the actual site of the lesion spreading there by means of direct fibre pathways. As the shock effect subsides there is a gradual improvement. In 1958 Kempinsky found support for such an effect as his recordings from cortical areas distant from the cerebral lesion showed transient depression followed by normal functioning. Hoedt-Rasmussen et al (1964) showed that in strokes there is a marked transient decrement in metabolic rate in brain areas opposite a lesion.

Simple examples of such a recovery would include concussions, little strokes, or transient ischaemic attacks (TIA), and the remarkable recovery seen after several weeks or months from a more severe stroke. The extent of the original lesion determines the residual dysfunction.

Substitution

Here particular functions are not necessarily linked to set locations in the brain. When a part of the brain is damaged the remaining parts adapt to take over the functions for which the damaged area was responsible, or in which it was involved. New strategies would be substituted and behavioural processes would assume responsibility for restoration. It is possible that redundant mechanisms, already present in the brain, could be employed. Several workers have found an indication that 'recovered' behaviours are not identical to those exhibited by normal animals used in their experiments. As explanation it is suggested that some neural structures failed to act as perfect substitutes for the original ones (Finger et al 1973). Gazzaniga (1974) suggests that diachisis is insufficient alone to account for recovery from massive brain damage. He states: "I believe recovery in the adult, resulting from non-physiological improvement, is the result of pre-existing behavioural mechanisms not necessarily routinely involved in a particular act now covering for the mental activity under question".

In his opinion the restoration is due to 'other existing behavioural strategies that are capable of handling the job but have previously been involved in the other more supportive roles'.

This implies that a previously little-used system with the capacity for carrying out the specific function can take over when necessary.

Radical re-organisation

This theory holds that there is a radical re-organisation of the destroyed activity. The function is restored by means of different and unaffected neuronal structures assuming the role of the damaged one. If primary structures have been damaged then secondary areas can be brought into use. However, if a secondary area is destroyed the whole functional system will suffer. In order to restore function in the latter instance it may be necessary to employ new methods. These may 'lead to the creation of new functional systems, and almost any area of the cerebral cortex may be included in a particular functional system in order to reintegrate the disturbed activity of the brain' (Luria 1963).

The degree to which neural tissue is able to take up new function (neural plasticity) remains controversial. The extent to which new links can be formed rather than the preserved links being re-organised is still unclear. Readers are referred to Luria (1963), Blundell (1975), LeVere (1975), Finger et al (1973) and Hècaen & Albert (1978) for more information.

Regeneration

The recovery is seen as due to actual restitution of tissue. In the last decade research findings have shown, quite clearly, that various forms of regeneration do occur. Several accounts are valuable as reference (Finger et al 1973, LeVere 1975, Hècaen & Albert 1978, Bowen & Davison 1978, 1980). Axonal sprouting following damage has been found in cortical and sub-cortical structures, but studies (mainly in animals) have shown that recovery is most effective in early youth. There have been doubts as to the possibility of regeneration in adult brains, but recent work is throwing more light on the probability of plasticity of the mature brain. New dendritic growth in aged animals was first noted and then found in normal ageing human brains (Buell & Coleman 1981). Such growth does not seem to occur in the brains of Alzheimer patients. The implications of these exciting findings require further investigation and new developments are being reported frequently (Wilcock 1984).

Comments

This discussion of four possible mechanisms of 'reactivation' of neural pathways is necessarily inconclusive, and it is beyond the scope of this book to indicate a preference for any of them. They are presented as intriguing possibilities, rather than as well-established processes (for more detail see Miller 1984).

To return to the questions posed as a result of Stephens' statements about neural pathways, some can be answered and some remain tantalising problems yet to be solved. Cells *can* regenerate, not only in extreme youth, but, because of dendritic growth in normal ageing brains, plasticity is possible in maturity. There *are* suggestions in the literature that function can be maintained by using other routes or strategies, or by using by-pass systems. The possibility of parts of the brain suffering from disuse and 'wasting' as disused muscles do is fascinating and seems quite likely for highly localised functions; some theorists would argue that such little-used areas might be called upon to take over functions in damaged regions!

The theories that have been outlined may not be mutually exclusive. They point the way for intensive research evaluating the effects and mechanisms of rehabilitative techniques. Workers like Gazzaniga et al (1971, 1972) are having success in retraining after strokes and Luria demonstrated how function could be restored to the brains of war-wounded patients with head injury. Other improvements can occur without specific intervention. Thus where RO is successful in producing changes in stroke patients or elderly people who have suffered other actual brain injury, then the adaptive capacity of the brain should not be discounted as a possible reason. There is no evidence, however, that these changes do occur as a result of RO intervention – indeed this aspect does not seem to have been systematically investigated.

In the context of dementia related disorders it is conceivable that some of these mechanisms *could* occur. Diachisis might occur in multi-infarct dementia, for instance. Regeneration would be valuable in any disorder! Re-organisation and substitution are likely, however, to require more time and retained capacity than might be available once a deteriorating process is under way. Again no link has been established between RO and restitution of neural structures as such in dementia. Whatever the form of brain injury Stephens' suggestions must remain speculative – although in the light of current theory not completely far-fetched.

INCREASED ATTENTION AND STIMULATION

Any form of research carried out in an attempt to change behavioural patterns should be questioned as to the effects of added attention. This has been called the Hawthorne Effect after the first researcher to be concerned about such a variable. All investigators need to be aware of the inevitability of some degree of change arising simply because the system is the focus for much more attention than usual. Attempts to allow for this variable include the use of control subjects who, while not receiving the actual therapy, receive all the other extra attentions which arise due to the experimental situation. Untreated control groups have been used in several studies, but they do not allow for these non-specific effects of any intervention. For instance, Harris & Ivory's (1976) comparison group was on a separate ward from the RO group. The RO ward had 'special' status; as well as the researchers' input there was interest from outside the hospital. Staff morale was reported to be raised by this increased interest in the ward. This could then have been a major factor in the changes reported. Given that elderly people are often in institutions that are characterised as unstimulating, with little attention or variety for the patients and low staff morale, any innovation of a therapeutic nature might produce positive changes regardless of actual form and content of the treatment.

Brook et al (1975) did control for these factors. As the control groups also went daily to the RO room both groups received added variety and exposure to a more stimulating environment than on the ward. Ward staff may well have felt involved in a 'special' project but this would have affected both groups equally as group membership was unknown to the nurses, and so could not have affected their ratings of ward behaviour. This study, therefore, gives support to more than innovation, or the provision of stimulation, being responsible for the greater changes produced by RO than the control procedure.

However, the extra attention given to the RO groups by the therapists might account for the improvement. The control group in marked contrast to the RO group received no encouragement or direction from the therapist – they simply sat in a circle. Efforts have been made to control for this additional staff attention by Woods (1979) and Reeve & Ivison (1985) who both used 'social attention' comparison groups. These group sessions aimed at encouraging conversation in group meetings held for the same amount of time and meeting as frequently as the RO sessions. In Woods' study RO methods were not used in these groups and rambling or confused talk was not corrected. It will be recalled that both these studies found RO to be superior in terms of cognitive change, suggesting that the form of attention is of importance. Generalised attention may not be as beneficial as attention that specifically encourages and reinforces orientated behaviour. These findings are not an artifact of staff realising that 'social attention' was a form of placebo. In Woods' study the same care staff led both groups and as previously mentioned, preferred the 'social attention' believing it to be more effective. These results cannot then be related to the fulfilment of expectations. Non-specific effects do not seem to be sufficient to account for all the changes produced by RO. Staff attention is almost certainly an important and effective therapeutic tool but it needs to be directly focussed on appropriate behaviour, rather than supplied in an indiscriminate manner.

In Chapter 2 a number of general and sensory stimulation programmes were outlined. These can be seen as attempts to ameliorate the sensory deprivation that some elderly people are said to undergo. In practice RO may involve both an increase in general stimulation and increases in sensory stimulation so it is possible that these are some of the factors which make RO effective. However, a firm conclusion cannot be drawn as to the extent of their contribution to RO. Only in the single-case studies of Greene et al (1979) and Woods (1983) have these effects been removed to any degree. The success of these interventions suggests that stimulation itself cannot be the only therapeutic factor leading to change, but it could certainly account for part of the changes noted in other studies. In the practical situation, for the present, the best strategy may be to use general stimulation and attention in the context of RO to maximise the gains produced.

GENERAL COGNITIVE EFFECTS

If RO produced a general increase in the person's cognitive functioning – in alertness, concentration, and new learning ability etc., as well as in verbal orientation – then performance in a number of other areas could be facilitated. These general effects could also result from practice at and reinforcement of being attentive and concentrating on cognitive tasks as are usually carried out in RO sessions. If, in RO, stimulation is varied and the sessions are carried out in such a way as to be enjoyable and rewarding to the participants, then motivation, attention and concentration can be maximised.

There is some evidence for general cognitive changes occurring, although most studies have only assessed verbal orientation. Woods (1979) showed improvements in concentration and new learning ability in RO subjects compared with social attention controls. Similarly, Reeve & Ivison (1985) report improvements on the Mini-Mental Status Test (Folstein et al 1975), related to RO sessions. This test does cover a range of areas of cognition, but whether the improvements were mainly on the verbal orientation component of the test was not reported. Hanley et al (1981) found changes in verbal orientation, but not in other aspects of cognitive function. At present, the occurrence of general improvement in the level of alertness and concentration of elderly people is open to question. If this could be established there would be the fascinating task of relating it to possible changes at a neural level, or to motivational aspects.

RE-LEARNING

As discussed in Chapter 2, elderly patients with severe memory disorders are capable of some new learning. RO may be seen as providing good conditions for their limited learning to take place. Appropriate behaviour is elicited and reinforced in RO which may be viewed as a behaviour modification programme for orientation.

There is some evidence for this point of view. Hoyer et al (1975), for instance, report an unpublished study by Hoyer & Spitzberg which demonstrated reinforcement effects operating in RO sessions. The single-case studies described in Chapter 3, carried out by Greene et al (1979), Woods (1983) and Hanley (1986), also demonstrate clear-cut learning of verbal orientation under appropriate conditions. Studies of ward orientation training also demonstrate clear specific learning of information taught to the patient. The comparisons of RO sessions with 'social attention' sessions have emphasised that attention has to be given to desired behaviour for improvements to be obtained.

All this strongly suggests that re-training and re-learning must almost certainly form part of any account of how RO operates. The approach is bound by the limited learning ability of the elderly person with dementia, and this may be a factor in the relatively small gains that are made with RO. Clearly where capacity is limited it is important that it is used as efficiently as possible – perhaps by learning to use memory aids as suggested by Bergert & Jacobsson (1976). Single cases reported by Woods (1983), Hanley & Lusty (1984) and Hanley (1986) show this is feasible for some patients with dementia. The patients involved were all able to learn to use a notebook or diary to assist in the recall of personal information or of appointments. Similarly, with regard to ward orientation the value of signposting as a memory aid, in conjunction with training, has been demonstrated by Hanley (1981).

Hanley (1984) has particularly emphasised the importance of cued recall, and in Chapter 2 we reviewed the evidence showing that dementing people are less impaired when cued recall is used. However, Downes (1987), drawing on the extensive research on cued recall in amnesia, argues that the higher levels of performance in cued recall do not reflect *knowing* the day, place or whatever in any real sense. The person may well be literally *unknowingly* giving the correct response to the cue. Being correctly orientated for the day of the week usually involves recollecting the activities of the current day and the previous day (Brotchie et al 1985), for example. The person with dementia does not go through such a process when cued to say 'Today is Wednesday' by giving the first two letters of the answer. The person achieves the right answer, but the process is completely different from the normal one.

In relation to verbal orientation it may be that rather than talking about re-learning, we should see RO as an approach which helps to compensate for dementia-related impairments. The 'correct' responses are arrived at from external cues, provided by the physical and social environment, rather than from the self-generated cues that we all normally employ. For tasks that can be less dependent on verbal reflections, as in finding the way around a ward, 're-learning' may be a more appropriate description.

Downes points out that a crucial test of the value of any 'improvements' is whether they can be observed outside the standard test situation. Does the person find his or her way around the ward better when on his/her own following ward orientation training? Does he or she use improved verbal orientation outside the RO session? There is, unfortunately, little evidence for this sort of impact on the person's everyday functioning. However, in the case studies reported by Hanley (1986), there are interesting indications of some clinically significant changes. If we see change as less about the person learning and more about the environment compensating for deficits and cueing appropriate behaviour, the question of the generalisation of learning from the test situation becomes more of an issue of to what extent the environment can be adapted to replicate the conditions found helpful in the more structured situation.

OVERCOMING DEPRESSIVE WITHDRAWAL

Seligman (1975) argues that repeated trauma can lead some people to adopt a position of 'learned helplessness'. The person then fails to carry out tasks of which he or she is capable. There is withdrawal from active participation and a belief that control over the environment is lost – that nothing can be done to make any difference to the situation. Self-esteem becomes lower as everything seems more and more hopeless and useless.

These considerations are relevant for at least two major groups of patients. Firstly, those with a dementia or other organic damage will be faced with many failures at tasks that were previously extremely easy and straightforward; for some of these patients this failure will be distressing and perhaps traumatic. One way of dealing with this is to do less and less, and thus avoid failure by not attempting any sort of task. As a result they will function at a much lower level than their true degree of impairment necessitates.

The second group of patients are those who have also become depressed and withdrawn, but with only minimal, if any, cognitive impairment. They may have had a number of experiences of rejection, suffered losses, isolation or other trauma. They may even have been diagnosed as having dementia as diagnostic errors do occur (see Chapter 1). Studies indicate that such people may be placed in an institution for physical or social reasons.

RO by its repeated exposure to success may begin to combat the helplessness and assist the person to function at a level more in keeping with his or her full potential. Increased self-esteem could be a powerful mediator of generalised improvement.

If an elderly person has withdrawn because of shame, depression, feelings of inadequacy and lowered self-respect and is then placed in a situation where the aims are so simple that it is guaranteed that some response will receive praise, self-esteem will improve. When someone is faced with the realisation that memory is failing and that abilities and status are also suffering, self-doubt and depression seem almost inevitable. Failure is the factor which becomes the focus of attention, not only by the self but also by others. If instead of concentration on the many failures – inability to wash and dress, inability to move about freely – these are minimized and there is praise for simple things confidence can return. To praise a person for the positive things that he or she can do is an effective method of approach. To know what day or month it is is a simple memory task, to be able to tell a story about a past experience is always possible to some extent, to be able to recognise a smell, to know the name of a flower or a fruit, these are simple aims on which to build. It is easy to say 'That's right' with some enthusiasm. To an elderly person becoming used to being always wrong this is an achievement which will encourage further attempts towards self-expression and help.

However, evidence for this theory is limited. MacDonald & Settin (1978) included a measure of 'adjustment' – The Life

Satisfaction Index (LSI) – in their study. They found that RO patients tended to deteriorate on the LSI, whereas patients in a sheltered workshop reported increased life satisfaction. It has been suggested that RO was used rather inflexibly in this study, with the RO being set at too low a level for the elderly people involved. Clearly, if hopelessness is to be overcome RO has to be used in such a way that the person experiences success rather than boredom!

More recently, Baines et al (1987)) used the LSI in their comparative study of RO and reminiscence sessions. Here again the trend was for attendance at RO sessions to be associated with lower LSI scores, although there was not a significant difference between the groups. These authors suggest that an apparent lowering of mood may relate to a more realistic self-appraisal; both positive and negative feelings were expressed openly in the RO sessions as they progressed. Both RO and reminiscence sessions were reported to be enjoyed by the residents involved.

There are difficulties in assessing mood in people with severe cognitive impairments. Both the above studies have relied on the person's self-report based on answers to a brief questionnaire. The reliability of this procedure with more impaired patients is open to considerable doubt. Another approach would be for someone who knows the patient well to rate the patient's mood using a suitable scale. This method was adapted by Greene et al (1983) in their study of people with dementia attending a day hospital. A relative living with the patient completed a number of ratings regarding the person's mood and behaviour. During the period of the trial when RO sessions were taking place an improvement in the patient's mood at home was noted. This is possibly the strongest available evidence for RO having a positive effect on mood.

Other evidence has to be anecdotal. Certainly a large number of patients with a diagnosis of early dementia may in fact have a depression or may have depression plus early dementia. Our impression is that such patients often do well on RO. Mrs B sat in her chair for some months, declaring that she was incapable of doing anything. She felt that she was useless, a nuisance and frequently wept with despair. She believed that she would not do anything right in RO, but, on the contrary, once there she found that she could do things she thought impossible. She required a great deal of re-assurance and encouragement, but smiles began to appear as success after success occurred. Her self-care improved, and she was well enough to be discharged within a few weeks.

Clearly this possibility needs systematic exploration. The absence of general changes may be against it as being the overall mechanism of change, but it may be important in some cases. The difficulty in pursuing it further is the problem of assessing feelings, mood etc. in a memory-disordered person.

FINAL COMMENTS

There has been little in the way of satisfactory evidence in this chapter, and much speculation. This reflects the currently unresolved and often apparently unconnected progress and research on both the ageing process and the effects of positive approaches to care. In the case of RO most effort has been applied to establishing whether or not it works, and very little attention has been given to *how* it works. In many ways RO seems to have developed as a practical coming together of methods and ideas, rather than having from the start a firm, reliable conceptual base. On the available evidence, and from our experience of using RO, the behavioural retraining model and the combating of depressive withdrawal seem to be the most useful models for its operation. Indeed the former may largely account for the small changes usually found in group studies, and the latter for the more dramatic changes which also occur.

PART | # TWO

Positive approaches in practice

'How I long for a little ordinary enthusiasm. Just enthusiasm — that's all'. *John Osborn.*

5

An integrated approach

Chapter 1 ended with the hope that readers would take from this book an integrated, individualised, value-based means of working with and communicating with elderly people with dementia. Most of the research that has formed the basis of the intervening chapters has focussed on specific techniques, rather than on developing an overall approach. Does RO, on which the larger part of the research has been conducted, provide the integrated approach that is required?

Several recent critiques of RO would suggest it does not (Burton 1982; Schwenk 1981; Powell-Proctor & Miller 1982). Reisberg (1981) suggests, for example, that RO 'appears to be little more than a sensible, scientific-sounding modern ritual' and that 'challenging their fantasies or attempting to educate and continually re-educate dementing persons is probably of no value'. Hussian (1981) argues that RO has taken the place occupied by custodial care before the 1960's as 'a "treatment" approach of less than empirically supported efficacy'. He asserts that premature complacency about the effects of RO could be damaging, if it prevents the development of improved approaches to helping people with dementia. We agree that approaches should never be static, they must continually be subject to review and development, with the benefits of research and experience. There is still, however, a tendency to equate RO with Folsom's original, innovative description, and to give new titles (e.g. Memory Development; Carroll & Gray 1981) to approaches with a similar basis. We concur with Powell-Proctor & Miller's (1982) comment that RO be seen as a starting point, for further innovation, adaptation and refinement, rather than the end point, the answer to the complex, pervasive problems to which RO is applied. Burton (1982) criticises RO for not being appropriate to the people and settings in which it is used, as well as for its failure to produce behavioural change apart from in orientation to the environment. Burton suggests the behavioural ecology approach as an alternative. Rebok and Hoyer (1977) in their discussion of behavioural ecology, make a point of the need to draw in the beneficial aspects of the various approaches. Similarly, Hussian (1981) describes a modified form of RO that incorporates more explicitly behavioural principles.

What should an integrated approach incorporate? Which findings from the various studies are essential to any approach? Here we describe those that, in our view, are most significant.

a. Attitudes

The first feature we would emphasise, and to which we give over-riding importance, is that the approach should be based on an explicit set of values regarding the elderly person with dementia. Any approach can be misapplied if it is applied with inappropriate attitudes that devalue or patronise the elderly person.

Gubrium and Ksander (1975) have illustrated this point clearly in relation to RO. They observed RO in two nursing homes. Their findings led them to doubt the 'reality' of RO. One particular interchange they report is indicative of what they observed. The aide leading an RO group had indicated on the RO board that it was 'raining'. He asked the patient what the weather was; she looked outside, saw that the sun was shining (the rain having abated), and said it was sunny. The aide disagreed with her until she read 'correctly' from the board that it was raining, whereupon she was praised warmly. Buckholdt and Gubrium (1983) similarly point out the danger of RO being applied in a mechanical, depersonalised fashion.

Other approaches too can be misapplied. For example, in the behavioural approach to incontinence reported by Schnelle et al (1983), social disapproval for wetting was given e.g. 'I don't understand why you wet on yourself and didn't ask for help. I come round every hour'. It is not difficult to imagine how such a statement could be turned into a vindictive reprimand with a particular tone of voice and inflection.

The dangers are clear. An explicit value system can go some way towards ensuring that bad practices do not slip through

Table 5.1 Key Principles (from King's Fund 1986)

1. People with dementia have the same human value as anyone else irrespective of their degree of disability or dependence.
2. People with dementia have the same varied human needs as anyone else.
3. People with dementia have the same rights as other citizens.
4. Every person with dementia is an individual.
5. People with dementia have the right to forms of support which don't exploit family and friends.

and that uncertainty is reduced. Staff have a clear yardstick against which to compare their interactions with those with whom they work. Attitudes are discussed in practical terms in Chapter 7. Here we list five principles set out in a recent King's Fund publication on working with elderly people with dementia, which provide a sound basis for work in this field (see Table 5.1).

b. Individualisation

As well as its justification as a basic principle, there are ample pragmatic grounds for developing individualised approaches. These include the great variability in people with dementia, the variability in response to treatment approaches, differences in appropriate target areas for intervention and differences in interests, preferences and attitudes. Any approach must take account of this individual variation, be flexible enough to ascertain and respond to individual needs and to build on the preserved abilities and interests of the person with dementia. Thus two patients with the same 'problem', might be best approached in quite different ways. Generalised treatment approaches to, say, incontinence or wandering will have less effect than approaches which recognise 'the same problem may occur in the same person at different times for different reasons' (Hodge 1984). A good illustration of this is provided by Snyder et al (1978) who identified at least three different patterns of behaviour that could all be described as 'wandering'; single individuals showed different patterns at different times. Detailed individualised assessment is needed to reach a sufficient depth of understanding of the person with dementia in order to really tackle their special needs.

c. Learning is possible

We reviewed evidence in Chapter 2 concerning the learning ability of people with dementia. The RO literature provides confirmatory support for the view that some learning is possible. Re-learning to a small extent has been demonstrated with both verbal orientation and ward orientation. Obviously, new learning is not one of the major strengths of the person with dementia, but it is by no means impossible. There is little in the way of generalisation from one area to another, so it is important to focus directly on training the skill in question. Hanley (1984) suggests a number of ways in which the chances of learning occurring could be increased (see also Carroll & Gray 1981). These include:

1. Increasing the person's motivation by using relevant, interesting materials.
2. Providing a number of opportunities for practice.
3. Providing a number of retrieval cues in the environment, reducing the emphasis on free recall, using the person's limited learning ability to make use of further prosthetic aids which will reduce dysfunction further.

d. Selection of targets

Among the most often voiced criticisms of RO is the lack of real clinical relevance of the changes produced. Either the size of the effects are deemed too minimal to be of use (Powell-Proctor & Miller 1982), or the 'reality' of the effects are questioned – the similarity of the assessment measures to the training procedures being cited (e.g. Hussian 1981). The emphasis of RO on verbal orientation has also been suggested as reducing its clinical relevance. Does the dementing individual really need to know what day it is? Is there any benefit in knowing the name of the Prime Minister? These considerations must lead towards the development of approaches where targets for intervention are selected for the individual patient such that a small realistically attainable change would actually make a difference to that individual patient's quality of life. For one patient, this might involve learning to find the toilet on the ward; for another, improving dressing skills. For others, increasing social contact may be an important target. For some patients in the community who receive different services on different days, learning to keep touch with days and dates may be a priority. The often noted lack of generalisation of learning (reflected in Hussian's critique), means that targets have to be very carefully selected to be precisely and specifically relevant and appropriate.

e. When to stop

The poor maintenance of changes produced by all the various

therapeutic approaches means that an approach must be developed where intervention is not simply for a fixed period of time. It must be continuous, and targets need to be regularly reviewed as the person's condition changes. An approach that assumes stability in the dementing person's function is doomed to fail. The approach must then have a built-in monitoring and review procedure, to allow the maximum flexibility. It must be seen as an overall long-term approach, not as a short-term intervention.

f. Effects on staff and carers

Schwenk (1981) asserts 'it is not clear whether RO is therapeutic for the staff or the elderly'. The impact of any approach on those caring for the dementing person day by day must be considered. If it is positive, staff or carers may usefully be aided in their difficult and demanding task – a worthwhile aim in itself. Improved morale, less strain and burden are likely to lead to more positive interactions between carers and patients, and so will be of benefit for all concerned. This area has attracted too little research attention so far, as we discussed in Chapter 3. The improvement in carers' mood reported by Greene et al (1983), coincident with their dementing relatives attending RO sessions at a day-hospital, is one of the most interesting positive indications. The increase in staff knowledge of individual patients reported by Baines et al (1987) is also important. An integrated approach must take into account the needs, strengths, perceptions, commitment and abilities of carers if practicable, realistic care-plans are to be developed. It is not sufficient simply to produce positive change in the patient's behaviour. As Tarrier and Larner (1983) discovered, staff may not perceive objectively measured change. Sometimes, interventions have to be developed in situations where carers' and patients' needs are discordant. Resolution of these differences is not always possible; approaches which fail to recognise them are likely to run into difficulties.

g. What can you expect?

What should be expected from psychological approaches to dementia? There is clearly no miraculous 'cure-all', no return to complete normality. It has been suggested that the term 'therapy' is inappropriate, in view of its curative connotations: 'management' has been preferred by many workers (e.g. Miller 1977b). Yet Schwenk (1981) argues that approaches other than RO should be explored 'in view of the lack of strong evidence that RO is *universally* beneficial to the elderly' (emphasis added). Indeed great expectations! Could any approach in any sphere claim universal benefit? If workers in this field blind themselves to what they know about dementia and build up their hopes expecting to see massive improvements in their patients when they begin RO they will almost inevitably be disappointed. RO is then likely to be consigned to the pile of approaches that have been tried and found wanting. What will be the next approach to follow the same path? People with dementia *are* likely to show overall deterioration; people with dementia *do* differ greatly from each other; people with dementia have many *different* strengths, retained abilities and resources, needs and disabilities. Changes are generally likely to be small, probably in specific areas. Even when there is not an improvement in function, there could be important and valuable achievements in involving the person in a positive experience – a feeling of success, a moment of contact with another human being, a smile of appreciation. . . . . If targets for change and development are individually set, the rate of expected achievement of these targets can also be individualised. By setting it at a level where small successes are being achieved, staff do not become disappointed and the patient is not over-pressured. It is not universally effective approaches that are needed, but an approach geared to individual needs. Here potentially useful changes can become a reality.

An integrative approach

These considerations lead us to recommend an approach that has been described as 'individual programme planning' (Woods & Britton, 1985), 'goal planning' (Barrowclough & Fleming, 1986), and which is closely related to most applications of the 'nursing process' (e.g. Stockwell 1985). This approach flows easily from the principles and values previously outlined, and which we believe are vitally important for any worthwhile approach. At the heart of this approach is the individual plan. This should cover all aspects of the person's life. A multi-disciplinary team is a good setting to develop such plans, to ensure that medical, social, physical, emotional and psychological aspects are not artificially separated.

It is useful if certain staff members develop close contact with a designated group of patients. Such contact provides the opportunity to really get to know and build relationships with a more manageable number of elderly people. As there is less staff change, staff are recognised by patients more readily. It is easier to spot the areas where something may be achieved in individuals that are known well by the staff member. It is easy to be discouraged when thinking about a ward of 30 dementing people, but once they begin to be seen as individuals new horizons become apparent. There may be practical difficulties in allocating nurses to particular patients, but in many settings these are being overcome. A key-worker system is often established, giving one member of staff responsibility for ensuring individual plans are drawn up, carried out and reviewed regularly for a small number of patients. In some places two staff, on opposite shifts, may share this responsibility.

Developing an individual plan begins with careful and thorough assessment of the person's strengths and needs. This should include assessment of any medical conditions and sensory deficits. One of the first goals of the plan should be to correct and alleviate these as much as is possible. The assessment should include efforts to elicit the views of the elderly people themselves and of their relatives or other carers. As far as possible, the person with dementia and his or her family should be involved in this planning process. Finding out the wishes of the elderly person may not be easy, especially when communication is poor. Guidance from the person's past life and experiences should be helpful, together with information from relatives, friends of long-standing and so on. Getting to know the dementing person in the context of his or her whole life is vital. Reminiscence-based activities may also help.

The assessment stage will include attempts to *understand* as well as to define the person's behaviour. The reasons for difficulties must be examined, including consideration of specific neuropsychological deficits. Generalised descriptions of behaviour such as 'attention-seeking', 'confused', 'incontinent' and so on must be replaced by detailed descriptions of the person's behaviour, the exact circumstances, its frequency and intensity. The assessment process is described fully in Chapter 6, where particular emphasis is given to straightforward methods for identifying specific neuropsychological deficits. The discovery of such deficits should not lead to therapeutic despair, but should concentrate energies on finding ways of overcoming the effects of the problems and ways of compensating for the disability.

Once the initial assessment phase is complete, the plan is drawn up. The strengths and needs that have been identified are used to form the plan. The person's strengths and resources are used to help meet particular needs selected for intervention. These are not selected simply for the convenience of staff, but in relation to the quality of life of the person. It may be that where a particular problem behaviour has been identified the targets will include the encouragement of activities that are incompatible with or which will reduce the frequency of the 'problem'. For instance, the target for a person who is frequently incontinent might be for the person to learn where the toilet is on the ward.

Goals for the person are broken down into smaller manageable steps. Which people will take what action under what circumstances is clearly specified. The criterion for successful achievement of the goal is made explicit, and is set to be realistic, attainable and observable, so that confusion over what has been achieved is kept to a minimum. An indication of the actual frequency of the behaviour and the desired change may prove useful, e.g. 'improve dressing' would be an imprecise target; it would be hard to say when it had been achieved. 'Increase frequency with which patient puts on his shirt with only verbal assistance, from present level of once a week' might be better.

Accurate recording of the patient's behaviour is very useful indeed; e.g. if the target is to increase the patient's rate of self-initiated visits to the toilet then each visit should be noted on a record sheet. Recording is invaluable in providing staff with both a reminder of the target and reinforcement for their efforts. In order to monitor change, it is of course essential to have an initial measure for comparison purposes. This could be done by daily recordings of the particular behaviour, until a fairly consistent picture of the person's function is attained. As different people tend to interpret observations in an individual manner, it is advisable that staff should discuss any discrepant findings so that a high degree of consistency is obtained. Some patients may benefit from having their own chart, showing their progress in graphic form.

Having established a plan for the individual patient consisting of targets and procedures for achieving them the task is not complete. The plan cannot be an inflexible and unchanging statute for all time; it has to change to meet the changing events that occur once it is put into action. Responses may be unexpected or even undersirable; some targets may be quickly achieved, others may take longer or show no progress at all. The next stage is to review progress and to establish fresh targets where necessary. If previous targets have been realized then more diffficult ones can be set; if progress is slight then the level of difficulty must be lowered – using, perhaps, intermediate goals. Realistic, attainable goals are important in all work with elderly people. The ideal aim is complete independence, but to be realistic more independence of functioning in a particular area would be a desirable improvement. Small changes can be of real practical value, but are too often overlooked. Their occurrence indicates a positive move forward. If encouraged, they can increase self-esteem, confidence and effort on the part of the patient and have a real effect on staff morale while also releasing more time for rehabilitative work.

EXAMPLES OF INDIVIDUAL PLANS

Obviously these examples are much abbreviated – with a range of goals sketched out. They are presented here to illustrate the points outlined above.

Mrs A

This 78-year-old lady was a resident in an EMI Home, (a

residential home for the elderly mentally infirm). Her diagnosis was senile dementia. She reported that she felt a bit of
a failure as she could not remember things and often felt
useless. She liked to be kept busy and to socialise with other
residents. She had a family, and previously had been a fit,
active person with a warm personality. As regards her abilities, her self-care was largely independent, her mobility and
dexterity good. She socialised well, making relationships with
particular residents, but had difficulty in learning their names,
and in recognising relatives when they visited. She knew her
way around the home, but tended to get lost outside. She
only rarely took part in domestic activities such as preparing
food etc.

Mrs A caused no specific problems in the home. Although
her memory was poor and she tended to ramble on in
conversation, her behaviour only fluctuated when she
suddenly became unhappy and weepy.

Mrs A's strengths include: good mobility, good dexterity,
independent self-care, ability to find her way around the
home, her interest in being active and sociable and her excellent social skills.

Mrs A's needs include: needing to feel useful by being busy
in a way she would see as helpful; needing more opportunities to socialise – perhaps in settings outside the home;
needing to learn to use memory aids and supports to overcome memory failures. A tentative plan would aim to use
some of Mrs A's many strengths to meet her needs. Her good
skills and mobility and her interest could be harnessed to
increasing domestic and cooking activity; her warmth and
social skills would make it feasible for her plan to include
socialising outside the home; the same strengths would be
an asset in RO sessions of a suitable level, geared towards
helping her use memory aids.

Plan	
General	*Specific*
Increase domestic activity	(These are *aims* not orders)
	To make her bed at least two days out of three
	To tidy and dust her own room at least one day in three
	To help with laying the table once a day
	To help drying up after meals once a day

Increase cooking activity	To make a pot of tea daily To make a snack (e.g. sandwiches) one day in three To cook a meal one day in seven
Increase social activity outside the home	To attend an Over-60s Club once a week
Improve and support memory	To participate in daily RO sessions Pictures of relatives to be obtained for use in RO sessions To use memory aids about the home To keep a diary as a memory prop

Record-keeping would indicate the degree of success in reaching the targets and what level of prompting was required – with the aim of eventually reducing prompting.

Mrs B

Mrs B was another resident in an EMI home with the diagnosis of dementia. It was difficult to obtain a clear picture from her of exactly what she wanted. It seemed that her major goal was to be with her daughter – she had previously lived with this daughter and had been very dependent on her for physical care. The daughter's marriage had been jeopardised so she was unable to continue to care for her mother at home. Previously Mrs B had been socially very active and very much involved as an organiser in various charitable bodies.

The care staff completed a detailed behaviour rating scale which showed that toileting and eating were normal; that she communicated well and that orientation about the home was good. Poor mobility curtailed domestic activities. She lacked confidence in walking and would desperately hang on to people and things, sometimes so fiercely that people would fall over with her. She refused to dress herself and was resistant to looking after her personal cleanliness.

The major problems the staff reported were her constant demands for somebody to come to her, her continuous shouting and her resistance when being helped. Her daughter spent a great deal of time at the home and whilst there her mother persuaded her to do everything for her. The daughter was so concerned about her mother that, as she told the staff, her marriage was still under strain, despite the fact that Mrs B had been removed from the scene.

The staff felt extremely angry with Mrs B – she played one off against the other – and made them look uncaring in front of visitors. It was as though she was trying to exercise over them the same enormous power she had over her daughter.

Fluctuations were noted in Mrs B's behaviour; for some staff she would dress herself, sometimes. When not being overtly observed it was felt she walked slightly better. When her daughter was present she lost all semblance of independence in her behaviour.

Mrs B's behaviour had been labelled as 'attention seeking' and – as is so often the case with such difficult patients – staff who were genuinely caring and warm to their residents were extremely angry with her. It would have been only too easy in what had become a tense home situation to establish a punitive plan; the suffering that other residents were undergoing in being deprived of *their* rights of attention could have made this seem justified.

Mrs B clearly had a number of strengths and resources, although the 'problems' being experienced by the staff threatened to obscure them! Her strengths included: an evident interest in social activity and in being an organiser; good ability to communicate, orientation, eating and toiletting; the concern of her daughter; some ability to dress and walk, in certain situations.

Mrs B needs to become more confident in walking, and to regularly dress more independently; she needs to have more opportunities to socialise (and so to receive 'attention') appropriately; finally Mrs B needs to develop more mutually satisfying relationships with her daughter and the staff at the home.

The plan below aims to use Mrs B's strengths to help meet some of her needs.

It aims at building up positive behaviour, whilst not ignoring the negative feelings of the staff which it was important to have in the open to be discussed and acknowledged.

Plan

General	Specific
Increase mobility to unaided walking in home	Brief walking practice to be given, but staff support to be gradually withdrawn

Increase social interaction	Staff to employ 'chatty' conversation when she is sitting quietly – perhaps concerning past activities; Mrs B to be invited to take on organisation of small tea party with three other residents
Improve dressing to self-care level	Staff to encourage her to do a little more for herself each morning, providing lots of time, only a few prompts which are withdrawn as soon as possible, but praising every effort made.
Increase physical independence from daughter	Daughter to be counselled to withdraw physical care and provide attention in alternative ways
Staff to feel less angry with her	Care for Mrs B to be shared among staff – staff to be free to hand over to someone else if they feel under stress with her. Staff to discuss her difficulties and her qualities and seek to understand her point of view

Notice that no specific attempt is made to stop Mrs B shouting. One might consider ignoring her shouts, but the problem with this is that even if the staff manage this consistently other residents or visitors will respond from time to time and thus spur the shouting on even more. The plan aims to meet Mrs B's needs for her daughter's attention and that of the staff by increasing her positive behaviours and providing some attention for these. Mutual staff support is important too; not all patients are easy to love and yet care staff can feel guilty if there is an inward feeling of distaste, anger or active dislike for a particular person. Open discussion of these feelings helps to see that other people can experience the same emotions and negative feelings. Together it may be possible to see beyond the problem to more likeable attributes; here a previously highly competent lady, faced with the frightening reality of failing abilities, found a way of maintaining great power by taking on a demanding, dependent and manipulative role.

Mr C

Our third example is a man with a moderate degree of dementia, also resident in an EMI home. He had previously been interested in music, lived alone and had been an avid reader. Socially affable, he would willingly join in group activities, although he had yet to form any real relationship with any particular residents. Mobility and eating skills were generally good but his problem was that he became completely lost in the home. Occasionally he was incontinent, at night in particular. He joined in some domestic activities but required some verbal prompting for dressing and washing.

The one problem which concerned the staff was his temper and they reported that he 'was prone to temper outbursts and some aggression'. This was usually verbal, but at least once a day a blow was struck. These incidents occurred about once a day; usually they were when staff had *told* him to do something, upon which he would become angry and impatient. Afterwards he would be a little apologetic and then act as if the incident had never happened. There was no real evidence of fluctuations in his behaviour.

Mr C's strengths include his interest in music and in reading, his sociability, his good mobility and eating skills; his ability to be continent most of the time during the day and his ability to wash and dress with only verbal prompts.

A clear need for Mr C is to be able to find his way around the home, and to improve his dressing and washing skills so even fewer prompts are needed. More opportunities for pursuit of his interests and for developing relationships are also needed. Finally, Mr C needs staff to ask him to do things – not to give him orders. A preliminary plan for Mr C might then include the following:

Plan

General	Specific
Develop recreational interests	Explore Mr C's previous interests – obtain some of the music or books that he likes. Draw him into daily recreational activities.
Develop home orientation: aim to achieve independent ability to find his way	Guided tour of home-pointing out his room, toilet, dining-room, lounge etc. Indicating signs on doors, using colour as a clue, special pictures and particular characteristics as memory aids. Repeat this at least twice daily, gradually asking him to do the guiding, prompting with clues only when he is uncertain.
Develop independence in dressing and washing	Give praise to each phase of these performed correctly.

	Ensure there is an order in laying out the clothes. Gradually fade the prompts as the sequence is learned, eventually use mime as a clue until hopefully no prompt is needed.
Develop relationships with other residents	Introduce him to other residents. Slowly and appropriately – those sitting near him in the lounge, at the table. Ask him to repeat the names when introduced.

Basic approach to Mr C. Ask and do not tell him what to do. Praise him for co-operation.

Again there is no specific resolve to deal with the problem behaviour, instead attempts are made to avoid situations in which it might occur. This is achieved by the staff consistently adopting an approach that Mr C is able to accept.

Mr D

Mr D is 68 years old, he had a mild stroke which left him with some weakness in his left hand and leg. He has recovered from this weakness very well but there are other signs which cause his wife and family some concern. The cerebro-vascular accident has affected the right tempero-parietal areas so that although his speech is unaffected he does have difficulty in finding his way about, shows evidence of dressing apraxia, and has problems with maps and spatial organisation. Sometimes he has a little difficulty with finding his way around the house. He used to have a fairly responsible job with the Gas Board, used to drive one of the vans and was required to travel around the region. He had been a member of several clubs and Sports Associations and was regarded as an outgoing person. He has insight into the changes and is becoming increasingly depressed. His wife still works and so he is alone in the house during the day except when he goes to a day centre twice a week. He has some difficulty remembering important information, or what he is meant to be doing, especially when he is on his own.

Mr D has many assets and strengths, despite his disability. His speech is good; he has always been a sociable person with interests in various sports and clubs. He has a concerned wife and family who may be able to help in his plan, as may staff at the day centre he attends twice a week. His own insight may be used for him to take an active role in finding ways around his disabilities.

The list of needs is shorter – he needs to learn to find his way around, to dress more independently, to use memory aids and to be engaged in activities and interests that lift his mood. The plan might tackle these needs in the following way:

	Plan	
General	*Specific*
Help recent memory	Notice board (or chalk) in kitchen – Day, Month, and Weather every morning. Important information to be remembered. Also notebook always in top pocket. Memory games – name of newsreader on TV last night, one main headline from news, then increase in number of things to remember as successful. Items from paper, TV, visitors etc. Games related to interests – cards, bought games etc.
Help dressing	Clothes placed in order. Tags denoting Front, Back, Left or Right. Practice with buttons, encouragement, written instructions if necessary. Modelling, verbal instructions, as little actual help as possible in order to build routine.
Help him to find his way about	Use of three dimensional games useful – 3D noughts and crosses. Drawing maps of increasing difficulty – starting with home, then street, then shopping street. Using words as cues, i.e. names of rooms, street names, house names, any signposts, shops names and commodities. At home use colour and words to denote toilet, bedroom etc. Play games e.g. Scrabble to increase confidence. Slowly move on to shapes, house colours, postboxes, buildings etc. Routine of putting away in set place – washing up, clothes etc.
Assist depression	All successes to be noted and encouraged. Bouts of 'low' behaviour to be ignored, but alternatives to be offered – 'let's go to the club'. Interest to be encouraged, friendships used. Routine way to the club, involvement in activities outside and at home.

Guidance should be given here to all the family (grandchildren included) on the use of RO, and a booklet can be helpful here. The overall aim is to use preserved abilities in order to increase function in the more impaired areas.

In each of these four cases fairly lengthy plans have been suggested: in the real-life situation these would be likely to evolve over a period of time, with particular parts of the plan being reviewed, changed, extended, or abandoned according to circumstances. In our view, the decision-making progress outlined above should be followed through, even if the ultimate decision is to attempt no change at all to the person's functioning or their environment. In this way patients are seen as individuals, and not just as part of a large group.

CONCLUSIONS

In this chapter we have sought to go beyond RO and outline an approach seeking to produce effects in specific areas of functioning. RO may be seen as one aspect of an integrated approach and the plans outlined above show they can mesh well together. We suspect that the behavioural principle of rewarding appropriate behaviour also plays a part in the successes of other types of general treatment programmes outlined in Chapter 2. For RO this has been demonstrated (see Chapter 3); for the other approaches it is a reasonable assumption. This approach makes explicit what is often implicit in other programmes: this must help to bring about desired changes in a more efficient manner.

The setting of specific objectives tends to simplify the process of evaluating results and the ever-growing volume of knowledge of human learning, from experimental psychology, will in years to come generate techniques to be developed to facilitate learning further.

A danger of the 'individual plan' approach is that it may focus attention on changing the individual patient's behaviour and ignore the wider context in which that behaviour occurs. The behaviour is always an interaction between the person and the environment and we cannot ignore this interaction.

The environment is of course made up of many parts – the physical surroundings, other patients, the staff and their behaviour. Often in our individual plans we are changing aspects of the environment e.g. by changing our response to the patient in different situations.

Whenever we come across a person with a deficit of those skills needed for independent living we need to make a decision to try to at one extreme retrain these skills, or at the other end of the spectrum, change the environment so that these skills are rendered unnecessary. Thus for a dementing person living at home who cannot care for herself any more, do we retrain cooking skills, or provide meals on wheels so that the skills will not be required? The behavioural approach in the community would seek to identify those skills that are and are not retained; only supports that are necessary should then be provided. A general package of services should not be given; it may not meet specific needs and may in fact deny opportunity for expression of some skills that are retained. For the elderly person living alone at home it is this environmental modification that will be of prime importance as there is no one present to repeatedly reinforce appropriate behaviour. What is needed is a prosthetic environment, an environment that fills in the gaps in the person's skills and abilities. The use of memory aids is part of this, as are home helps and meals on wheels. In the not too distant future the deteriorating person's environment could be monitored by a control system so the flat is kept at an even temperature, cookers are turned off automatically if left on or if saucepans boil dry and help is alerted if the person has a fall. Those controls the person can operate would be made as simple as possible. In this way risks to those living alone could be diminished, which would allow both personal choice and relief for worries of relatives.

This is similar to the application of the Community Care Scheme (Challis & Davies, 1985, 1986) discussed in Chapter 10, to people with dementia. A package of care is established which seeks to reduce the risks of both gradual self-neglect and the risk of accidents, establishing a regular pattern of prompting to maintain the person's function.

In a residential setting, the environment should be enriched with features that tend to prompt appropriate, valued behaviour by the dementing person. Thus the environment should be arranged physically to facilitate social interaction, and appropriate materials should be readily available for valued activities. Where particular themes occur again and again in individual plans, e.g. orientation, domestic skills, social activity, a case can be made for establishing groups to work on these areas. Groups should always arise from needs identified from individual care plans, rather than trying to fit patients into existing groups which may not meet their particular needs. Within any group there is still a need for individualisation, according to the person's capabilities, interests and personality.

This integrative aproach is founded on three central components: an agreed, explicit value system; a careful, thorough holistic assessment of the person; an individualised care-plan, with clear, realistic, regularly reviewed goals. From this base there is scope for work with individuals, for work with groups and for environmental change. In the remainder of the book we will describe the practicalities of assessing and working with people with dementia in this way.

'We care what happens to people only in proportion as we know what people are'. James Henry

6

Assessment: some possibilities

WHY ASSESS?

In this chapter we are concerned with the type of assessment that would be helpful in the individual planning process discussed in Chapter 5. Assessment for its own sake, or which produces scores or labels that do not add to an understanding of the patient as a person, are of dubious value and relevance. Test batteries applied without sensitivity and thought regarding the aims and purpose of the assessment and without consideration for the level of stress produced run the risk of 'battering' the older person (Holden 1984a).

There are a number of cogent reasons for making an assessment of an older person. These include:

1. Finding retained abilities.
2. Isolating particular disabilities.
3. Selection for particular purposes, e.g. group work, research, placement.
4. Monitoring change.
5. Diagnosis and prognosis.

It should be appreciated that assessment methods which are excellent for one purpose, e.g. in contributing to the information required in making a diagnosis, may be of little use for others, e.g. monitoring change. Here, we will not be supplying a full account of test procedures for the elderly or discussing their relative merits or demerits, nor will we examine the issues involved in diagnosis, prognosis or placement (see Woods & Britton 1985). The focus here is on holistic assessment leading to individualised care and support for the older person.

Without intruding on a person's right to privacy, it is important to have a wide knowledge about the individual with whom we are working. To know that there is a particular problem is not enough. In order to set realistic goals for improvement, to correct deficits – medical or sensory – and to gather relevant information about life-style, interests and abilities it is necessary to involve a variety of disciplines. Nurses, doctors, occupational therapists, physiotherapists, speech therapists, social workers, clinical psychologists, care workers, friends and relatives have all something to contribute to the store of information which will provide guidelines for intervention best suited to that individual. All the different disciplines that are available in a particular setting or team can feed into this wide ranging assessment. A first goal of any plan should be always to alleviate and correct any medical condition or sensory deficit as far as is possible. A competent medical evaluation is a vital aspect of a holistic evaluation.

The team needs to collect information, ideas, views and opinions in order to address the following questions:

1. What does the elderly person want?
2. What assets, abilities, skills, resources and interests does that person have?
3. What problems does the person experience? What needs does he or she have? What difficulties for others does his/her behaviour cause?
4. Are there any behavioural inconsistencies?
5. What are the person's previous daily routines and social history?

1. What does the elderly person want?

What are his or her objectives? What are seen as problems? What does he or she want from us? It is hard to believe that the necessity of posing such questions can come as a surprise. Those 'in charge' sometimes take it for granted that they know best and so ignore the wishes and needs of the person whose life is being organised. Even if poor memory, poor decision-making capacity or other problems exist the right to be heard must be retained. Respect does not imply complete subservience to the needs and demands of the elderly. There are wishes which are totally unrealistic, practically impossible or even encroaching on the priorities of others. However, the views of the individual must be considered when any decision is being discussed. This question is placed first deliberately.

To make a decision about what an elderly person wants based on 'when I'm 85 I will want to . . .' is to impose our own, possibly faulty conceptions and fantasies on the individual. It is essential to discuss the situation with the individual concerned, and to take into account biography, abilities and personality in order to fully appreciate the situation. To accept at face value expressions of helplessness and weakness can lead to further misunderstanding about real needs and feelings. These can be signs of depression and withdrawal which can prove misleading and which may well recede as the person becomes more active and more in control of life once again.

2. What are the person's strengths?

Detailed observations of behaviour are of importance. There are various methods available to assist in achieving this, for instance rating scales (see Woods & Britton 1985). These can provide information on a variety of functions. It is vital to ascertain what a person can still do, what skills are retained – self-care, social, other acquired skills, capacity to perform domestic tasks and so on. The emphasis is on assets not deficits. It may be that tasks are carried out slowly, or some prompting is needed; what is important is to recognize that the person does have some skills and abilities and the eventual plan will seek to capitalise on these.

It is equally important to know what the person's interests have been, what was enjoyed and some idea of background and life history. This provides valuable information in building up a picture of what the person would be like without the present disabilities, in individualising recreational and constructive activities, in providing guidance as to topics for conversation and in selecting suitable rewarding items and events.

The question of the very deteriorated patient is often raised. What skills, abilities, and interests can possibly be retained? Here a more basic level must be considered; perhaps the person cannot use utensils for eating, but succeeds well with fingers; perhaps verbal communication is poor, but a smile is offered in response; despite apparent total withdrawal a sudden noise elicits a turn of the head; music and rhythm lead perhaps to joining in a dance or a song. Under these conditions very careful observations are necessary. There is a need to stand back and allow the patient to attempt something for himself or herself before automatically doing it for him or her. This permits the expression of whatever remaining skill there may be. Above all else a patient must be seen as a living being who must not be 'written off' no matter how deteriorated appearances suggest him or her to be.

3. What are the person's needs? What are the areas of difficulty?

Again the placing of this question is deliberate. Too often it comes first – understandably enough – as it is the problem behaviours that make life difficult for those in the caring role. It is placed low down the list of questions to avoid the possibility of perceiving individuals only in terms of problems. Frequently patients are described as personifying particular behaviour. As a result they become known as 'the screamer', 'the wanderer', 'the hoarder' etc. In any plan the emphasis must be on the person's assets if the problem behaviours are to be improved at all. Negative aspects of behaviour cannot be seen in isolation from neutral or positive features. If the aim is to reduce the frequency of a problem behaviour e.g. wandering, the aim should be to increase the frequency of other – preferably incompatible – positive behaviours. In this example, the amount of sitting, reading a magazine, or joining in a group singing session could be usefully increased.

In specifying the possible problems of each patient several issues need to be examined:

a. the problem should be stated clearly

b. the frequency of its occurrence

c. the situation in which it occurs

d. any clues about events preceding its occurrence, or which could act as a catalyst

e. What follows as a result of the behaviour. In other words what are the reactions of staff and others in the situation, what benefit or gain does the person obtain and what are the losses?

It is necessary to say much more than 'Mr Jones is aggressive'. A more correct account might be 'Mr Jones hits other patients once a week. This occurs when someone sits in his chair in the living area. The staff try to restore peace by removing the other patients from the lounge so that Mr Jones can have his seat back'.

Specific descriptions of behaviour are required; this is essential for an individual plan to be developed. Abbreviated notes such as 'confused', 'attention seeking', 'demented', etc., are insufficient and may have quite different meanings for different staff members and disciplines. The word 'confused' can be used by one member of staff to describe continual wandering about the ward, whereas to another it would imply an inability to name the day and time of year. Particularly misleading is 'attention seeking' which can even be used as a derogatory term for unpopular patients. It rarely proves informative; after all, human beings are all seeking some form of attention! Problems can arise over the nature of the attention seeking and the amount demanded. Once again the nature of the problem in each case should be explicity specified.

Mrs R and Mrs S were both described as 'attention seeking'. Mrs R was an obese diabetic who found it impossible to stick to the prescribed diet and so had a constant thirst. She would call for water whenever a nurse passed within earshot – even though she might have a glass already in her hand. Her call was loud and insistent. Enumeration of this behaviour indicated that she shouted 'Nurse, nurse' approximately 30 times in an hour. The appearance of a nurse acted as a trigger. Reactions varied – she was ignored, told to be quiet, some attempted to calm her down and others provided her with more water. Reactions of other residents were consistently negative, urging her in the strongest terms to 'pipe down'.

Mrs S complained of nausea in order to 'seek attention'. She felt sick at the meal table and invariably had to leave halfway through. Her nausea was worse with difficult-to-digest foods. The other patients responded negatively and objected to being put off their own food, and although initially sympathetic the staff eventually became matter-of-fact in their approach. Medical investigations showed a partial oesophageal obstruction and so treatment plans were directed towards a special diet.

Two quite different situations and yet the same label – 'attention seeking' – illustrate the point that greater detail is necessary in order to avoid the consequences of what is undoubtedly pejorative terminology. Careful medical investigations are usually indicated when there are complaints of physical symptoms which may not appear to have a physical basis. Even when these are negative it should be borne in mind that some studies have shown that the elderly patient's self-evaluation can be a better predictor of survival even than that of the doctor's!

Finally, several studies have shown that there is very little

staff-resident interaction in some long-term care environments. To those rebelling against routine and not being
'model' residents the label of 'attention seeking' can be
attached and natural independence can be stifled. To be a
'model' resident often seems to mean sitting quietly, asking
for nothing and accepting without question. Rather than
attempting to suppress the 'problem' by achieving an undesirable state of depersonalisation, such 'problems' should
indicate a need for the environment to be modified. Attempts
should be made to provide the residents with more scope for
personal contact, more choice, more individuality and more
opportunities to be individuals in their own right with reasonable control over their own lives.

Listing needs rather than problems is a powerful way of
developing ideas for care plans. 'Incontinent' may become
'needs to go to the toilet when prompted', or perhaps, 'needs
to learn the way to the toilet'. 'Cannot dress' may become
'needs to put clothes on in the correct sequence'. Detailed
descriptions of exactly where the difficulties arise are
required, and of what the person positively needs to do for
the problem to be overcome.

4. Are there any behavioural inconsistencies?

This question should provide further clues as to capacity for
change. It highlights aspects of behaviour that vary from situation to situation, or behaviour that depends on the presence
of a certain staff member, or is inconsistent within an area of
function.

An example of a situational variation in behaviour would be
the person with dementia who sits alone and withdrawn in
the lounge of an old people's home but in the pub becomes
sociable and chatty (this precedes the ingestion of alcohol!),
or the lady who is able to cook a meal at the day centre but
never at home. These variations demonstrate the retained
capacity but suggest that some situations lack sufficient
stimulus.

Different reactions to different staff are commonly
observed. One nurse will say Mrs Brown cannot dress herself,
another will say she can. Such inconsistent observations are
extremely valuable and should not be concealed; they

provide clues as to the best ways to help the lady concerned. On this occasion perhaps one nurse may have stood back a little more, allowed Mrs Brown more time and managed to find the right way to help her. Other staff could then benefit from the discovery of the particular 'trick' in their own inter- actions with the lady.

It is in examining the inconsistencies of behaviour that 'excess disabilities' may be identified. These are deficits that seem worse than the person's level of actual impairment would suggest. Here multi-disciplinary assessment is particu- larly valuable; some specific deficits e.g. in dressing, eating, language and so on may be related to damage to particular areas of the brain. Knowledge of these kinds of deficits will help staff understand the patient's difficulties, enable suitable aids and adaptations to be provided and realistic goals to be set. Excess disabilities are identified where staff have some evidence to suggest that given the right conditions the person could perform a task which currently he does not. An example of this would be a person whose language functions are clearly intact, but who never initiates a conversation; or someone who has been observed to use a knife and fork once or twice, but who usually uses fingers.

5. Previous daily routines and social history

It is equally pertinent to enquire about the person's previous history and normal routines. Here the help of the social worker, neighbour, friend and relative is vital. So many apparently disruptive behaviours can be better understood with the help of such information. Was this person very independent, a bit of a hermit or socially very active? A professional client who has been accustomed to respect and responsibility could react forcibly to being addressed as 'Love', 'Johnny' or 'Maggie' by all and sundry. The person with minimal education and a simple job could be over- whelmed by close association with people whose past experi- ence was broader. To be expected to participate in groups whose social and intellectual levels are totally different is unrealistic.

Some clients wander. They may be searching for lost freedom, friends of a similar background, or, commonly when there has been a recent bereavement, for a lost partner. A person who has lived a solitary life could be looking for the peace and quiet to which he or she is accustomed as the noise and activity in the home or hospital is totally alien to him/her (Stokes 1986, 1986a).

Routines of many years are part of all our lives. Taking the dog out for an evening walk, having a late night cup of cocoa or even a glass of beer are common practices. Reading in bed, seeing the late night film, having a sleep in the morning, tidying up before going to bed, putting the cat in or out are others. These simple routines can be severely disturbed by the policies and systems of a care-setting. However, to ignore them or not to be aware or their existence can lead to apparently disturbed responses from clients, resulting in misunderstandings all round. It is not too difficult to find measures to coincide with the old routines. If tea is served at night, those who prefer cocoa, or whatever they have usually, should be able to inform staff of their preference. Choice of bedtime is not a great upheaval and perhaps one of the staff has a dog that could enjoy taking Mr Jay for an evening stroll around the grounds!

Attempting to answer these questions will rely a good deal on the first two possible purposes of assessment listed above. Finding retained abilities and isolating disabilities help to identify strengths and needs. Difficulties with speech, reading, writing and visuo-motor skills could be possible hindrances. Enjoyment of social interaction might be one of many factors which could prove of great value.

In using assessment for selection purposes, the most important issue is to match the person's abilities and needs with the demands and supports of the group or treatments being considered. It could be detrimental, for instance, for a person to be included in a group that was too high powered, too demanding or too active for that individual. A group might be irrelevant to that person's needs, skills or interests resulting, at best, in boredom for that individual, at worst in their feeling insulted by the low level of activity offered. So in order to achieve, say, a well matched group some questions must be asked, some areas explored. Are the demands on the person's ability to understand too great, too small? Are expectations of concentration greater than the person can sustain, or not high enough? Usually tests are of less use in this evaluation than careful observation of the person in particular situations. Equally important is a good all-round knowledge of the person's abilities and interests.

Monitoring change is essential to the individual care plan. Plans should be reviewed regularly and progress, or lack of it, should be recorded. This not only helps you to see what is happening as a result of the plan, but it also provides feedback for the staff. Even going on a diet requires an initial weight to be recorded so that loss in a week can be measured and the person encouraged to continue. When working with clients it is important to be clear about which areas of functioning are being monitored, and where change can be expected. There is little point, for instance, in assessing incontinence if the retraining programme is not directed at toileting skills. As emphasised in Chapter 3, evaluation of change also involves looking at changes in staff behaviour and attitudes, relatives and the environment as well as the elderly people themselves.

HOW TO ASSESS?

Staff – trained and untrained – are observing and assessing patients continually. These assessments are based on the staff's perception of the patient and are coloured by their reactions and their attitudes to the patient. Most often they are 'stored' in the staff-member's memory, to emerge in discussion and conversation. 'I'm sure Mrs Jones is more confused today' or 'Mr Smith didn't dress himself this morning – he usually does'. Problems arise when staff-members use the same words to mean different things 'I had to help Mrs Brown with her dinner' could mean anything from actually spoon-feeding Mrs Brown to helping her cook it, to take an extreme example. The introduction of the nursing process has facilitated recording and individual responsibility. Where this system is used, a member of staff takes on special responsibility for and interest in a particular patient. Aims, or targets, are agreed at weekly or daily meetings. Records are carefully kept, changes are noted and any misunderstandings are referred back to the nurse in charge.

Where this system has been established it can work well and prove invaluable. It is important to ensure that targets are not too vague or set at too high an initial level. Relevant information about the person's previous life-style should be an essential part of these notes.

In situations where the nursing process is not in use – e.g. many residential homes – notes are kept but are limited in the information they provide. For instance, different staff place different emphasis on different aspects of behaviour and functioning, so that comparisons with previous behaviour and with other clients may prove difficult.

More formal assessment methods have been devised to overcome some of these difficulties. They provide a structure for the observations; they make more explicit how the person functions; they involve less subjective and potentially biased opinion from the staff-member; they provide results easily compared over a period of time or with other patients. It is for these reasons that the use of formal assessment procedures is to be recommended. They do have their limitations and drawbacks, which will be pointed out, and they need to be used with common sense. They do not replace the care-staff's observations, but can enhance them by providing structure and the opportunity to highlight the problems of particular residents.

WHAT TO ASSESS?

As stated earlier, it is not our purpose to provide a critique of test materials as this has been done elsewhere (e.g. Woods & Britton 1985; Gilleard 1984a, b). However, the important areas to cover are:

1. The person's cognitive functioning – concentration, memory, orientation and so on
2. The person's specific neurological difficulties if any – speech problems, visuo-motor deficits etc.
3. The person's general functioning and behaviour – self-care, socialisation, activities and so on. What the person actually does
4. How the person feels – is he/she generally sad or happy, satisfied with life or depressed?

5. The environment and its influence. Staff attitudes and the kind of care provided.

COGNITIVE FUNCTIONING

In most cases a simple Mental Status Questionnaire is most appropriate. There are a considerable number of these available. A frequently used example is included in the Clifton Assessment Procedures for the Elderly (CAPE – Pattie & Gilleard 1979). A composite set of items devised by Woods (1979) covers much the same ground as the CAPE and the Blessed et al (1968) test – this is included in Appendix I as an example of the type of test in use. The items usually cover current orientation, personal information, current information, personal and non-personal memory. The questions are asked in a one-to-one situation; no assistance is given to the patient, but usually it is permissible to re-phrase or repeat the question. Scoring usually presents few problems – answers are easily checked and if anything other than one point for each correct answer applies the criteria for 2 or 3 point responses are laid down. In short these tests are intended to be objective and to produce a reliable score, regardless of the tester, which is indicative of the level of memory impairment.

If the aim of testing is monitoring change then there is much to be said for devising a more personalised test, with questions relevant to the patient's family and circumstances. It is advisable to assess the person several times before the rehabilitation or retraining programme commences. Preferably the assessment should be at the same time of day, and should continue until the result is consistent from day to day i.e. within two to three points at the most. If selection or identification of assets or deficits that will affect the care plan is the aim, then the reason for any failure on the test should be examined thoughtfully. A low score does not in every case indicate a severe dementia. Other factors that can lead to low scores are life-long low intelligence, deafness, poor eyesight (for reading and writing tests), severe depression and/or anxiety leading to slowness of thought or distractibility, and speech difficulties – expressive or receptive. Thus test scores need to be evaluated in the light of other information about the person. Specialist help for sensory deficits, and any possible amelioration, is a necessity. Likewise depression and extreme anxiety – if reassurance does not help – need appropriate treatment. Speech difficulties and their assessment are discussed in the next section. Life-long low intellectual difficulty may be suspected from the person's educational or occupational history, and from a low reading level that is not part of a visual or dysphasic problem. Reading level is a good predictor of previous intelligence, and the National Adult Reading Test is a useful tool to clarify this issue (Nelson 1982). Of course, these factors can occur in combination, adding further complications! It is important to realise then that there may be multiple explanations for poor performance on such tests. The converse occasionally happens also, and a person of superior intelligence, who has deteriorated from a previously very high level, scores so well that the true state is overlooked. Careful screening and retesting are advisable in such circumstances.

As was clear in evaluating the results of RO (Chapter 3) the person's cognitive functioning and performance in other areas are not completely correlated. Thus improvements on cognitive tests have no wider implication until changes in other areas are also found. Given the aims of RO however, this is certainly a direct means of examining whether it is having any effects at all, even if ideally more general changes are desired.

NEUROPSYCHOLOGICAL ASSESSMENTS

This could equally be entitled 'Misinterpreted Behaviour'. When confronted with what appears to be unusual or disordered behaviour the observer naturally interprets it according to personal experience. If a person uses foul language, is socially objectionable or insulting in some way it is not surprising to find he or she is labelled as 'psychopathic', coarse or socially unacceptable. If a person looks much like anyone else, has no apparent disability and seems to be generally capable, the observer cannot be blamed for an inability to see inside that person's head. Brain injury and disease change behaviour. The behaviour may be an indication of brain disorder.

In practical terms staff may see a patient eating only half a plate of food and will assume that the person is apathetic or has anorexia nervosa. Someone will walk into objects or trip over them and is regarded as forgetful, clumsy or going blind. Onlookers, or listeners, can believe that because a person has problems with words or reading he or she has completely deteriorated. Lack of recognition of objects or faces is classed as blindness or stupidity, and the inability to perform a task on request has many implications. The patient who is capable of dressing but who will not get dressed, no matter how often he or she is told to do so, is often viewed as a nuisance or attention seeking or uncooperative. The person who repeats words, phrases and gestures is seen as deliberately irritating family or staff. There are many behaviours which cause staff to conclude the worst about a person, and which, in practice make life very hard for everyone.

Lack of knowledge about the relationships of brain and behaviour can also lead to the setting of inappropriate targets and the use of inappropriate methods to obtain improvement. If someone no longer knows how to speak, simply being praised for making a noise will not improve communication. Although even the very young who have sustained a closed head injury can suffer 'hidden' neuropsychological deficits – e.g. an outspoken teenager with frontal lobe damage ostracised by his old friends – some of the more subtle effects of brain injury and disease seem to be less likely to be identified and understood in older people.

It is important to appreciate that an apparently generalised dementia can be made up of a number of particular dysfunctions. Specific impairments do occur in dementing processes as well as in trauma (e.g. head injuries), stroke or physical disorders. In the early stages these impairments may be minor, but as the deterioration in function becomes more severe, obviously, the problems become more apparent. Awareness of their implications and presence – for whatever reason – can assist staff in planning management and treatment programmes in a realistic manner.

This is a complicated field which we will attempt to simplify as far as possible. Abilities and functions are not necessarily linked to a particular location in the brain. Although certain major functions – such as speech – may be associated with a specific location, other centres may also be involved in some way. These main centres will be mentioned, but it is the resulting behaviour which is of importance and which plays a vital role in management and treatment. Readers are recommended to consult Walsh (1987) for a more detailed account of neuropsychology.

Disorientation

This is the most obvious and most frequently tested problem. Disorientation for time, place and person signifies some degree of confusion. It may occur with any illness, with delirium and at any age. Investigations for this are mentioned above. In addition to asking the person where he or she is, it is worth asking to be escorted around the ward or home to check if spatial orientation is intact. Some people with memory problems fill in the gaps in their memory, perhaps from a past experience or some plausible account *confabulating* about where they are and what others are doing. The person may be convinced that the time is ten or more years earlier than it really is, as if he or she were still in a previous phase of life. Some forms of brain injury or disease, e.g. Korsakoff's syndrome and other amnesias, specifically impair a person's memory and learning ability.

Aphasia – speech disorders

Relatives and friends as well as a number of staff are often under the impression that speech disorders resulting from strokes indicate a progressive deterioration and assume that reasonable comprehension no longer exists. There are many forms of speech disorder which occur for many reasons. This is an outline of the fundamental divisions for general guidance.

Dysarthria

This is often confused with true language disorder. It is an impairment in the actual production of speech due to a lesion in the upper or lower motor neurones, the basal ganglia, or in the cerebellum which results in weakness, paralysis or incoordination of speech musculature. The usual definition in dictionaries describes dysarthria as imperfect articulation. Problems of oral communication can be due to impairments not only in articulation but in one or more of the following: respiration, phonation, resonance, volume, rate, voice quality, intonation or rhythm. The use of word or sentence construction may be correct, but, to the listener, speech may sound indistinct.

Receptive dysphasia

Receptive dysphasia occurs as a result of damage to the part of the brain concerned with comprehension – usually the Wernicke's area of the dominant hemisphere, where the temporal lobe joins into the frontal and parietal lobes. This is called the posterior part of the superior temporal gyrus (see Fig. 6.1). In most right-handed people the dominant hemisphere is the left half of the brain. The situation is more uncertain in left-handed people.

The patient fails to understand what is being said to him.

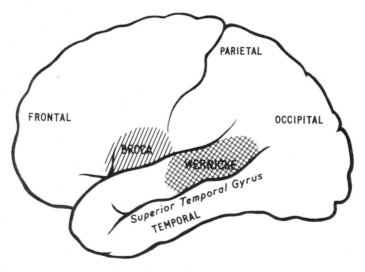

Fig. 6.1 Main areas of the brain including speech centres.

He has difficulty with verbal communications. His speech, superficially, may sound normal, but often there is a 'press of speech' – using too many words, bits of words, or even made-up words; when this is put together speech is often unintelligible and is called jargon. Contact with others is difficult or impossible. Associated problems can include difficulty in naming objects and in reading and writing. With such difficulties a person may even appear psychotic. However, the degree of impairment can vary from person to person, and because of apparently normal, though slow, speech the situation can be overlooked. Any doubts with regard to hearing should also include questions about the possibility of a receptive dysphasia.

Expressive or Broca's aphasia

This takes various forms. The damaged area is the posterior part of the dominant frontal lobe called the inferior frontal convolution of the temporal lobe (see Fig. 6.1). A stroke patient who is right-handed can have damage around this area of the brain, which causes a paralysis or weakness of the right side and produces an expressive aphasia. This impairment of speech can vary from complete loss to mild word-finding problems, grammatical errors, hesitancy and shortened sentences. Usually understanding is preserved as are automatic phrases – 'one two three', or 'good morning'. Writing is affected, and reading and calculation may also suffer.

There are many other varieties of aphasia, including global aphasia which affects all forms of language. For those who require a more detailed account a textbook such as Darley (1982), Albyn-Davis (1983) or – dealing specifically with older people – Ulatowska (1985) would be appropriate. The two forms of aphasia mentioned (or dysphasia – the two terms are often, if incorrectly, used interchangeably) do overlap in severe cases, and so may be predominantly expressive or receptive. Guidance from speech therapists can enable relatives, friends and volunteers to assist in practice and in the constant encouragement that is required to obtain improvement. Special forms of therapy, such as Melodic Intonation Therapy (a use of melody and rhythm), have been described and have proved successful in selected cases (Albert et al

1973, Sparks et al 1974) but require a great deal more development.

Apraxia

This is an impairment of voluntary and purposive movements which cannot be attributed to muscle weakness or defect, nor can it be attributed to lack of comprehension. Quite simply, the person is able to perform movements, knows what he wants to do, but if consciously trying to make a gesture or a required movement cannot organise and co-ordinate both the thought and appropriate action. This disorder is fairly common, and is often misinterpreted as uncooperativeness. Clumsiness, 'He's all fingers and thumbs' and 'She doesn't remember what to do with her fork' are usually noted. There are several forms of apraxia the principal ones being Constructional, Ideomotor, Ideational and Dressing.

Constructional apraxia

This form of apraxia has been particularly in the province of neuropsychology as it is difficult to elicit clinically. Special tests are required to isolate it. Although movements are possible the patient has difficulty in assembly, and the parts of an object cannot be put together correctly in order to achieve the whole. There is a defect in the transmission of information to the limbs concerned with the action. For example, a motor mechanic would develop problems in putting an engine back together. Arguments have arisen as to whether the difficulty results from a motor impairment for complex, sequential activities or a defect in visuo-spatial perception (how one sees spatial relationships). Studies have shown that right hemisphere damage (parietal and tempero-parietal lobes) causes visuo-spatial perceptual defects, so that even with a model to copy the patient cannot construct or draw a simple geometric figure (Warrington et al 1966, Gazzaniga 1970, Dimond 1972). Patients with known damage in the left hemisphere (parietal or tempero-parietal lobes), can perform the tasks once supplied with visual clues, and, furthermore, can improve with learning (Warrington et al 1966, Hécaen & Assal 1970). It is now accepted that left hemisphere lesions cause a motor defect – an inability to establish a programme for the required action – and right hemisphere lesions show visuo-spatial disturbances which may even be aggravated by visual cues and learning situations (Hécaen & Albert 1978).

Constructional apraxia can be demonstrated quite simply by asking a patient to draw a star, a cube and a clock face. Construction of a star with sticks or matchsticks is also useful (Fig. 6.2). Even with a hemiplegia it is possible to construct with the unimpaired hand. If the shapes produced are disoriented or inaccurate a model can be provided to copy. For less educated patients the cube might be too difficult, and drawing a house could be more appropriate (Moore & Wyke 1984). With elderly people it is rarely necessary to provide a complicated and undesirable test battery, but with younger and fitter over-60s it may be possible to introduce the Block Design Test – or Koh's Blocks – which provide more information.

Star

Without copy　　　　　　　*With copy*

Cube

Without copy　　　　　　*With copy*

Clock face saying 10 to 5

Star construction with match sticks

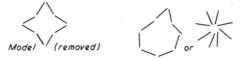

Fig. 6.2 Drawing showing spatial or apraxic disturbances.

Ideomotor apraxia

This condition is an inability to perform simple, single gestures. More complex gestures may be possible. Automatic or incidental gesture is performed perfectly. This may be thought of as a loss of memory for the pattern of the action – or engram. Although the pattern is preserved it is not under voluntary control. A Catholic can go to Mass, where he can make the sign of the cross without any difficulty. When asked to repeat it in the clinic he is totally unable to do so.

Simple gestures can be tested by asking the person to:

Wave goodbye. Pretend to stir the tea. Imitate a series of hand and arm poses (Christensen 1975).

Responses to imitation are usually better. Generally ideomotor apraxia results from bilateral brain damage.

Ideational apraxia

This is noticeable when a person attempts to carry out a complicated gesture or action. There is full understanding of what is to be done, the physical capacity to perform the action is preserved, but there is a disruption in the order and sequence of the total action and in the ability to plan properly.

In ideomotor apraxia the plan, or engram, is preserved, but the gesture is not. In ideational apraxia the single gesture is preserved but the overall plan is lost. The classical example is to ask the patient to take a match from a box, strike it and light a candle. The patient can repeat and understand the instructions, but when responding becomes very confused. The match may be struck upside down, or on the candle, or the candle may be struck on the box. The correct, logical sequence cannot be performed. Once again, well-established and automatic actions can be normal, as they do not require conscious thought. However, once the patient has to think about the response, or there is some stress, errors are multiplied. Imitation is usually more successful.

With such a complicated disability, explanations can become equally complicated! Both ideomotor and ideational apraxia are associated with lesions in the dominant parietal and temporal regions, but there is still controversy about instances of bilateral or even diffuse damage causing such impairments. Practically speaking the problem of location is irrelevant here. What is relevant is the need for an awareness of these disabilities as a sign of actual damage, so that suitable plans can be made for rehabilitation which will take the resultant behavioural problems into account. A detailed account of the apraxias can be found in Hécaen & Albert (1978).

Dressing apraxia

This seems to result from lesions in the non-dominant parietal and occipital areas. It is a visuo-spatial defect and the degree of impairment varies. Inability to dress, slowness, confusion as to which piece of clothing goes where, and inability to fasten buttons are all common complaints which can be related to a number of physical problems as well as to a dementing process – dressing apraxia is one of the more frequent reasons. The patient just cannot find the right gesture to associate the clothes with his or her body. The mental plan for an almost automatic action has been lost. Sometimes, when a patient suffers from one side neglect (anosognosia) and actually ignores one side of the body (see below), there will be difficulty in dressing that side. This form of apraxia usually is associated with damage to the right parietal and occipital areas.

There are a number of other forms of apraxia; for instance buccofacial – the inability to perform voluntary movements such as sticking out the tongue; limb and gait disturbances and even whole-body apraxia can occur. Apraxia for speech is a common disability in the speech therapist's day. A patient may be able to eat and swallow correctly, or even produce involuntary speech, but there is an inability to make the correct movements of the tongue and lips in order to produce voluntary speech. Once again there is no physical reason for this and comprehension usually is normal. The patient may produce the same automatic phrase when trying to speak e.g. 'I don't know what to say, I don't know what to say' or 'Do, do, do, do'.

Treatment

Treatment of the apraxias varies. It is often based on using preserved function and adapting it to compensate for the loss, practice of a graded programme of related tasks or the use of rhythm. For instance distraction can assist a patient to speak or complete an action normally. Concentration on a rhythm instead of the actual words can be enough to allow speech to come. Simple sentences like 'It's a ni – ce day' can be sung to a beat. The patient is amused, distracted from the real problem and then delighted to find that the words have been produced. Similarly with actions, by distracting attention from the movements the required action can be made. For instance, teeth brushing may be impossible until the chant of 'up, down' is used or a beat is tapped out. Grasp reflexes which will not release from a handshake can be resolved by distraction – stroking the back of the unwithdrawing hand. The graded programme could be used in retraining, for example an apraxic hand. A series of large, medium and small beakers are of use. Aiding the person to grasp the largest beaker, aiding movement in order to place it in another large beaker would be the first step. Encouragement to repeat this, then to try it alone would constitute the next phase. When this is successful the next size can be introduced, until by practice, and with reinforcement by praise, the actions are relearned. Tasks with meaning – helping with the washing-up – are usually the most successful.

Agnosia

This is:

An impairment in the accurate perception of objects which is not due to a defect in the sensory systems, ignorance of the nature of the object, defective intelligence or to confusion.

It is a condition which is generally unknown, almost impossible to elicit by clinical methods and the subject of much neuropsychological investigation. The commonest and best-recognised form is Visual Agnosia, but there are a number of others.

Visual agnosia or object agnosia

This is:

An inability not only to name, or demonstrate the use of an object, but an inability to appreciate its character and meaning, or to even remember ever having seen it before. Obviously it is necessary to distinguish this from aphasia and visual memory loss. Other sensory input is required. Usually if another sense is used the clues lead to recognition. A characteristic smell, noise or feel provide these clues. A patient while recognising the colour, shape and size of a lipstick remained unable to name it. She stated that the object was a maroon and gold container, cylindrical in shape and about three inches in length. Only when encouraged to remove the lid, smell the perfume and rub the contents across the back of her hand was she able to identify it. The problem appears to be associated with damage around the lateral ventricles extending into the occipital lobes. The Popplereuter's test (included in the Luria investigations, Christensen 1975) is useful in identifying this impairment. It comprises of a set of pictures of mixed-up everyday objects – a jug apparently containing a paint brush, an axe, and a pair of scissors is one example. Another test from the Luria investigations comprises sets of photographs – an object is vague in the first picture and later becomes quite distinct.

Colour and Auditory Agnosia are other forms occasionally found which can cause problems in treatment and management. A patient with auditory agnosia has word deafness. He cannot grasp normal conversation and becomes very distressed. Usually slow, distinct speech helps the problem considerably. With colour agnosia colour not only cannot be named, but matching and association of colour are impaired.

Spatial agnosia

This disorder is fairly common and is a spatial disorientation, a defect in finding the way even in familiar surroundings. A young navigator who had a mild stroke was unable to understand maps that had been given to him as an amusement during recovery. This happens in older people too. There is loss of appreciation of right and left, incapacity for drawing simple maps of the house, or the ward. Recognition of indi-

vidual objects in the environment is preserved though localisation of them is disordered. Under this heading there is the
not uncommon phenomenon of autotopagnosia – a failure to
recognise or localise parts of one's own body (related to
parietal damage). Body agnosia is also associated with
another, fairly common disorder – anosognosia. One side of
the body is neglected or denied. The patient may say her left
hand does not belong to her, or even that it belongs to
someone else. It is not rare to hear that a patient believes that
there is a strange hand in her bed, and she can require some
persuasion to accept that hand as her own. Dressing the
neglected part of the body is also a problem, and food on one
side of the plate will not be touched. The affected side is
almost invariably the left one. From a management viewpoint
it is important to be aware of this state. Simple measures can
be instigated. At mealtimes the plate can be turned around
so that a full meal is obtained. The wanderers who get lost
on the way to the toilet or who get into somebody else's bed
could have this complaint. The toilet is invariably approached
from the wrong direction and the bed on the wrong side on
return. A simple solution is to transfer beds to the most
convenient side.

Fig. 6.3 Reproduction of actual drawings by a 70-year-old lady with
anosognosia – left-sided neglect.

A drawing of a clock face, or the assembly of one of the educational variety will easily demonstrate the problem, as will the drawing of a house. (Fig. 6.3).

Other tests for body agnosia are to ask the person to point to various parts of his body and to use the Finger Agnosia tests. After a demonstration of the task the patient is asked to close his eyes, or is blindfolded. The examiner presses one of his fingers and requests the person to 'show' that finger on the other hand. There is a further test to see if the person can say 'how many fingers are there between that one and that one'. The examiner will press gently on, for instance, the forefinger and the little finger of a hand, and expect to receive the answer 'Two fingers' and so on.

As has been stated, unilateral spatial agnosia is almost exclusively related to the left half of space. Obvious exceptions would be people with right hemisphere dominance – usually left-handers. Other forms of agnosia include:

Tactile, or astereognosia, which is discerned by requesting identification of objects, particularly coins, by the sense of touch alone.

Prosopagnosia, failure to recognise faces. Testing for this problem is through the use of photographs of familiar and unfamiliar faces. Occasionally, the person cannot even recognise self-reflection in a mirror.

Simultanagnosia, is an inability to perceive a whole while being able to interpret the parts. If a picture of, for instance, a floral festival is presented and the person asked to supply a suitable name for a picture, the task will prove impossible. Each single flower will be pointed out, even each blade of grass, but the scene will be too difficult to grasp. There appears to be some association with reading problems, for although a sentence can be written correctly it can only be read back letter by letter.

Awareness of agnostic factors has very practical implications. To use 'left' and 'right' as meaningful concepts for someone with spatial problems is obviously inappropriate. Words either written or spoken – depending on the impairment – are more valuable to those with such difficulties. A picture above a bed, a name in large print and verbal directions using colour or some meaningful symbol are more useful in retraining than spatial directions.

Acquired knowledge

There are other factors which should be checked in any neuropsychological investigation. Impairment of acquired knowledge may have more implications than that of global deterioration.

Agraphia – an inability to write properly. This includes spelling, letter construction and word organisation and is related to aphasia and tempero-parietal problems.

Acalculia – or difficulty with numbers, can also be related to parietal lesions, reading difficulties (alexia) and spatial disorders.

Alexia or dyslexia – inability to read, is a disturbance in the relationship between visual and language functions, and can occur in association with a number of other conditions. From the management viewpoint, if someone cannot read it is hopeless to expect him or her to cope in situations where such ability is vital. Directions on medicine bottles, street or directional signs will prove meaningless.

The magazine method of testing (Fig. 6.4)

A useful and unthreatening method of investigation is to use an ordinary, colourful magazine which can provide a wealth of information without stress. Using a suitable selection of advertisements from the two open pages of a magazine it is possible to test:

Reading – Can the person read, can only large letters be meaningful, can smaller ones be read or is reading impossible?

Comprehension – Can the implications and meaning of pictures be understood, as well as words? Are comments and memories produced, with encouragement, from the content?

Aphasia – Can the person use the right words and name the objects on the page with ease?

Agnosia – Has the person any difficulty in seeing the pictures, appreciating what they are? Is colour meaningful, can faces be noted, or parts of the body? Can the whole of a picture convey meaning, or are only parts of the picture seen?

Fig. 6.4 The Magazine Method. Using pages from a journal with clear, distinct pictures, words of varying size, columns, and colour in order to apply simple investigations of ability.

Anosognosia – By watching the person's way of reading, and the initial direction of gaze it is possible to tell if there is one-sided neglect. If the farthest column on the right hand page is the first to be noticed there is a possibility of anosognosia. Check to see if there is difficulty in recognizing the existence of a left hand page and a column on the farthest left of that page.

Apraxia – Can be suggested by difficulties in turning pages and in pointing.

The 'magazine method' is by no means conclusive, but it is certainly very helpful and completely painless. It provides staff with information, useful interaction and the patient with some stimulation. It is not vital to have strict assessment procedures with sick elderly people, what is important is to find out as gently as possible if there are impairments in certain functions. Using material from the natural surroundings provides a comfortable, unthreatening and easy way to screen for any possible difficulties which can be looked at in more detail, if necessary, later.

Frontal involvement

Though there are symptoms and signs associated with many locations in the brain, and much to suggest that localisation is not complete, discussion of these aspects is not appropriate here. However, some of the personality changes and function impairments associated with frontal lobe damage are of importance in understanding some of the behaviour frequently observed, and also helpful to the design of suitable therapeutic intervention. The frontal syndrome recognised in post-traumatic injuries usually shows some, if not all, of the following signs: impulsiveness, aggression or apathy, poor planning and logic, and an inability to monitor or control what is said or done. The person may not be able to end a letter or a conversation and may appear rather garrulous.

Emotional lability can be very upsetting to relatives and staff. It is often the result of a stroke or other neurological trauma. Euphoria, inappropriate laughing and/or crying, the use of undesirable language, sexual exhibitionism and erotic behaviour are disturbing and they are usually out of character. The mechanisms of control have been lost and emotions can run riot. If the involuntary nature of this emotion is understood it is easier to use distraction than inappropriate sympathy which aggravates the situation. Lack of initiative is another common feature. This is not caused by paralysis, apraxia or confusion but an inability to voluntarily and spontaneously initiate a desired or automatic motor task. Recently it has been found that thought processes can also suffer from this inertia. Quite simply the victim cannot get going. There is a disorder of attention. Questions must be repeated over and over in order to elicit a response. This is linked to initiation difficulties. Similarly the patient forgets to remember. The information has not been forgotten, but the ability to start the necessary 'wheels' turning to make the memory process work is impaired.

Perseveration is common. On long-stay wards patients can be heard repeating the same phrase all day, or seen performing the same action again and again.

Writing and drawing show repetitions for instance:

The girl has a nice hat – can be reproduced as – The girl has has a has or when asked to copy MNMNMNMN – MNNNNNNNN is produced.

This form of perseveration has a bearing on the difficulty in changing set, or in progressing from one idea to another. When asked to complete a series of sequential tasks errors occur – such as the pattern in Fig. 6.5.

 please repeat across the page

The response might be, for example:

△△□□□++OOOOOOO++++++

Fig. 6.5 Sequential Pattern Completion. One of the tests to help in assessing frontal lobe, or operational thought, impairment.

Similarly a set of wooden or plastic shapes which are also in sets of different colours can only be sorted into either colour, or shape groups; the alternative group cannot be found.

Luria (1963) has many suggestions for aiding rehabilitation programmes that are in difficulty because of this perseverative process. Though time-consuming they are effective. Distraction at the right moment is the key. The second an error in movement is commenced the action can be interrupted and distraction introduced. A comment on the weather or flowers or some nearby incident would be suitable. To ensure that the next movement in the task is correct physical guidance is used. To make a stitch with a needle, for instance, a hand guiding a hand can ensure the correct path and so help to stop perseveration of an incorrect action. Phraseology can be interrupted in a similar manner and reinforcement, usually praise and attention, can be given to non-repetitive talk. However, long-standing perseverations are very difficult to eradicate and early intervention is more successful.

Final comments

Understanding of some of the behaviour resulting from specific damage can improve the aims of programmes and rehabilitation. Relatives need to understand some of the changes that they see and cooperation from them can be increased. Examinations need not be threatening or stressful and the 24 hour RO approach can be used in aiding assessments. If the person's problems are related to damage, more appropriate measures of retraining can be used in conjunction with RO and with the reinforcement of behaviour modification methods. Goals can be set at a suitable level, the right kind of attention and encouragement can be discussed and applied, and simple management measures introduced. Furthermore such understanding will assist in better appreciation of such behaviour patterns that have been incorrectly attributed to a dementia or to disruptive or uncooperative personalities (Table 6.1).

Table 6.1

Neuropsychological deficits		Simple tests
Language problems		
Expressive dysphasia	Difficulty in conversation	Listen. Word finding, odd words and sentences, little speech, or complete rubbish
Receptive dysphasia	Comprehension difficulty	Lack of appropriate response to questions
Agraphia	Writing difficulty	Write a simple sentence
Acalculia	Difficulty with numbers	Write numbers, add, subtract, multiply and divide simple sums
Alexia	Reading difficulty	Read notice on ward, on TV or from a magazine
Apraxia		
Constructional	Difficulty in putting things together to make a whole	Use matchsticks to make a star. Draw a star or a cube. Also use model for copying
Ideomotor	Difficulty in making a single gesture	Ask to be shown hair brushing, waving, clenching teeth etc.
Ideational	Difficulty in making complex gesture	Pretend to get out a cigarette, light it and start smoking
Dressing	Difficulty in dressing	Put on a coat, button it and take it off again
Agnosias		
Visual	Difficulty in appreciating meaning of objects	Use a letter or a number made up of other letters

Table 6.1 (*Cont'd*)

Neuropsychological deficits		Simple tests
		or numbers, e.g. a large 2 made of tiny 4s and see if both are recognised
Colour	Difficulty in appreciating colour	Naming, matching and association
Spatial	Difficulty in finding the way Unable to understand maps	Draw a plan of home
Autotopagnosia	Difficulty in recognising parts of own body, or another's	Point to parts of own body, and that of examiners
Anosognosia	Neglect of one side body	Watch dinner plate Draw clock-face or house
Astereognosis	Difficulty in recognising objects by touch	Name a selection of coins by touch alone
Prosopagnosia	Difficulty in recognising faces	Naming familiar and unfamiliar faces from photographs
Simultanagnosia	Difficulty in perceiving a whole	Name a picture with something suitable to describe its content
Frontal involvement	Personality change Euphoria or apathy Disinhibition Lack of initiative Perseveration Inability to plan	Watch Ask relatives about previous personality Use sequence of shapes or figures. Watch how games such as cards are played

ASSESSMENT OF GENERAL FUNCTIONING AND BEHAVIOUR

Three main approaches have been used with the elderly:

1. Rating Scales, where staff who know the person well assess the person's functioning from their general unsystematic observations of them in their own environment.

2. Direct observation in a structured situation, where the person is requested to carry out particular tasks, and then assessed on his or her performance.

3. Direct observation in natural settings, where a large number of systematic observations of the patient in his or her natural environment are made.

Rating scales

These have been the most frequently used form of behavioural assessment – perhaps because they are the most economical in terms of time. There are so many different scales that have been used with older people that their various advantages and drawbacks cannot be covered here. The interested reader is referred to Woods & Britton (1985, ch 6) and Gilleard (1984b) for reviews. Hall's (1980) review of rating scales in general use is also helpful for its advice on the development of new scales.

One of the major problems with rating scales has been the difficulty in measuring small changes in behaviour. Most scales cover change in relatively large steps and are rarely sensitive to small changes or improvements. For instance, a person who is incontinent 10 times a day has made progress if the frequency drops to only 5 times a day. A scale which asks if incontinence occurs frequently, occasionally or never will not reflect such improvement. As a result, the ability to monitor fine change is limited and further assessment is normally required to identify specific targets in goal planning.

The Holden Scale (Appendix 2) was first used in Holden & Sinebruchow's study (1979) and is concerned with communication and social behaviour, rather than self-care skills, on which most of the other behaviour rating scales focus. Despite its different emphasis respectable correlations have been reported with the CAPE Behavioural Rating Scale and the CAPE cognitive scale (0.78 and 0.75 respectively, Merchant & Saxby 1981), supporting the validity of ratings on this scale. As a rough and ready guide, it has been suggested that scores above 25 indicate the person may well do best in a group where expectations are at a fairly basic level; scores between 15–24 reflect a more moderate degree of impairment, and a probable response to a slightly more demanding group; scores less than 15 suggest milder problems with less support and direction being needed in a group situation. As with all total scores, where widely ranging areas of function are added together, these scores should only be treated as a general indication. The Holden Communication Scale is being widely used in RO and reminiscence programmes to good effect. Its content is more relevant to these approaches than other scales. It would, of course, be of little use in assessing progress in a self-care re-training programme!

More practically, how does one go about selecting and using a rating scale? The first and most important consideration is to select a scale that is acceptable in the particular situation. It needs to be short enough so that time is available for it to be completed – rather than it being left half-finished. It needs to be easy to use and understand, without difficult terminology. Scoring and interpretation should be simple also. It needs to be relevant to the situation; e.g. in many situations an item on 'regular work assignments' would be inappropriate. Item definitions must be clear and precise (Hall 1980). There must be no ambiguity or misunderstanding about the meaning of an item. Interpretation of behaviour reduces reliability e.g. different staff have different criteria for a term such as 'restlessness' unless it is defined more specifically. Items should have single definitions; items like 'misidentifies persons and surroundings but can find way about' cause problems for the person who cannot find his way about, identifies people, but not his surroundings! Where items are ordered the sequence needs to be carefully examined, so there are no anomalies. On one scale a person who walks independently with a stick could receive a score of 2 or 4 on mobility depending on the staff member's interpretation of the item. Few scales have none of these faults; they are exceptionally difficult to avoid, particularly if a fresh scale is devised.

In using the scale, consideration needs to be given to who will make the ratings. The person who has most contact with the patient is the ideal choice; often trained staff members have less patient contact, so they may not be in the best position to carry out ratings. Training in the use of the rating scale should always be given. Making independent ratings of the same patients and then discussing reasons for any

discrepancies is a useful exercise. The rating procedure needs
to be clear; is the person rated as they are today, over the past
week, month? Can the rater only use his own observations,
or can he make use of what others have observed? What is
the procedure for commenting on aspects of behaviour not
covered by the scale?

It can be seen that there are many problems inherent in
reducing the whole range of behaviour of the elderly person
into a brief rating. Added to these are the difficulties brought
about by fluctuations in the person's behaviour – sometimes
related to different staff. None of the scales available is
perfect, but used with common sense and again in conjunction with other available information they can play a useful
part in assessment.

Direct observation – structured setting

This is a well-established assessment method, where the
person is asked to perform certain tasks in the presence of
the assessor, who then rates their competence in this structured setting. The best example of this approach is the
Performance Test of Activities of Daily Living (PADL),
described by Kuriansky & Gurland (1976) and used extensively
in studies of psychogeriatric patients in New York and
London. This consists of 16 tasks, all easily demonstrated in
an interview situation. These include drinking from a cup,
combing hair, eating, making a 'phone call so on. Most need
'props' e.g. a cup, comb, spoon with sweet, 'phone etc., and
it is recommended that these be collected into a portable kit.
Performance on each task is broken down into component
parts and whether or not the person carries out each part is
recorded. Simple tasks are given initially to reduce anxiety,
and the whole test takes around 20 minutes to administer.

Independent ratings of patients' performance by the inter-
viewer and an observer showed high inter-rater reliability
(0.90). Evidence of validity – in its relation to physical health,
mental state and prognosis – is presented by Kuriansky et al
(1976). The test is reported to be generally acceptable to
patients.

There are advantages to this approach, particularly in as far
as the person's capabilities are revealed, whereas in the ward

setting opportunities for some skills might not be available or necessary. In developing an individual plan, this test might be useful if it revealed more ability than shown on the ward, providing potential areas to encourage and work on. However, this possible discrepancy between ward and test situation makes it less useful for monitoring changes on the ward. When specific programmes aim at particular targets included in the PADL, the sub-division of each task may be helpful in planning treatment and assessment of change. Unfortunately, the restricted range of items detracts from this application. There is no assessment of communication or socialisation.

Discrepancy between ward and test performance is also possible where the structured situation fails to elicit the person's best performance, which may occur more easily in some cases in a natural setting. Comprehension difficulties could lead to this, as could anxiety and insufficient motivation. Reasons for failure need to be explored carefully; the person may not have grasped what he is intended to do or may be too anxious or apathetic to carry out the task correctly.

The test may be useful for selection of patients, establishing a dependency level, and for monitoring of some programmes focussing on specific aspects of the person's functioning. It could be utilized alongside ratings of the person's functioning on the same tasks in the ward setting.

Direct observation – natural setting

This is where the patient's actual behaviour on the ward, old people's home or day centre is observed and recorded. On the face of it if the aim is to change the person's performance within this setting, this should be the assessment method. It has been used extensively with children and the mentally handicapped, and to some extent in behavioural studies with the elderly.

Two initial issues concerning direct observation both relate to producing manageable data from a potentially massive amount of observation. Firstly some method of sampling the person's behaviour must be chosen. By time sampling, a snap-shot picture of the person's behaviour over a longer time period is obtained. Thus observations might be made of the person every three minutes or every 10 minutes or every 30 minutes and so on, depending on the frequency of the behaviours being observed. A further decision must be taken as to whether to record over a short period (10–30 seconds, say) all the behaviours the person exhibits. If a very frequent discrete behaviour (smoking and shouting can be examples of this) is being observed then all the occurrences in a certain time period (say 15 or 30 minutes) might be counted at different times of the day. The second issue is to decide on what areas of functioning to observe, and at what level of precision. Often social behaviours or other readily accessible areas are chosen. The range of precision extends from the relatively crude categorisation of a person's behaviour as 'engaged' or 'disengaged' to the level of fine analysis of behaviour – for example, recording the person's direction and duration of gaze.

Some complex problems can arise. Readers are referred to Hutt & Hutt (1970) for a full exposition of direct observation. If it is desired to monitor a range of behaviours, the problem of the observer having to use too long and detailed an observation schedule will have to be faced. If behaviours occur infrequently, say once or twice a day, then they may be missed entirely by most time-sampling methods; direct frequency counts are preferable here. The observer needs to fit unobtrusively into the surroundings, so that his or her influence on the patients' behaviour is minimized. An adaptation period is needed for staff as well as patients. Staff may either keep well clear or arrange special events, which bias the picture obtained. Behaviours to be observed need to be defined carefully, without ambiguity, and a second observer making observations simultaneously but independently is helpful in ensuring this has been achieved. Time sampling is easiest when all patients are together in one place and very difficult if they are scattered throughout a number of rooms.

The simpler the observation method used the more reliable results will be. Jenkins et al (1977) used the concept of 'engagement' in their study of activity in old people's homes. Residents are said to be engaged if they are interacting with people or materials; non-engaged if they are doing nothing; a detailed manual is available with full definitions. The method is to enter the room where patients are being observed, count the number of people who are engaged and then count the total number of people present. A percentage is then calculated of the proportion of those present who are engaged. This is then a group method, which may be useful where changes throughout the home or ward are being monitored. McFadyen et al (1980) and McFadyen (1984) have extended the method by recording engagement for individuals, and by breaking the types of engagement and non-engagement down slightly. The definitions of Jenkins et al are given in such a way as to make this analysis quite straightforward. McFadyen et al made observations on each patient every half-hour over a $2\frac{1}{2}$ day period. They found greater than 90 per cent inter-rater agreement on simultaneous observations of 20 patients. Their results showed a non-significant relationship of engagement with memory and information test performance, although ratings of self-care impairment did correlate significantly with active engagement in both a psychogeriatric ward and an old people's home.

This type of assessment, which because of its restricted range is reasonably manageable, would be useful in monitoring treatment programmes. It also makes possible the monitoring of staff-patient interactions, which are the basic therapeutic method in 24 hour RO. The necessity for ensuring changes do occur at this level has already been emphasised. This method would enable patients to be identified who have low levels of engagement or social activity; the reason for this could then be explored. It has been suggested that engagement is an indication of the 'quality of life' in an institution; if this is so then this method could help to identify the need for environmental changes of every kind in institutions for the elderly and help to monitor them.

ASSESSMENT OF THE PERSON'S AFFECTIVE STATE

So often it seems that the last people to be asked about the effects of treatment programmes are the elderly people themselves. Few studies of RO have included a measure of the effects of treatment on the person's feelings; MacDonald & Settin (1978) and Baines et al (1987) used a Life Satisfaction

Index. The difficulty with this and other similar measures is that they are questionnaires that the patients fill in themselves. Their validity is doubtful in more severely demented patients, who may not be able to comprehend the self-report format.

For patients who are less deteriorated and can complete a brief questionnaire a number of mood, morale and life-satisfaction scales are available. Lawton (1971) and Woods & Britton (1985) review many of these.

An alternative strategy is for an observer to rate the person's apparent mood or level of depression. Kochansky (1979) describes several such scales. However, little attention has been given to the assessment of mood in demented patients. Generally the emphasis has been on differentiating people only suffering from depression from those only having a dementia. The overlap – which certainly exists – is usually ignored. For the present it seems that there is very little available to enable mood to be evaluated satisfactorily in people with dementia. Assessments of an informal nature, based on close knowledge of the elderly person and efforts to form a relationship with them, may be the most practical approach available.

STAFF ATTITUDES AND ASSESSMENT OF THE INSTITUTION

This is another extremely important area – though assessment of attitudes remains difficult. Attitude change appeared to be measured successfully in a study by Smith & Barker (1972) who used an adaptation of the Oberleder Attitude Scale (Oberleder 1962) to measure staff changes after training in using RO. However, when an attempt was made to replicate this by Bailey et al (1986) the scale proved of little value despite the staff's agreement about improved morale.

This is one of the most difficult areas to assess and monitor. It may be possible to create an atmosphere for change (see Ch. 10) but to evaluate and monitor how this is achieved and maintained is a considerable challenge. Staff responses to attitude scales, where the expected 'positive' answer is fairly obvious, may not relate well to actual staff behaviour (Saxby & Jeffery 1983; Adelson et al 1982).

The MEAP (see below) does throw light on some aspects as it looks in depth at the enforcement of rules, policies and practices in institutions. The degree of tolerance and leeway allowed to residents can be estimated. The MEAP provides some indication of a particular institution's concern for its staff – but it does not throw light on their feelings, their conception of their role, how they spend their time, where priorities lie or factors such as job satisfaction or attitudes to age.

Most training centres are becoming increasingly aware of the problems of staff 'burn-out' (Quattrochi-Tubin et al 1982). The implications of this state of exhaustion and demoralisation are obvious and probably most common in isolated, unsupported homes and hospitals where encouragement, relief, staff and resources are at a minimum. Staff turnover and sickness rates will be high. It is probably even more common with caring relatives, alone in what can be a demanding and stressful situation. However, the concern may well lead to improved assessment procedures for morale and job satisfaction in the near future. Scales evaluating stress and strain in carers are already available (Greene et al 1982; Robinson 1983; Gilleard 1984c)

The environment, as discussed in Chapter 7, plays an essential role in influencing independence, stimulation levels, maintenance of personal identity and needs. An environment in which a person can exercise no control will encourage institutionalisation. It thus becomes important to be able to evaluate an environment, and the questions of how this can be done, what should be examined and how changes can be monitored all require an answer. It is necessary to look at both the physical and psychological environments in order to obtain as full a picture as possible.

Psychological environment

Here we would be assessing level of activity, the degree of choice, interaction between client and client, and client and staff and considering the amount of engagement. Meeting individual needs, privacy, preservation of dignity and self-respect, retained abilities that are being used, help being available when required and the encouragement to achieve goals are all areas which are too rarely assessed. Some could be covered by Life Satisfaction Indices, but such ratings require a greater ability to judge, respond and be critical than most people with dementia retain. The direct observation methods mentioned above could be relevant. For instance, Jenkins et al (1977) rated residents as engaged when they were interacting with other people or materials, and not engaged when they were doing nothing. Others, such as McFadyen (1984) and Baltes et al (1980), have employed an individual recording system rather than the group one used by Jenkins et al, and have broken down the definitions of engagement into the component parts of self-care, social activities and the interactions between clients and between staff and clients. Using methods like these and others outlined by Woods & Britton (1985, Ch. 6), it is possible to obtain some insight into the quality of life provided by a particular care-setting. Unfortunately, present measures cannot provide more than a sample of what it is like to live in these places and there are many aspects about which more should be known. In measuring activity levels, for example, it is also important to know the amount of choice residents have; are they allowed *not* to participate! How relevant are the activities to the person's interests? How much does each person value the activities in which he or she takes part? Similarly, with interaction *quality* is as important as *quantity*.

Physical environment

The effects an environment can have on an individual have been recognised for many years, and various attempts have been made to develop check-lists to evaluate whether the architecture and internal layout provide relevant facilities and meet reasonable standards. In recent years there has been an increase of interest in this area, particularly for the mentally handicapped and the elderly. Lemke and Moos (1980, 1986) have developed the Multiphasic Environmental Assessment Procedure for the elderly (MEAP) (Moos & Lemke 1980). Although not standardised for British settings it is not difficult to adapt, and many of its components can be used singly to evaluate a particular aspect. They break the environment down into 5 specific parts, each part forming a sub-scale of its own. Each of these parts can be assessed and scored separately, with a total score to provide an overall picture. The MEAP covers architectural and physical features of the building and surroundings; the policies and programmes; information about staff and clients; a Rating Scale – possibly the most interesting as it covers the living environment in detail and looks carefully at the grooming of the clients, their clothing and activity levels, and at staff interaction with them, and it also examines organisation and possible conflicts. The Sheltered Care Environment Scale forms the final part. This is in a simple 'yes' and 'no' format designed to be completed by both staff and patients. It is open to the criticism that the 'right' answer is obvious, and clients may respond with caution, doubt or may not even understand or be capable of completing it.

The whole MEAP takes an age to complete! At times it poses problems as to who is responsible for completing it. It takes a careful and thorough investigator to obtain valid responses. Undoubtedly, it provides a very useful overview and can highlight problem areas. It has especial value in comparisons between units, in setting up new centres and in finding targets for change. Additionally, it provides a system for re-evaluation. It is, of course, impossible to change or improve everything – buildings are hard to move and additions are sometimes hard to supply! An old unit can be modernised, but the fabric will be the same.

When examining the MEAP in detail there are many omissions – despite its length – and for many, the time required to complete it is daunting. A shorter version which could be used as a screening device for most institutions or units was devised by Holden (1984c). The ORIF (Orientation Facilities Check-list) concentrates on some of the more salient features of internal planning, sensory stimulation and facilities to encourage independence. It is divided into two parts – architectural and sensory stimulation. Each part has 20 questions which are scored on a four point scale. As with the MEAP, each sub-scale has its own score and the combined scores provide an overall picture. An old setting may score low on the architectural aspects, but may be active and stimulating; the converse is also possible. The ORIF has been used in practice to good effect. Bailey et al (1986) showed that despite the age of the hospital unit, the changes made by the staff to the environment were clearly demonstrated by changes in the scores on the ORIF. In looking at residential homes and hospital wards it is designed to draw attention to areas which could be improved and in monitoring changes taking place.

Useful measures of the environment would then provide a guide as to what to change and the success of change, would help to define the type of institution in reports of research studies and perhaps clarify some of the conflicting results obtained in studies which may be related to differences in institutional structure, policy and priorities.

CONCLUSION

In the use of assessments it cannot be stressed too much that to employ any test requires that the examiner should have the individual, as a whole person, in mind. Anything which causes distress or is irrelevant is of little value and of a doubtful ethical standard. The person's needs, wishes, strengths and weaknesses are of prime importance. Not only is the individual to be considered but also there should be investigation of those aspects of living which can affect his or her ability to live and function at an optimum level. So the people around, the staff and the relatives, must be involved in the assessment, and the environment carefully observed and evaluated. The needs and feelings of those closely involved should also be considered. There are still several areas for which there is a dearth of appropriate measures – attitudes for instance. There has been an increasing awareness of the gaps in knowledge and much work has been done and is continuing to improve our pool of information and resources.

'There is great beauty in old trees
Old streets and ruins old.
Why should not I as well as these
Grow lovely growing old.'
(Seen in old churchyard in Cornwall)

7

The basic approach – RO in everyday use

INFORMAL OR 24 HOUR RO

Reality Orientation in its broadest sense is a basic informal communication approach. As such it is used by many staff, perhaps unknowingly. In principle it could be used by all those in contact with elderly people with dementia. In essence the method is simple, obvious and practised automatically by many caring people. In this chapter will be discussed – in practical terms – how communication, even with elderly patients with dementia, can be facilitated using 24 hour RO. As the name implies, this is an approach to be used throughout the person's waking hours; in fact, every interaction is an opportunity for RO. In addition the approach demands certain environmental changes that will be described in this chapter also, together with techniques for making the most of the person's learning potential, however limited this may be.

It is likely that difficulty in communicating with elderly patients is one factor in the frequent reactions of distaste, repugnance and rejection that occur in younger people faced with working with them. The barriers to easy communication may be many; some, at least, are potentially soluble. If they can be overcome then care-staff will find their work more satisfying and enjoyable, and patients will feel less rejected, frustrated and distressed.

Sensory deficits

The normal process of loss of acuity provides difficulties for both staff, relatives and friends as well as those involved in the actual loss. Eyesight is not as keen, nor often is hearing. The skin is less elastic so gesture is limited. Ageing bones, joints and muscles cause a decrease in mobility so fluency of action and movement change. As a result social contact and communication change (Bromley 1978). Because they do not hear, see or move as easily as in earlier years the elderly are often less aware of events occuring around them. A nurse can appear on the ward before breakfast and her general, cheerful 'Good morning' will elicit no response. Quite naturally she may feel upset and rejected. The patients may wonder why she becomes less friendly and helpful. A serious misunderstanding has occurred! The nurse was too far away, too impersonal, and spoke too quickly and too low. Even if standing fairly close to an individual a greeting or question may not be observed. If relatives mistake this lack of response for mental deterioration they begin to talk to each other as though their ageing parent was not present. The reaction of many patients in such a situation is withdrawal. Another misunderstanding!

Severe sensory loss is easier for staff and relatives to accept and understand; efforts are always made to help the very deaf and blind. The normal loss of sensory acuity, coupled particularly with any form of infirmity, is often overlooked. The attitudes of others caused by unawareness of the situation can lead to withdrawal which together with sensory loss has serious psychological implications.

In Chapter 2, the possible role of sensory deprivation in increasing the degree of confusion in elderly people was discussed. Sensory deprivation is the loss of sensory input for any reason; loss of sensory acuity and withdrawal are two ways by which a person's sensory stimulation may be reduced.

Two other processes by which withdrawal may be related to loss of acuity are probably common. Firstly, some patients may feel embarrassed about their failing senses, and suffer loss of self-esteem. A reaction to this may be to cut off from potentially embarrassing social situations. Secondly, some environments for elderly people may lack interest for particular patients; if they have a loss of sensory acuity 'shutting off' the unpleasant, boring situation is easy. In each case further sensory deprivation, and probably increased confusion, will result.

To combat these problems the barriers to communication should be attacked. Eyesight and hearing should be tested. When aids are required they should be used and checked regularly. Dentures should fit well, be comfortable and in their owner's mouth not in a glass or box! Thus the person's sensory and speech functions are aided as far as possible. Environmental help is also needed – lighting should be bright (but not glaring), extraneous noises damped down to a minimum. Staff need to remember that conversation should be at close range. It is better to be beneath the older person than to speak looking down at her. Slow, clearly enunciated speech is more appropriate than most quick-fire remarks. Shouting is usually unnecessary; clarity is more important.

To avoid sensory deprivation, as many of the senses as possible should be stimulated in conversation; the person is encouraged to feel objects, smell them, and taste them where appropriate. Particularly where one of the senses is impaired this sensory enrichment of the more intact senses is crucial in helping the person keep in touch with his or her surroundings.

Non-verbal communication

Non-verbal communication, or 'body language', is important in facilitating interaction. To join in a conversation people will move forward, or move away if they wish to escape. Gestures are vital in some cultures and have their place in every language. Not only limbs, but eyes, eyebrows, lips and the head can be used to express emotions, reactions and other messages. Close relationships have their own private system which is completely meaningless to outsiders. The movement of an eyebrow can mean anything from 'That's good' to 'Let's go' or, 'What a funny man'. Eye contact can be used to encourage the shy, to embarrass or to console someone. It can imply concentration or interest and many other factors depending on individual ability and expressiveness.

Elderly people with sensory loss will be less sensitive to non-verbal communication; in normal conversation many of the signals given are subtle, and easily missed if eyesight or hearing is impaired. Staff need then to make their non-verbal messages slightly more clear-cut than usual. Thus a slow approach from in front of the patient is less likely to be misinterpreted as aggressive than suddenly appearing at the patient's side from behind. In face-to-face contact a warm smile expresses friendliness; eye-contact expresses the staff member's desire to interact and is useful in gaining and maintaining attention. The use of gentle touch should be encouraged – a hand over the other's hand, a soft stroking of a cheek with the back of the hand. These and other gestures are warm, reassuring and imply concern and friendship; touch is also helpful in attracting and keeping the person's interest and concentration. If the nurse, by these means, appears to the patient as calm, warm and friendly then the patient is more likely to respond and be relaxed and re-assured. The nurse's aim is not to put on an act, but rather to express clearly, minimising the danger of misunderstanding, whatever he or she is trying to communicate.

In listening to elderly people, attention must be given to the messages they give non-verbally, as well as to what they say. Here it must be remembered that the ability of elderly people to give out messages may be impaired as well as their capacity to receive them. This is due to the decrease in mobility and dexterity mentioned above. However, as will be discussed later, the signals that are given can be important in making some sense of what the person says. It may take a little longer for the non-verbal signal to appear or to sink in – good reasons for adapting the pace of the interaction to the individual's speed.

Personal distance

The distance between people effects interaction to some extent. This varies from culture to culture, from situation to situation and from person to person. Generally, total atten-tion is required at a distance of about 18 inches; at four feet some communication is indicated and a distance of up to twelve feet still provides the possibilities of social interaction. Over twelve feet allows for public space so it is possible to sit in a park, or on the beach or in a waiting room and main-tain privacy even in a crowd (see Fig. 7.1). Sometimes, however, distance cannot be controlled and difficulties arise.

Problems caused by the need to manipulate distance are fairly common. For instance, the train is late, the station is very cold; to the relief of the passenger there is a fire in the waiting room. Before rushing to the only available seat the passenger notices that it is adjacent to one occupied by an undesirable, objectionable being. The need for warmth is greater than scruples, but precautions are essential. Non-verbal communication provides the answer. A newspaper is raised, a shoulder is turned to cut off direct view and any form of self-sufficiency is employed to illustrate the wish to preserve anonymity. How different the situation would be if

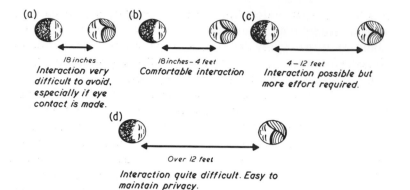

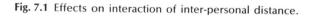

Fig. 7.1 Effects on interaction of inter-personal distance.

both persons were attractive!

Elderly people can be lonely even in a residential home; the lounge can be like a waiting room, with little interaction occurring, and residents remaining strangers to each other. Staff need to bear in mind that some chair arrangements help, and others hinder, social interaction (see Chapter 2). It is difficult to converse side-by-side, it is much more comfortable to be facing the person (see Fig. 7.2). A lounge with many

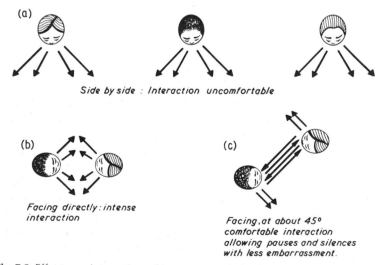

Fig. 7.2 Effects on interaction of inter-personal angular orientation.

people in it will inhibit interaction; it is difficult enough for younger people to get to know 25 or more people at once; the problem is immense for the person with memory problems whose awareness and recognition of others grows very slowly indeed. A smaller group will help the development of relationships and interaction, particularly if there are common interests and a shared task or activity. In this situation staff-resident interactions are made easier and more natural than when residents are dependent on staff for most opportunities for conversation. Staff do not have to search for topics of conversation, as they are provided for them by what is happening in the group. This does not imply that all homes with large lounges have to be rebuilt; it is possible with room-dividers, partitions and careful furniture arrangement to achieve a great deal in encouraging the development of small groups (see Chapter 2 for references on and more details of the 'group living' concept). Table 7.1 gives a summary of the practical steps recommended so far to aid communication.

Table 7.1 Overcoming barriers to communication

1. Correct sensory deficits
2. Speak clearly
3. Use all the senses
4. Use eye contact and touch to maintain attention
5. Arrange furniture to assist conversation
6. Reduce size of groups

The whole person – basic attitudes

Far too often the need to treat the Whole Person is forgotten. Treatment programmes, either at home or in care, provide for the physical needs but ignore psychological and emotional needs. On hospital wards individuals can become medical diagnoses and the physical cure pursued vigorously. It is as if the identity of the person is forgotten. The patient in Bed 4 becomes a broken femur, the occupant of Bed 10 a heart condition instead of Mrs Anne Brown or Mr Peter White with their personal concerns relating to their rent, their possessions or their own individual personalities. The use of the Nursing Process, with its emphasis on careful individual assessment, can help to ensure that patients are persons in their own right. If the staff and friends know how to communicate they will know more about the whole person and be able to meet his or her individual need.

Elderly people have had longer to develop, and perhaps are more different from each other than younger people. Their psychological needs can only be heeded if they are seen and treated as individuals. They have had adult status for 50 or 60 years or more; to be then treated as a child will be potentially deeply upsetting. Even elderly people who are extremely impaired may have an awareness at some level beyond that which they are capable of expressing. Interaction should then be attempted at an adult-adult level, however child-like the response may seem. Where it is obtainable, information about the person's background can illuminate present functioning and even help to make more sense of apparently random behaviour. Attempting to write a brief biography of the person can be a useful aid here. Compiling a scrapbook about the important experiences, events and people of the person's life, with the help of relatives as well as the person's own reminiscences, is a marvellous way of really getting to know the whole person.

Preservation of dignity and respect play a major role in assisting the elderly to cope with their problems. To lose independence suddenly due to hospitalisation, or by being placed in a home is disturbing in itself. When dignity is further upset by total strangers presuming (for instance) to use familiar Christian names, status is lost and self-esteem jeopardised. Some people do prefer to be addressed by their Christian names but some do not. For example a retired surgeon was taken ill and admitted to hospital where he became confused and difficult overnight. It was noticed that the staff were addressing him as 'Joey'; he was completely bewildered by a situation of unprecedented equality, as surgeons of the 'Old School' were notorious for their concern for personal dignity and aloofness. Once the staff began to call him 'Sir' he promptly regained his composure: within a few days he began to order everyone about in his customary manner and was quickly discharged!

Similarly a lady in her 80s was called 'Lavinia' by the staff. The younger nurses arranged her hair in pigtails and tied it up in pink ribbons. Until shortly before her illness she had been a very independent, arrogant spinster and a much feared and respected Justice of the Peace. In hospital she began by preserving her authoritarian demeanour but slowly lost her ability to dominate the scene. She stopped thinking for herself, lost independence, deteriorated into a confused institutionalised, childlike waif and simply faded away.

There are innumerable situations in which dignity and self-respect can be stripped from a person – often by lack of thought. Examples are: talking about a person in their presence, as if they were not there ('she doesn't understand'); leaving toilet doors open while occupied; doing something to a person (combing their hair, lifting them and so on) without first explaining to the person what is about to happen. The reader will be able to add many more instances; in short, any situations where the person is to some extent made to feel small, worthless or is humiliated are to be avoided.

Dignity and respect *can* be maintained. The individual's experience, standing in the community, achievements, and knowledge of the past are all aspects that can be used to retain his or her self-esteem. Explanations of what is happening, or will happen, are necessary. Day-to-day events, from the immediate environment or from national and international news, should be discussed. A concern for privacy, personal likes and dislikes shows courtesy which is appreciated by all age groups and preserves self-respect. Politeness is noted and invariably merits a response, particularly from people who grew up in a culture which valued good manners.

The attitude involved here might at first glance be characterised as behaving as if the person were not impaired at all, as if the memory and behaviour problems did not exist. In fact, the approach is, firstly, to treat the person with dementia as a *person*, and to recognise that because of this, dignity, respect, individuality and so on remain important. Secondly, however, the person must be accepted as he or she is now. This involves recognition of current limitations – but to see these as a starting point, as being possibly modifiable and not necessarily fixed. By doing this expectations and demands can be sensitively set at a level which does not place the person in a position of failure, whilst at the same time they are gradually increased as and when the person's functioning improves. Failure is avoided, as it leads to loss of self-respect, particularly when the tasks involved are still perceived as extremely simple. The avoidance of failure is not to be the passive 'if I don't do anything at all I can't possibly fail' variety. It is instead an active avoidance where those areas that the person can succeed in are emphasised. Too often the presence of dementia is unnecessarily demonstrated and made obvious by the use of direct questioning of memory, rather than allowing the patient to succeed by the skilful use of cues and prompts.

In summary, allowing dignity and self-respect is not achieved by pretending that any dementia is absent when it clearly is not; it is achieved by removing the focus from the disability onto preserved areas of functioning. This is of course exactly what happens with physical disabilities, and the same should apply to mental disabilities also.

Two further related aspects of the *whole person* need to be discussed, particularly in relation to the elderly person in institutional care. The first is choice; it is only too easy to remove choice and to place elderly people in a situation where they have little control over even the small – but none the less significant – features of daily living. For example, a cup of tea may be provided at breakfast time, when the patient had always been accustomed to coffee; or clothes may be laid out for the patient without any consultation about the selection. Complete freedom of choice is of course available to hardly anyone. In a communal setting inevitably there are restrictions; the approach here is to discover what choices can be made available and to present these to elderly patients. Encouragement may be needed to help them make their own choices, especially when they have become apathetic and accustomed to the staff deciding. This is an important part of being an adult, dignified, self-respecting individual.

The final aspect to be encouraged and developed is independence. Again, no-one is ever truly independent; we are all interdependent to a greater or lesser degree, and inevitably in communal settings particularly it is more difficult to be less dependent on other people. Once more though, many instances occur of patients being more dependent on staff than is necessary; thus patients are sometimes completely dressed by staff for the sake of speed when the patient can manage slowly with much less help; or sugar is put in the patients' tea when they are capable of adding it themselves. Self-help is important to a patient's self-esteem; the success of doing something for oneself, albeit slowly, can be rewarding. Interdependence was mentioned above; a neglected aspect of the whole person is often the extent to which they can do things for other people, the extent to which other people can be dependent on the patient. By helping the patient have a meaningful role, be it clearing the table, sweeping up, telling a story about the past, singing a song or whatever is appropriate and possible, again the patient's self-esteem is built up. The option of having privacy must be provided also. Hospitals and homes need to allow some space for privacy, plus the necessary arrangements to ensure it. Screens or curtains, the ability to display some personal items, personalisation of clothing, storage, thinking and entertaining space are vital to the quality of life.

Those aspects of the whole person that staff attitudes need to develop are listed in Table 7.2. These attitudes underly the whole RO approach. Without them any approach will fail at a human and emotional level. It is no easy task to apply these attitudes. For instance, providing basic physical nursing care for a severely impaired person that preserves real dignity calls for a high level of skill, consideration and creativity. Using Table 7.2 as a yardstick to look at and evaluate our own practice will help in developing such qualities.

Table 7.2 Basic attitudes

Staff attitudes must allow the elderly person:
1. Individuality as an adult
2. Dignity
3. Self-respect
4. Choice
5. Independence

These attitudes are a central feature of the normalisation approach, which is being applied increasingly in relation to other disabilities. This involves allowing the person access to experiences and life-styles valued in society.

Thus a physically disabled person would work at a conventional job, despite being confined to a wheelchair; he might drive to work in a specially adapted (but otherwise conventional) car and live in an ordinary (but adapted) house. This is in contrast to a person living in an institution with other physically disabled people, driving an invalid carriage and working in a workshop for the disabled. Similarly mentally handicapped people are increasingly integrated into 'normal' society, rather than being placed out of sight and out of mind in a large country hospital.

We saw in Chapter 1 that 'normal' for elderly people is largely a continuation of previous patterns of living. If we apply this to the person with dementia the implication is that independence in self-care should be encouraged. Previous activities and interests, social, recreational, domestic, occupational, etc., adapted where necessary, should be facilitated. Adaptations to the person's living arrangements so that previous life-styles can be continued are entailed.

It is, of course, quality of life that is the prime concern. This rather nebulous concept in this context could be assessed by the extent to which the person's life-style can continue despite the dementia, memory difficulties and so on. If this seems a far cry from the average long-stay ward, the normalisation principle does have its implications there also. Personalised, rather than shared, clothing; choice of food from a menu; space for personal possessions; choice of activities and so on all help to form the fabric of an existence comprising more that is valued and generally agreed to be desirable.

Three commonly quoted implications of the normalisation approach (e.g. Woods 1987) are:

1. People with dementia should be accorded full respect and dignity as people with human worth and rights.

2. People with dementia should be treated appropriately to their actual age.

3. People with dementia should be helped to participate in good social relationships in the ordinary community.

The first of these is clearly embodied in the attitudes discussed above. The second is an important consideration in selecting activities, recreational materials etc., though, as Woods & Britton (1985, p 273) discuss, this can be a complex issue. It is important to define 'age-appropriate' without accepting the devalued conception of elderly people and their activities prevalent in society. We should be guided by what was valued by each individual over their life-span, rather than by what is seen as the 'norm' for elderly people. Attaining the third implication may be aided by the growth of positive approaches, of which RO is one, emphasising the assets, strengths and resources of the person rather than his or her weaknesses and deficits.

24 HOUR RO – METHODS

Having covered barriers to communication, non-verbal communication and the attitudes underlying communication, the next section considers much more the content and form of communication with the elderly patients. It is what the staff member actually says that is to be considered here. The guidelines are summarised in Table 7.3.

Table 7.3 Guidelines for 24-hour RO

Remind the person:	Useful tips:
A. Who he or she is	1. Use short simple sentences
B. Where he or she is	2. Encourage response and repetitions
C. What time of day it is	3. Use past experiences as a bridge to
D. What is happening in the	the present
person's surroundings	4. Keep conversation specific
	5. Encourage humour
	6. Provide a commentary on events

The aim is for each interaction that the elderly person has to be used for 24 hour RO. There are numerous opportunities during the day when even a short contact between the young and the old can be used to advantage. Waking people up, helping them to the toilet, serving meals are all natural situations for conversation.

Simple methods of disguised repetition, and attention to everyday, simple matters such as the weather, the day and the month, and the time encourage awareness in the elderly person. This can be done by drawing attention to what is happening indoors and outside the window; all the senses can be involved, as for instance by remarking on the lovely smell of breakfast or the feel of cold hands just come in from the snow.

Some examples of simple interactions are as follows:

'Hello, Mrs Smith; this place is called —— Hospital; yes, that's right, —— Hospital.'

'Mr Green, it's 12 o'clock now; time for lunch; that's right, the dining room is through that door there.'

'Your bath is ready for you, Mr Brown. Take off your jacket, then your shirt. .; when you've finished undressing there's a nice hot bath for you.'

'My name is Jean; yes, Jean. I'm a new nurse here at —— Hospital. What's your name? I'm pleased to meet you, Mr White. Have you seen what an awful day it is today? Come and look out the window. Yes, it's pouring with rain; I suppose we can't expect good weather in November. It's good to be indoors today. At least —— Hospital is warm and dry, isn't it?' Note the frequent use of names (patients and staff) and the relatively short, simple statements and questions, which are intended to encourage a response and repetition, wherever possible, and *not* to make the person fail. The more opportunities for repetition that can be made the more likely is the learning process to be reawakened. Disguised repetition is necessary as elderly people are not children and naturally resent being patronised or treated as though they are inferior in any way.

There is a need to be aware of a short attention span or wavering concentration. In order to hold attention a number of related items which stimulate the senses are useful. For example, when waking Mr Smith in the morning one may say 'Good morning Mr Smith; it's eight o'clock, time to be getting up for breakfast'. After a short time a further comment on the time can be followed by 'Have you looked out the window yet? It is really spring-like today, the sun is out and it's quite warm for March'.

At breakfast this can be repeated, 'Look, we've daffodils on the table. It's almost spring, don't they smell nice?'. Later in the day a calendar can be produced, the day and the month indicated and further reference to spring can be made. Repeated presentation of information may sound like a broken record to staff, but to the person with memory problems it may be only vaguely familiar!

The use of past experiences in comparison with the

Fig. 7.3 Using reminiscence as a means of developing communication.

happenings of today allows reminiscence to play a vital role in a conversation.

The elderly know more about the past than their children or care staff. To capitalise on their experience helps to provide an opening to talk about the present. The old folk are aware of their superior knowledge and do not feel threatened by a possible exposure of inadequacies. Past experiences are used to help the person become more aware of the present – contrasts and similarities can be emphasised. When talking about past events it should be made clear to the elderly person by the use of past tenses of verbs, and so on, that current reality is not being discussed. For example: 'You used to work in a coal mine didn't you Mr Green?' or 'Before you came into hospital, you had lived in South Avenue for 30 years, hadn't you, Mr Brown?'. Note the attempt to provide a temporal context here.

One difficulty of communication with an elderly person suffering from some impairment of function is the frequency of 'crossed wires' in a conversation. The staff member is continuing on one subject, the patient drifts on to another, perhaps related topic, until the two diverge completely. The problem of many conversations is that they rely on memory of the words that have just been spoken a few sentences ago – this is very difficult for most patients with dementia. A way around this is to have a focus for the conversation. Words are spoken and then have gone, but if both the participants in the conversation have their attention on something specific – a picture, an object, an odour, a view from the window etc., – then it is more likely that the patient will remain on the same topic as the staff member. Although inevitably there will be some repetition at least both parties will be talking about the same thing! Avoidance of vagueness by the staff will also aid communication. In everyday contacts it will be of value if they are kept specific and concrete.

If a discussion of current events arose and one aspect, for example the Prime Minister, was chosen for discussion, rather than simply using words relevant items could be employed as a focus. A picture, television programme or a book about him or her would help. If the time of day is the subject a clock or a watch could be used. Conversations about relatives can be facilitated by the use of photographs from the past and present. Without such references the person could be talking about her daughter aged three, but the staff could be discussing the 50 year old lady whom they meet regularly!

Humour is to be encouraged. Laughing *with* the elderly person, never permitting the person to feel that he is being laughed *at*, are vital aspects. Humour breaks the ice, helps the patient to relax, and perhaps, makes it easier to cope with the reality of disability and impairment. No examples can be given, as what is funny depends on the situation, the people concerned and the timing. Its occurrence is a positive sign, especially when patients begin to initiate the humour and make gentle fun of the staff!

Conversation does not have to concentrate on major events; a straightforward comment on the day's happenings, however mundane they may seem, is important for the person who is having difficulty keeping in touch with reality. Physical care need never be given silently. Even if the patient is withdrawn and unresponsive the nurse can still talk about what is happening. It is not a rare occurrence to see two people attending an old person and talking to each other as though there was no third party present. 'I was at a party the other night. The band was great'. The friend will ask 'Was it punk rock?'. The discussion will continue as a duet. The older member of the trio could be included quite simply by enquiring 'What kinds of music do you enjoy?', or whatever may be appropriate to extend the conversation. Normal conversation is not impossible!

In hospitals or residential homes all staff and visitors can be encouraged to use 24 hour RO. The ladies who bring the flowers to the wards could make sure that the residents see the arrangements and touch and smell them instead of simply placing them on a window-sill or an out-of-the-way table. Flowers are beautiful, colourful, seasonal and smell delightfully. These qualities should be remarked upon and appreciated. Senior staff should watch the attitudes of regularly visiting services, as for example barbers, hairdressers and others, to ensure that dignity, choice and independence are preserved. No man should be shaved without being first consulted, and if he is being shaved should be treated like any other customer and not as an object. Similarly relatives and junior staff need to be encouraged to include the elderly in their conversations.

Finally, helping the person succeed is a major aim. In normal conversation questions are often asked to draw a person into talking and to elicit a response. If a question is asked of a person with dementia and that person cannot answer, the disability will be exposed. Prompts should be given so that the patient is able to respond and join in the conversation. The amount of prompting and clues needed depends on the person; just sufficient to produce the response should be given. Answers can often be given in the original question e.g. instead of asking 'What's the weather like today?', the staff member might say 'What a lot of wet, showery days we're having'. In other situations it is appropriate to give the first few letters of the answer. For example, if conversing about a record the younger person might ask 'Who's that singing? Isn't that Bing something – I think it begins with C . . . Yes, of course, Bing Crosby. What was that famous song of his, remind me, wasn't it White something or other . . .?'

In this way memories may be reawakened, the older person being unable to recall them freely without this help from the younger one. Often information is remembered by the elderly to some extent, but they are unable to recall it fully, or the memory is slightly vague. Thus many elderly patients are, for example, unable to name the current Prime Minister, but some recall the name, if a special clue is given, 'it's a woman' or by using letters from the name, perhaps even by giving the first name. By using clues and prompts sensitively the elderly patient's limited memory can be used to the fullest extent.

Night-time confusion is well known. A calm response full of simple, reassuring information is helpful. A statement such as 'Mr Jones, it's three in the morning. Look it's dark, everyone is asleep. What's wrong, couldn't you see the clock?', will help him to reorganize his thoughts without exposing his genuine confusion. Restoration of the missing information will assist his self-confidence and calm him. The effect of waking up in the dark on an elderly person with impaired functions may be compared to regaining conscious-ness after an anaesthetic when even personal identity is lost and short-lived total disorientation occurs. By providing the person with information, without questions which might expose the areas of difficulty and thus cause loss of face, confidence in the self and in the other person is restored.

Handling rambling talk

People with dementia often produce rambling, confabulatory talk. A person may chatter away talking apparent nonsense about where he or she is and what he or she is doing, or may seem to live in the past. 'Oh, I just baked a lovely tea for this picnic. We're in the park I used to play in as a child. That's my sister over there eating chicken.' This kind of statement is commonly heard in the midst of a ward and possibly in the midst of winter. The only thing in keeping with reality may be the fact that it is mealtime. Rambling talk like this shows that the person is mixing past events, experiences and present events indiscriminately. Reactions can include impa-tience or sharp correction, acceptance of the remark as indica-tive of a dementing mind, or agreements with the incorrect statement to 'humour' the elderly person.

It is sometimes thought RO always involves 'putting the person right'. As Table 7.4 makes clear the important principle is to never agree with rambling talk; after this there is a choice of strategies depending on the person and the situation.

Table 7.4 Rambling and confused talk

Do not agree

1. Tactfully disagree (on less sensitive topics)

or

2. Change the subject – discuss something concrete

or

3. Acknowledge the feelings expressed – ignore the content

The sensible use of tenses when responding to a statement such as 'I am a grocer and I must go and open up my shop' can preserve dignity, avoid contradiction and give recognition to the person's knowledge or skill. The reply could be:' 'Oh, Mr Zee, you *used* to have a grocery didn't you? It *must have been* good to know all your customers personally: not like the supermarkets today. *Did* you pack all the dried fruit in blue bags? *Was* it hard to fold them up so neatly?' Mr Zee is only too pleased to explain how it was done and will almost always use the past tense too.

Gentle correction is possible, particularly in situations where sensitive topics are not involved. These corrections should be tactful, so that they can be accepted without loss of dignity. For example:

'Actually it's Tuesday today – but one day does seem much like another here.'

'This is a hospital in fact, but we like to think that it is as good as any hotel.'

'That's Jim Smith, one of the other nurses, perhaps he looks like your son Bill.'

Such statements could be possible corrections for confusions of day, place and person. Where more sensitive areas, such as a bereavement, are concerned it is wise to first ascertain the type of response which occurs after correction to errors on a more general plane. If these responses are usually reasonable then it would be feasible to attempt open discussion about the more emotionally loaded situations. The important point is to choose appropriate occasions for correction – when the person is calm and there is time available. If a bereavement is to be discussed, it may appear fresh to an old person, almost as if it was new information. Therefore the same procedure should be followed as when it is necessary to break bad news to someone. Time, also, should be allowed for this and for sitting with the person as he or she grieves. It is not such a terrible thing if the person cries – indeed it may be more abnormal not to cry in the circumstances.

It is seldom, if ever, useful to correct a person in such a way that a head-on confrontation ensues. Indeed, a direct confrontation may result in the person becoming *more* fixed in his or her mistaken belief, or agitation will become so intense that further information simply will not 'go in'. What are needed are ways to calm and reassure the person, without agreeing with any of the confused talk.

On many occasions – where time is limited or there is already some agitation or confusion and talk is vague and incoherent – it is better not to correct confabulatory state- ments. Instead of emphatically denying that such a thing is possible it is better to ignore the content of the rambling talk and use distraction. A gentle touch on the arm, eye contact and an attempt to attract attention by speaking in a firm, clear voice should be followed by a distracting statement. The use of an interesting item such as a flower accompanied by a suit- able comment 'Ellen, Ellen, what do you think of this?', will usually suffice to promote a definite response. If proper direction of attention is enforced rambling will stop. Moving the person's focus of attention onto something in the surroundings is important in any attempt to change the subject of the conversation – everyday objects and pictures can be used to achieve this.

The final possibility for responding to confused talk is relevant when it seems that a statement or remark is an attempt to express a feeling. This feeling is hidden, perhaps because the appropriate words are not available. Possibly non-verbal methods are used to convey the message e.g. 'I'm sorry, I must go home now and get my Dad's tea.' The lady is 84 years old, had been hospitalised for three years and her Dad died 20 years ago. Pointing out these facts to her would be inappropriate in many situations. The 'hidden' meaning may well be the simple one that she is expressing boredom or a feeling of insecurity for the moment and wishes to escape. The response is to acknowledge the feeling – but not the actual words. Here it might be 'We've done enough for today haven't we, let's get a cup of tea on the ward', which allows the person to retire with dignity.

A further example would be 'My mother is coming soon' – when the patient's mother had died several years previously. The response to this might be 'It must have been a good time of life when you were with your parents, and they were there to look after you.' The feeling communicated was again one of insecurity – a need to recall the time of life when the patient was very dependent, but had her mother there to provide security for her. Here background knowledge of the patient is important as there are homes where both mother and daughter are residents!

Attempting to tune in to the person's feelings in this way has been developed by Feil (1982) as 'Validation'. Feil provides many valuable insights and techniques for facilitating communication with the person with dementia.

An interesting case of the 'hidden message' was an elderly lady who talked to her 'sister' in a mirror. She knew it was a mirror but had constructed a fantasy world when she was able to pass the time of day with her own reflection. Again responses like 'It's great to feel you have relatives near by', seemed more appropriate than outright correction, which the patient resisted. The point may be reached where one can say 'You know it is a mirror and I know it's a mirror but if you want to say you're talking to your sister, that's fine.' However, in situations like this the possibility of involving the person in activities and interests that were previously enjoyed should be seriously considered.

A refusal to cooperate often indicates a reaction to stress and an avoidance of a situation which might be threatening to self-esteem. Sudden deafness is an example of this! By smiling broadly and remaining silent, by being inattentive or by confabulating, anxiety is avoided. 'I don't want to answer any more questions', is an attempt to control a situation; once this is achieved cooperation usually follows. Old people may buy time in order to think, to control and to make sure that they understand the implications of a situation. 'Oh, I've forgotten my glasses' or 'I must go to the toilet' can be useful excuses to allow a delay. The importance of helping the person succeed, by not making demands or asking questions that will lead to failure, is clear. Helping the person to feel reassured, relaxed, and self-confident can thus reduce the amount of rambling talk.

ENVIRONMENTAL ASPECTS

Physical environment

An important aspect of 24 hour RO is to provide the means whereby clients can be as independent as possible and pursue their normal existence to the best of their ability. This can be provided if staff, and those working with the elderly, can understand more about the impact of the environment on all of us.

Our home, our work, our friends, interests and possessions are all part of our environment. We choose our homes, or at least change them, to suit our purposes and needs. We organise our possessions so that we know where they are and so we can make the best use of them. We choose the colours with which we feel happiest; we place things in frequent use to hand and those of less importance we put away. Our home must run smoothly and fit in with our activities. Why else is it only the unwary who offer to 'put away' instead of 'help to wash up'?

If we recall our initial move to our present home we can remember the chaos, the priorities for unpacking and the difficulties encountered in finding our way about the un-familiar neighbourhood. It was vital to locate the right signs and cues . . . the pink house on the corner, the name of the pub, the big tree before we turned left . . . which, in time would all become automatic. Those first few days or even weeks in the new situation were filled with trauma and aggravation – trying to turn the key in the lock, reaching for a light switch that was not there and trying to decide how welcoming the neighbours were. All of this, no matter how difficult, was within our control, our choice, and the decision for change, organisation and inclusion were ours also.

Imagine what it is like for a person who has lived in the same place for many years to suddenly find him or herself in totally alien surroundings. Everything is under someone else's control. There are no personal possessions, no familiar things, routines or even faces: a place where wall and curtain colours are distasteful, which lacks privacy, contains too many strangers has too much noise or horrendous hush, and it is all unfriendly. There is no way to tell where things are, no personal chair, no familiar kitchen, no place to put anything and nothing to put there anyway. The culture shock, the realisation of the loss of control, the feeling of isolation or even imprisonment must be a devastating experience: one which need not be so traumatic if only it had been more carefully planned. *Any* move should be preceded by a few visits to get acquainted, although, of course, hospitalisation rarely permits this.

If the physical environment is designed to reduce disorientation and all the accompanying difficulties and traumas, an admission could prove less painful. Simple, common-sense measures could help. In the first place a guide is essential. Someone, even another resident, should be responsible for a guided tour. Even if the person is bedridden, some explanation of where and what could help. One tour or explanation is not enough. Attention and concentration will be stretched – the person needs to be told a number of times. Parrot-like repetitions are not necessary, or desirable, but opportunities – like a trip to the bathroom – will offer a chance to say again, 'Look, there is a notice saying where the Dining Room is', or the toilet, daily information board, or whatever.

There is a need to supply orientation aids. These will do little good if no one points them out, but with the help of a guide they can prove invaluable aids to independence. Some basic, but helpful aids are indicated in Table 7.5.

The aids must be large and clear enough for the elderly person to see; above all they must be accurate – or confusion

Table 7.5 Environmental aids: use orienting cues in the person's environment

Clocks		
Calendars		Large
Signs	*Ensure that they are*	Clear
Pictures		Accurate

will be increased! Getting these details right is an important – and inexpensive – part of RO.

Patients may need to be taught where the signs and aids are, and encouraged to make use of them. This initial effort is well worthwhile in view of the time saved later.

Colour plays a large role in creating an atmosphere. Bright covers on beds assist identification as well as looking pretty, toilet doors are easier to find if they are painted a special colour as well as bearing a printed notice. Attractive curtains, cheerful walls, interesting pictures, gaily patterned tablecloths and colourful crockery provide a varied environment with plenty of landmarks to aid orientation. The staff are helped by the memory aids too! They act as a reminder to use 24 hour RO in every interaction. Here as well as clocks and calendars, boards with clearly written information about the Day, Month and Weather, colourful pictures or collages of food, national leaders, places, children, seasons, occupations, maps etc. should also be on view. A daily newspaper and journals of particular interest should be easily available. There is always time in the day for comments on these, and they are valuable aids to communication, providing a visual reminder to the patient of the topic.

Common sense will dictate the important aspects of the environment that require emphasis. Why are toilet doors always so hard to find or identify? Why do they look like any other door so that the chance of finding the right one is limited and the chance of being labelled incontinent is so

(a)

Fig. 7.4 Signs, calendars and information boards can be extremely valuable in supplementing 24 hour RO. The dining room sign is the product of an RO session on food!

(b)

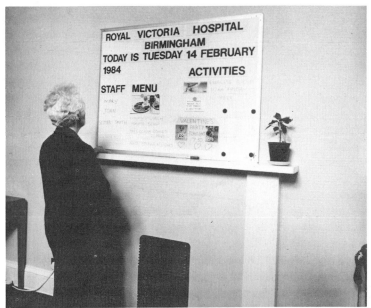

(c)

much greater. Why are corridors so long and threatening? Some indication of where the corridor leads might lessen the confusion and make the trip along it worthwhile. If individual bedrooms or areas had some significant picture, photograph or personal item on the door or bedside table owners could locate them so much more easily and unaided.

A home or ward should be concerned to encourage independence and the continuation of normal living as far as possible, but rarely is there a room for simple laundry purposes, or a kitchen in which basic cooking can be done. If it is normal to have only a cup of tea and a piece of toast for breakfast, why cannot the person do it for him or herself and get up at the chosen time? Not everybody will be capable of doing this for himself or herself, but are there other residents or patients who might enjoy helping?

Public space is necessary, but private space is equally important. Possessions, items recalling past experiences and successes, family souvenirs and personal momentoes are part of a person's private world. Interests can be pursued, letters can be read and so can books. Programmes on TV or radio which do not appeal to others can be seen or heard in private. Sometimes just to sit and look outside can be a pleasant relief from the activity on the ward or in the home. Everyone needs some personal space.

Lighting can often cause problems which are unnoticed by staff. Not only is it important to ensure that the elderly can see properly in order to read or write, but strange illusions can be caused by faulty lighting. One lady was thought to be deluded as she would insist that she could not leave her room at certain hours of the day because 'the hall is on fire'. Only when someone sat beside her did it become apparent that reflections from the lights produced a line across the floor that looked as though there really was a fire!

Only those who have had the experience of picking their way around on crutches can fully appreciate the importance of flooring! Anything that *looks* slippery, uneven or hazardous in any way can arouse anxiety. Too many floors seem to be problematic and often this too is caused by poor lighting, shadows and reflections. Contrasting colours of vinyl flooring meeting on a corridor may appear like a step to some patients. This has occasionally been a problem with the use of coloured lines on the floor leading the way to the toilets. This same sort of line is not helpful in encouraging older people to walk upright and to look ahead. A line drawn along the wall, or clear signposting is preferable.

Psychological environment

Anything which creates a feeling of worth or well-being is relevant here. Sensory stimulation should always be considered. Colours, good views from the windows, pleasant surroundings, peace and activity levels to meet the needs of each individual are all important. Information about orientation, forthcoming events, newspapers and journals should all be available. A simple library, relevant games, reminiscence aids – such as pictures of the old town and area, historical aspects of the locality, Then and Now books, Royalty, anything to prompt memories – these are all very useful for personal and group perusal. Just as important is some personal collection of photos and mementoes. Outings are an added stimulation, and again, may spark off personal memories – the church where they were married, the annual fête, the new buildings replacing the old shop or workplace.

Group sessions are important as a means to increase engagement, interaction and the establishment of good relationships with other clients or with staff. Understanding can grow. Visits from members of the local community and schools provide a link with local affairs. If the carers know their clients well, abilities, skills and experiences become more obvious and can be used to increase independence and confidence.

Lack of control over the environment coupled with lack of knowledge about clients can result in deprivation of many needs. For instance Mrs T. was an opera lover, but was in bed every time an opera was shown on TV. The radio blasted out pop music all day so there was never an opportunity to hear the classical music that she loved. Possibly others suffered from sounds and sights they did not appreciate either. This could have been rectified either by installing a radio in her room, providing a tape recorder or by ensuring that she could stay up and watch the programme in a quiet corner. There were many possibilities, but no one had bothered to find out about her interests and so no one knew that she was suffering!

There are so many aspects of living where the person loses control – from the room temperature to being able to lock away personal possessions. Helping the person exercise some control over their life-style must be a major aim of a home or ward, offering realistic choices appropriate to the person's abilities and interests. In some homes, with more able and articulate residents, Residents' Committees have been formed. Often they are rendered impotent by lack of attention to their requests and criticisms. Where they do have a say in policy and planning events they appear to be a responsive, lively group who make the staff's work much more stimulating. Independence does mean having opportunity to express opinions and make suggestions which are put to use.

Finally, there are some practices which, despite the growth of positive approaches, still appear to operate in some units. In assessing the good and bad points of environments, consideration should be given as to whether there are any environmental features which used routinely may cause acute distress and hasten the process of withdrawal. The use of cot sides is still, unfortunately, a common example of this. Restless patients, elderly stroke cases and others could wake up to a world cut off by bars. This must confirm feelings of rejection. If he wishes to use the toilet and no one is around he either attempts to climb over the bars – and has the accident the bars were meant to prevent – or is incontinent. Dignity and independence are lost – perhaps permanently. Similar problems are caused by the *routine* use of geriatric chairs, or even beds that are too high from the ground, or large open spaces, offering no aids to mobility.

A rich environment

The aim is to create an environment to which it is worthwhile to be orientated. The environment requires careful consideration and evaluation – both physical and psychological aspects – in order to ensure that it provides facilities and features which will encourage the person to live as independently as possible. Such aids would include activity levels which are neither too low nor too high for each individual, personalisation of clothing and possessions, and the opportunity to continue to cater for the self as far as possible. It also recognises the need for a group identity, either by providing a form of group living, or some degree of group activity, neither of which interfere with individual choice or need for privacy.

While a positive approach is urged, disabilities do exist. They too require aids and efforts so that the person can adapt to the deficits. Emphasis should be on regaining confidence by the continued use of retained abilities and skills, but the disabilities cannot be ignored. The retained functions can aid in retraining the lost ones, or be used in adapting to difficulties arising from the loss of function.

COMMUNICATING WITH DYSPHASIC PATIENTS OR THOSE WITH SPEECH PROBLEMS

People who have had a stroke, head injury or some neurological disorder resulting in damage to the parts of the brain responsible for speech will suffer from some form of sppech disorder. This is a complex field; fuller definitions are given in Chapter 6; here three major types of speech problems will be indicated.

1. Dysarthria

Here it is the actual production of speech that is affected; words and sentence construction may be correct, but the articulation is poor. The listener finds the speech indistinct and difficult to understand. Temporary dysarthria is familiar after a substantial consumption of alcohol!

2. Expressive dysphasia

This takes various forms; essentially the person's ability to express him or herself is impaired and the words and sentences do not come out correctly. There may be difficulties in finding the right word leading to a high frequency of 'thingumajigs', 'whatsits' etc. or to long-winded or circumlocutory speech when e.g. the person says 'a small piece for fastening articles that people wear' instead of 'button'. Words may be invented, reversed or omitted. There may be difficulty in reading, writing and calculation. Automatic speech such as 'Monday, Tuesday, Wednesday . . . . .' or 'one, two, three . . . . .' may be possible, as may be singing; these do not represent the overall level of functioning as they are so well-known to the person. The person may well feel frustrated at this inability to make others understand – such insight is distressing.

3. Receptive dysphasia

Here the patient has difficulty in appreciating what is being said. There is incomplete or even no understanding of conversation, directions or questions, which leads to a considerable degree of isolation. Some associated problems include reading, writing, calculation and spelling. The person is placed in a world which seems meaningless and he is likely to be bewildered, perplexed and frightened. The nature of the difficulties of comprehension is such that the person is also often unable to express him or herself clearly; a person's own speech is continually monitored by the receptive system, so expression is also likely to be affected by receptive difficulties.

Communication

Wherever possible a speech therapist should be consulted to guide, advise and treat. However there is a great deal that can be done by care staff – as the success of 'stroke clubs' and volunteer speech after stroke schemes has demonstrated.

The first step with these – and other – impairments is to recognise and accept that they are not within the person's control, that the impairment arises however hard the person tries to overcome it. Secondly, speech impairments may make people appear more deteriorated and confused than in fact they are. Here the basic RO approach of not writing anybody off, but continuing to treat them as a person, is of great value. Thirdly, particularly where a stroke has led to the impairment, improvement may well be possible. Where the speech problem is a feature of a dementing illness, more restricted aims will be appropriate.

More specifically the problem of communicating with the receptive dysphasic is the most challenging of all. They should not be included in group settings and communication should be on a one-to-one basis. The group situation aggravates their sense of worthlessness and frustration. Others appear to be enjoying themselves, but they do not understand what is so pleasing to the others in the group.

On a one-to-one basis communication must be simplified as much as possible. Non-verbal signals are very important; sudden movements, or an approach from behind may be misinterpreted as threatening and lead to aggressive lashing out. Gentle touch, an open and warm approach and voice tone should be employed to encourage a feeling of security and acceptance. Verbal messages must be simplified, avoiding complex concepts; sentences must be short and involve one idea at a time only. Words should be backed up with demonstrations, gestures, pictures etc. Every possible effort to understand the person's attempts at communication must be made; again non-verbal signals and gestures are important in making sense of what the person says. Any communication abilities the person does retain should be capitalised on, whether it be reading, writing, mime etc. With interaction being so difficult there is a tendency to avoid such patients; if only some feeling of warmth and acceptance is conveyed then something will have been achieved.

Patients with expressive dysphasia or dysarthria do well with RO both in groups or in informal interaction.

Mr D, a 79 year old who had a right-sided hemiplegia and severe expressive dysphasia resulting from a stroke, could say an occasional word, but more frequently said 'Five, five, five,' or 'Go to Hell!'. He was incontinent, negativistic, a little aggressive and cut himself off by burying his head in his arms. Though included in an RO group, he remained isolated for two weeks. Suddenly he began to write with his left hand and made several meaningful and distinct drawings. Gestures, eye-contact and interest in the materials used in the session began to increase. As his gestures and the therapist's understanding of them improved his needs could be interpreted. He showed his delight by increasing his efforts and warmth of response. His drawings became so meaningful that it was possible for him to give an account of himself and his past life. His intelligence was put to use in finding ways to tell his new friends about his experiences. His improvement was dramatic and his family were pleased for him to be discharged home.

Mrs V had a severe form of receptive dysphasia as a result of a stroke. She was extremely depressed and weepy, but there was little that could be done to communicate with her. Initially, before the problem was clear, she was included in a group. It soon became apparent that there were many problems and the situation was becoming intolerable for her. Individual therapy was instigated. Using warmth, information from her past, much respect and by introducing items that she recognised, it was possible to build up a happy relationship between her and the staff. Simple things, as for example bringing her a posy of the flowers with a similar name to herself, pictures of places she had visited and the use of gentle touch, all aided in at least improving her life on the ward. It also encouraged her to attempt to express herself non-verbally, so that the staff were able to learn more about the things which pleased or interested her.

Mrs F had a mild stroke one evening and in the morning was unable to speak properly. She was frightened and disturbed and the staff anxious. By using sentences which required the minimum of response – initially 'yes' and 'no' – it was possible to calm her and to gradually increase the span of response. For example 'Would you like some tea?', would become 'Would you like some tea or coffee?' Later, perhaps in a day or two, as she improved, a calm voice would enquire 'Would you like to get dressed this morning? What would you like to wear?' This permitted the use of 'yes' and 'no', but also allowed longer responses. These were aided by 'What about this?' or 'Do you like the pink jumper?' In an atmosphere of calm and of minimal demand on speech confidence can return and normal processes of recovery can be aided, with the minimum of stress.

These are some of many examples of how RO can be used to help those with speech problems. Special allowances must be made for them. Patience is vital and the patient should be given time and encouragement in order to appreciate that others are willing to help. The atmosphere should be one in which the clients do not feel that heavy demands are being made on them to express themselves, whilst being friendly and inclusive. As in other aspects of RO the person's disability is not to be exposed and demonstrated once more, but again help is given for the person to find success. He or she should be greeted, materials used by others should be shown, brought near or left in reach. Reactions such as eye contact or gestures should be noted and a response made to them. Again non-verbal responses are useful – touch, warmth, gesture and so on, but here there is more scope for verbal responses and reassurance. A reaction should not be forced, but any effort, however small, should be greeted with interest and attention. Too fulsome a response could be inappropriate, but warmth and moderated praise are indicated. 'What do you think of that, it's nice isn't it?' or 'You can do a lot with that left hand can't you? I like your drawing.' Lack of speech does not mean lack of intellectual ability, but it does mean that everyone has to try harder to understand and be understood.

Where some speech is retained but there is perhaps a word-finding difficulty then the patient may be able to indicate a choice from several alternatives; naming may prove difficult or impossible, but matching with an identical object or picture might be possible. Any communicative ability at all should be capitalized on, and the speech therapist may indicate certain aspects that are less impaired. The dysarthric patient may need to be taught to talk more slowly and precisely, and to use non-verbal means to provide a context for what is said. Words are easier to understand if the listeners knows roughly what is likely to be said. In all cases isolation and withdrawal are possible consequences of the speech impairment; the work of 24 hour RO is to ensure this does not happen, by helping the person feel accepted, and to some extent understood and – importantly – unpressured.

HELPING THE PERSON LEARN

People with dementia have considerable difficulty in learning, but as we have discussed in Chapter 2 learning is not impossible. Here we present some basic techniques for encouraging learning of new skills, re-training old skills, maintaining retained skills and for dealing with some of the problem behaviours that arise.

Reward

The fundamental principle in encouraging change is the use of a reward for desirable behaviour, and no reward for inappropriate behaviour. A 'reward' consists of something enjoyed by the patient. As individual tastes and values vary enormously it is vital to know what the patient's likes or dislikes include. Undoubtedly, elderly people most appreciate staff approval and attention, so good interpersonal relationships have a strong motivational force. The word 'behavioural' is often mistakenly equated with 'mechanical', but warm and affectionate relationships are of prime importance and preclude the possibility of mechanical and automatic responses being the rule in relationships. Apart from approval other practical rewards might include a favourite drink or food, a special event or outing, even cigarettes, any of which could be used to encourage new behaviour initially. Some studies have used tokens as a reward. The token can later be exchanged for rewards of the patient's choice. Token giving structures staff approval. If it is difficult for the elderly person to remember or to perform the necessary actions to exchange the token it is probably only a useful reward system for them in as much as it reminds staff to give their attention appropriately.

The use and relevance of rewards should be considered. It is illogical to reward a full stomach with food; a cigarette for a patient with a packet in his pocket is like coals to Newcastle; if someone wants to sleep he is not impressed by extra attention.

To delay a reward is to lose an opportunity. A very confused person forgets quickly and might not connect the praise with his/her own response: it is also advisable to make clear what is so pleasing. In the initial stages the rewards should be given virtually every time the desired behaviour occurs. If the behaviour becomes well established they can be slowly decreased, though continued, if only infrequently.

If rewarding the behaviour of elderly patients appears difficult and artificial it should be borne in mind that people are rewarding and failing to reward each other all the time – often without being aware of it. We all smile at those we like, listen attentively to what they say, yet ignore those to whom we are indifferent; these are examples of reward and lack of reward in everyday life. What is being advocated here is the use of these everyday phenomena in a planned, structured way to bring about specific changes in a patient's behaviour. Praise and encouragement are part of all good training programmes, and where the elderly are concerned many of the skills were previously in their possession and only require relearning.

One problem in using a reward system is to ensure that the behaviour to be rewarded actually occurs in the first place. For instance, if a patient never goes to the toilet without prompting how can he/she be taught to go on his/her own? There is nothing to reward. Clearly the behaviour must be elicited before it can be rewarded. Several strategies are possible. One method is to increase the probability of it occurring. The environment can be adapted so that the patient sits nearer to the facilities instead of a long way from them. The patient could be taken for a walk in the vicinity so that when the toilet is seen he/she might feel disposed to make use of it while close at hand. If social interaction is the target a patient could be invited to join a small group in order to play a game or have a drink in company. In such circumstances the desired behaviour becomes more probable, so then it can be immediately rewarded. Three other possible strategies are discussed in the succeeding sections.

Modelling

A second approach is to demonstrate, or model, the required behaviour. To increase recreational involvement an actual game can be shown; mime can be employed to show how to get dressed, how to wash, or how to eat correctly. A group already engaged in discussion can demonstrate to a withdrawn patient that by conversing they can obtain attention and praise from the staff.

Shaping

Here successively closer approximations to the target behaviour are rewarded, and as each stage is achieved the demands become a little stricter. If, for instance, the normal use of a fork and knife is the target the reward system could commence at a very low level:

> Any sort of self-feeding, even with the fingers, then reward only for an attempt to use a utensil, then only when a fork is used. Finally, only when the correct use of utensils is observed.

Similarly if the target is to be self-initiated toiletting:

> A visit to the toilet even when accompanied. Then managing with less and less help in getting up and walking there, then only response to verbal reminders is rewarded. Then these too could be faded into non-verbal cues – initially a mime, eventually perhaps a simple nod of the head. Finally the only reward to be given is for self-initiated toiletting.
>
> The entire procedure would consist of initial response to guidance, response to a verbal reminder, then a non-verbal prompt and finally no reminder at all.

Consistent use by the staff of the minimum prompt needed to begin or continue the behaviour in question is very important. When dressing a patient, for example, if verbal prompting does not get a response the patient's arm might be placed gradually in the sleeve of his shirt with firm pressure until he/she begins to continue the movement, when the pressure is relaxed and the patient praised. As soon as the patient stops the required movement the guiding hand of the nurse becomes firmer until he/she takes over again and can be praised once more. Thus small amounts of dressing behaviour can be reinforced and become more likely to occur again in the future.

Shaping involves the setting of intermediate goals in order to achieve the main one. If aims are set realistically it will enable the patient to obtain encouragement along the way and so increase the likelihood of complete success. Breaking goals down into small attainable parts is necessary in order to progress. If goals seem a long way off they discourage both patient and staff.

Backward chaining

The final related technique to be mentioned is backward chaining. Many target behaviours in fact consist of a sequence of smaller behaviours, for example toiletting includes:

Get up from seat in lounge
Walk to toilet
Remove clothing as necessary
Urinate in appropriate receptacle
Adjust clothing.

As the term implies, backward chaining involves starting at the end of the sequence, establishing that behaviour, and then going on to work on the preceding link in the chain, establishing that before going on to the next part of the sequence.

Thus, in the case of toiletting, the person's dressing ability should be checked, perhaps arranging for any necessary adaptations to clothing, and practice in dressing skills should be provided so that these parts of the chain can be performed. Next there is a need to ascertain if the person connects urination with being at the toilet. If when on the toilet urine is not passed, then this part of the chain requires assistance until the person reliably uses the toilet area (experience with mentally handicapped adults suggests that increased fluids and very frequent supervised visits to the toilet are useful at this stage). Then comes the 'approach response' which is the actual decision to go to the toilet, finding the way to it, walking to it and so on. As with any skill, the component skills of toiletting or dressing etc. may be learned (or here relearned), by repeated practice with rewards of praise for success.

In the case of a person who has lost the skill of self-feeding backward chaining might involve initially praising the person for mouth-opening to allow the spoon in, then letting the person help to carry the spoon the last inch or so into the mouth, then giving encouragement and praise when the person gradually takes over more of the complete sequence of actions that constitute independent feeding. The importance of backward chaining is that the completion of the chain has in it the reward of fulfillment – in this case food. This acts best on those responses closest to it, until these are well-established and can then be extended to include appropriate preceding responses.

Maintenance

The previous sections have concentrated on procedures for bringing about behavioural change, building up new behaviours, and re-establishing old ones. What must be understood, however, is that for change to be lasting the person's environment must maintain the new or re-established behaviour. When targets are set, maintenance of the targets must be considered. For instance, if we teach Mrs Jones to make a cup of tea for herself, will she continue to do so when there are six cups of tea provided daily in the Home? If we help Mr Smith to use the toilet independently will he continue to do so if most of his fellow patients are incontinent and so receive extra staff attention? Will Mrs Brown continue to dress herself if being dressed had been one way of obtaining staff attention? Having taught Mrs White to cook her own meals at home will she continue to do so when her neighbour provides her with a meal on most days? Although the emphasis may have appeared to have been on changing the individual's behaviour, behaviour-environment interactions are always present. How the environment must be modified to maintain the changed behaviour is as important as the actual change.

Reactions to problem behaviours

Sometimes the behavioural approach is characterized as 'reward good behaviour and punish (or ignore) bad behaviour'. The saying 'ignore it and it will go away' is only true in so far as the behaviour can be completely and consistently ignored – if it is rewarded at all, even infrequently, it will persist for a long, long time. To ignore a problem behaviour is usually an extremely difficult task for residents, relatives and staff. We are advocating an approach where the focus is on building up incompatible behaviours to take the place of those that are inappropriate.

Punishment is used in one form or another in everyday life – and not just with children. Everyone does or says things other people will not like, to get revenge for some real or imagined wrong. Withdrawal and moodiness may be used as punishments.

However, on ethical grounds we would not wish to see the development of programmes for the elderly (or anyone else for that matter) based on punishment. Care staff have – whether they realise it or not – a great deal of power over those in their homes or wards. Power to use wisely but also power that can damage, hurt and even destroy. The great majority of care staff use this power sensitively, responsibly and constructively. Inevitably there are those who do not; in institutions under pressure from poor facilities and resources, experience in other fields had shown that systems using punishment have lent themselves too readily to abuse. Too quickly the aims of treatment are forgotten and punishment has become a way of running a ward or home for the convenience of the hard-pressed staff.

How can problem behaviours be treated if they arise before alternative positive responses have been established? What reaction is appropriate if one patient literally throws another onto the floor because she has taken the chair she usually sits in? Obviously this would be difficult to ignore; clearly, if the offending patient reclaims 'her' chair she will have succeeded and may continue forcibly ejecting 'intruders'. One possibility would be to take the offender to one side (having ensured that help is being given to the patient on the floor) and reiterate in a firm, clear, calm voice, looking at her directly face to face, that violence to other patients is unacceptable. A good way of calming the situation might be to take her out of the lounge, or to her own room. However, the plan must not stop there. Positive preventive measures are required. In this instance a decision must be made on the contentious issue of ownership of chairs! If it is held that chairs are common property then patients should be encouraged to sit in chairs in different parts of the lounge; the pros and cons of each chair could be discussed – position, view and comfort for instance; a wider field of interpersonal relationships could be encouraged so that a number of chairs would be attractive alternatives. On the other hand if 'ownership' of chairs is accepted the 'owner's' name could be attached as an indication to others that this is 'reserved'. The patients could be encouraged to practise asking others, politely, to move and being allowed to call the staff for assistance if the chair was not vacated.

A second example could be the case of an elderly man who is incontinent of urine, but who is otherwise fairly good at self-care. His wetness cannot be ignored – some reaction is inevitable whilst his clothing is being changed. In this situation it is easy to make a critical remark which will only add to the humiliation of the whole event for the patient. The situation should be dealt with calmly in a matter-of-fact manner – so the patient is not given a lot of positive attention which might reward his being wet. The patient is prompted to get changed – as far as possible independently – and to take responsibility for the event – perhaps rinsing through the underwear, taking his trousers to the laundry room, or mopping up the puddle – as far as he is able. This does not constitute a plan for controlling incontinence and it is still necessary to train the person to visit the toilet as has previously been described. The desirable behaviour has to be established so that the problem of incontinence will decrease; the person is less likely to be incontinent if the toilet is used correctly.

It must be ensured that inappropriate behaviour is not rewarded – however unwittingly. The example of the person obtaining attention for being wet is clear, but in some situations a more subtle reward system might operate. Aggressive acts may be greeted by severe and critical responses which may prove to be rewarding enough to encourage further aggression. Even removing the aggressors to their own rooms may be rewarding for some patients; the accompanied walk, the peace and quiet of the room, the change of scene may be perceived as pleasant consequences of the aggressive act.

This area is one of great complexity and illustrates why problem behaviours can prove resistant to change. Considering the consequences for the particular event only and ignoring the totality of individual functioning can lead to errors. For any problem behaviour it is necessary to bear in mind that reactions to it may be encouraging its recurrence; in each case a consistent, humane response which minimises this should be planned.

CONCLUSION

Reality Orientation used as an informal or 24 hour approach should be used consciously by those in contact with elderly people. There is a need to be aware of dangers; sensory deprivation, neglect of the whole person, poor environment, poor communication and lack of understanding of individual problems are the main concerns. Awareness of these leads to better planning, more stimulation and increase in quality of life. It is vital to preserve dignity, self-esteem and an interest in life. Volunteers, friends, relatives and caring staff should use every opportunity to reassure and encourage the elderly by drawing their attention to everyday events. The use of simple forms of sensory stimulation – such as flowers, pictures, seasonal items – can be employed even by grand-children. The past, old experiences and knowledge with comparisons from the present are valuable aids to conver-sation and the reawakening of interest in the self and the environment. Social contact is equally important.

Efforts to understand the person's words and actions should be made; do they suggest anxiety or insecurity? Do they make sense in view of their previous personality, inter-ests, occupations etc? Is the person wandering along the corridor opening each door in turn really behaving aimlessly; perhaps he or she is looking for something that seems familiar (as many people do when lost); with a severe memory deficit everything looks new and fresh, nothing is familiar, unless known to the person before the memory problems began. Alternatively the person may be searching for the toilet!

Encourage and praise all the person's efforts at reality orien-tated behaviour; all their successes and achievements; their appropriate conversations. Praise and staff attention are powerful motivators where staff develop warm relationships with the elderly patients; they can help define that appro-priate non-confused functioning is the aim for the ward or Home, by reversing the common trend for most attention to be given to inappropriate, confused behaviour.

Above all, never write off the elderly person as a *person*: by getting to know and understand older people and all that has brought them to where they are now, communication on a person-to-person level becomes possible.

'If you really want to hear about it, the first thing you will probably want to know is where I was born, and what my lousy childhood was like, and how my parents were occupied and all before they had me, and all that David Copperfield kind of crap, but I don't feel like going into it'. *J D Salinger*

RO structured sessions

8

Groups
  Group identity
  Creating a group
Social atmosphere
Levels of RO sessions
  Basic group
  Standard group
  Advanced group
Final points
Summary

RO structured sessions consist of regular meetings of a small group of elderly people, when RO is carried out intensively for from 30 minutes to an hour. They are variously described as RO sessions, RO groups, RO classes or formal RO. Group leaders may include care-staff, nurses, OTs, speech therapists, psychologists, volunteers and so on; no formal qualifications are implied by the use of the term 'therapist' for these group leaders.

In many ways formal RO is the more immediately obvious and perhaps more dramatic aspect of RO. It usually seems to attract more attention than the more mundane hour-by-hour 24 hour RO described in the previous chapter. This is unfortunate as the RO session is intended to supplement 24 hour RO and not to replace it.

While informal RO assists in developing helpful attitudes and responses towards the elderly in any day-to-day situation, a formal session run by therapists provides an opportunity for intensive stimulation, guidance, and retraining. During the session it is possible to learn more about participants, to obtain an insight into their history, personality, individual characteristics, experience, likes and dislikes. Such information reinforces those working with the elderly and helps them relate with greater ease during the day.

As group member and therapist learn more about each other mutual understanding grows and becomes generalised into all contacts. Even difficult patients can become easier to handle because of this increasing awareness and greater insight which has developed between all parties.

Therapists become aware of the patients' capabilities and the elderly people feel more secure and closer to those who care for them. A bond is developed which can greatly aid rehabilitation.

This chapter will describe how to lead an RO session. Before RO sessions can be organised there are issues of staff-training and support, patient selection, programme co-ordination and feedback to be considered. These are covered in Chapter 10. In Chapter 6 assessment is discussed, and Chapter 9 includes many examples of possible equipment and aids to be used. However before describing actual sessions, we will outline some of the reasons why group work can be valuable for all concerned and describe the overall atmosphere at which groups should aim.

GROUPS

There are at least two excellent reasons for developing group work with elderly people with dementia. Firstly, it enables people who are unable easily themselves to develop relationships with others to feel some sense of belonging to a group, of *group identity*. Secondly, a group can provide a structured situation in which staff can directly help people to re-learn or adapt to difficulties and impairments, or to use their retained skills effectively.

Group identity

It is easy to forget how important belonging to groups is for people of all ages. Although a person may have grown old as a solitary individual, a hermit even, it does not mean that this need does not exist. From birth to death we are all members of some group. Initially the family provides sustenance, guidance, support, structure and rules. As we grow, other groups have an influence – the people in the locality, neighbours, friends and relatives are among the first. School – with its rules, sanctions and rewards – is the second major group we encounter. From then on our identities are further developed by a variety of groups – interest, sport, political, religious, occupational and so on. Even apparently distant agencies, like the law, government and unions, play their part in our lives.

All these bodies of people demand something of us and give us something in return. Our behaviour can change from group to group and the demands made on us are equally varied. Occasionally these demands do not meet with our approval, or fit with our values and principles. Then we are in conflict with the group. We can leave the group, 'fight' for our beliefs or needs, or give way and submit to the group.

A move or other event leading to isolation from the groups of our choice can cause a loss of part of ourselves. Most of us have experienced to some degree the ensuing feeling of loss, lack of support, consolation or encouragement which is normally taken for granted. This sense of isolation continues until new bonds are formed and we rebuild our lives, or return to the groups concerned. If a person lives in complete isolation, he or she will develop other ways of adapting to the new situation.

When one group is particularly strong it can enforce its will on its membership and, even more dangerously, on weaker external groups or individuals. Group conformity can at times weaken or threaten the opinions of even the strongest personality. Being ostracised can be a painful and confusing experience. Being overwhelmed by another group can be equally traumatic.

Institutions can form staff groups where the needs of staff become paramount to the service they are supposed to be offering. There is a reality in the idea that a new hospital with all its fine resources and highly qualified staff can be run like clockwork until patients are admitted! Staff can forget the reason for their employment. Without a customer there is no sale and no need for a salesperson. Hospital or institutional policy gets priority and the customer – resident or patient – becoms a cog, seen only as a part of the machinery of performing a job. The staff group, with its clear-cut role, its routine, the things to be done and the time in which to do them, is the efficient, powerful group of prime importance. Policy dictates that dinners are served at set times, that clients must be washed, dressed, watered and medicated, all according to the clock. The individual is lost and within a short time those who fit in well without complaint become the 'good' patients (no trouble, but well institutionalised!) and those who fight back and insist on recognition become the nuisances, the recalcitrants.

Patients and residents have a right to be part of a group too. They are in a weak position, faced by a strong staff group with clear-cut rules, strategies and aims. How can they survive the onslaught without support? Until staff appreciate how easily they can – perhaps unwittingly – manipulate their patients or residents into total dependency, they will find it hard to understand the responses of their clients and their tendency to become rebellious or like zombies. It should be a recognised duty of staff to ensure that their clients do have the opportunity of some form of group experience, of peer-support, where their position can be strengthened, and their identity defended.

Creating a group

If a person is impaired, fragile or limited in ability, help will be needed for a group to form. From the staff's point of view a group opens up many avenues for help, stimulation and self-care. It provides interest, livens up the day and allows people to get to know each other – staff included! In such a situation, it is possible to find out what the clients want to do and what they can do. A useful guide to setting up groups has been produced by Bender & Norris (1987). In this little book they suggest ways in which staff can consider their own skills, what they can offer, what realistic aims could be set and what kinds of groups would be possible.

It is too often the case that group work is set up on an ad hoc basis. Support from senior staff is not sought, careful planning is not undertaken and false expectations arise (see Ch. 10). Without careful planning projects are in great danger of floundering.

Clients do not always 'cooperate' and refusals do occur. Are the group sessions attractive and rewarding enough? Could more positive experiences be included – outings, tea-parties etc.? Are staff being supportive enough? Whatever the cause, attendance in the end must be voluntary, though the genuine degree of refusal needs probing carefully. It is surprising how factors like shyness, lack of confidence or reluctance to move from a comfortable chair can all prove the reason for a refusal, and evaporate after a little gentle persuasion! To miss something interesting or to be left out are both strong entice-ments and usually prevail.

Problems that are common to group work need to be recognised, and strategies planned to counter them. The garrulous person, the domineering member, the person who never speaks are frequently encountered and need to be handled with thoughtful leadership. It is important to have knowledge of the skills and experiences of group members so that they can be incorporated into activities. Very often these can provide strategies for helping the quiet person to become established.

SOCIAL ATMOSPHERE

As with 24 hour RO a basic aim is to help the elderly person succeed. For this to happen he/she needs to feel relaxed and unpressured. Many programmes in the USA use a classroom setting, with the nurse acting as a teacher, and possibly having, graduation' ceremonies when progress is made to a higher level of classes. Many elderly people in the UK in our experience find the classroom an anxiety-provoking setting, and they do not function at their best there. The classroom setting seems to emphasise the child-like level of knowledge and skills of the elderly person. Whilst recognising the good results often obtained with the RO classroom our preference is to emphasise the social aspects of the session. Clearly much depends on the cultural background of the elderly people involved; if adult education becomes more widespread the classrom may become more attractive!

Where should the session take place? Ideally a special room should be used. The atmosphere should be colourful, warm, sunny and relaxed and be designed to stimulate interest and response. Large external windows are an asset. The ward atmosphere is not conducive to concentration or relaxation. It is associated with ideas of Hospital, authority, routine and medical treatment. Even in community Homes the idea of a club or social activity room implies a change from routine and the possibility of being amused and diverted.

In the room a social atmosphere can be created with comfortable chairs, interesting and bright pictures and posters, small tables, flowers and plants, colourful curtains and so on. More elaborate settings can be devised. In Leeds RO rooms have been established with a 'pub' atmosphere. In Great Britain one of the most popular meeting places is the Pub. In this situation people relax, amuse each other and talk freely. There are inevitably those who take the drinking aspect too seriously, but the vast majority go for the company and some may only sip at an alcoholic drink or simply stick to fruit juice. In former years, when current elderly patients were in their youth, most pubs tended to be male preserves. However when female patients were asked if they would prefer a tea-room they unanimously chose the pub – perhaps feeling slightly wicked in so doing!

To produce a simulated pub at low cost is comparatively easy. It is often possible to find old cupboards with the correct elbow height. Beer advertisements are on posters, ashtrays and labels. Help may be obtained from a kind local

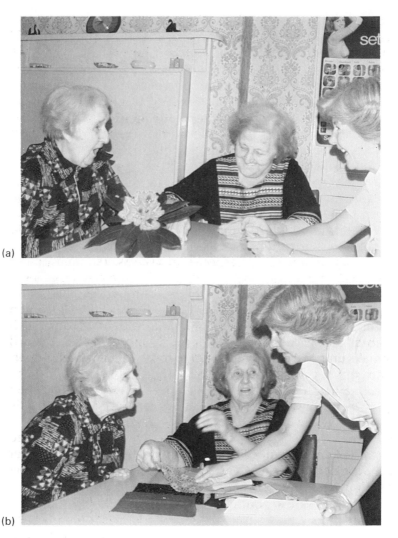

(a)

(b)

Fig. 8.1 Good interaction using (a) flower and (b) different types of material.

brewery. The hospital furniture store may have an old barrel and cash register. In everyone's home rests an object or two which would prove invaluable to such a setting. Enthusiasm and imagination on the part of the staff can work wonders! As most hospitals and residental homes have a little-used supply of beer, sherry and fruit juice for their elderly, there is generally no problem in finding the stock for the bar. It is more appropriate to have a drink in the right surroundings than by a bedside or simply at a meal table. Certainly it is more stimulating.

There are, of course, other kinds of suitable surroundings. One group in London is fortunate enough to have access to a swimming pool for their hemiplegic patients. They have instigated an RO type situation beside the pool where they can sit, relax and talk while not actually taking part in the water therapy.

Another ideal situation is an old-fashioned living room. The comfortable armchairs, old sideboard, table and dining chairs together with a real or simulated focal point fireplace provide a useful scene to stimulate social response. A family sitting room demanded social response to visitors, required politeness and involvement in conversation and the playing of 'host and hostess'. It necessitated the need to entertain and produce tea and some form of refreshment. Old well-learned reactions are allies to RO therapy and in a living room such learned social behaviours are much more likely. A small female unit in Leeds used such a room imaginatively. Apart from employing it for formal sessions each patient had the opportunity of occupying it at least once a week. This resulted in a greater awareness of the day of the week as each lady awaited her turn with eagerness. Once in occupation – usually in threes – each patient took over her chair, produced her crockery and utensils and adapted the room to suit her purpose and needs. Independence, interest and interpersonal relationships developed.

All is not lost, however, if a special room simply is not available. RO sessions can be carried out in a quiet corner of the day-room or in the dining room; the use of screens can partially remove any excessive distractions. If a special room is used the distance from the ward day-room is important as a great deal of time and effort can be expended simply getting the patient to the room if the distance is too great.

A further aid to a social atmosphere that should be considered is the avoidance of staff wearing uniforms in RO sessions. Uniforms, so often a sign of authority, can be changed or disguised suitably before a session. However, more deteriorated patients may find uniforms useful aids initially to the identity of staff-members; any change into everyday clothes should not change the staff member's appearance so much that she cannot be recognised as the same person by the patients! Also removal of uniform does not necessarily remove authoritarian attitudes; attitudes for RO sessions are identical with those for 24 hour RO (Table 7.2).

LEVELS OF RO SESSIONS

It has been argued that to divide people into levels of functioning for group membership is both patronising and demeaning. However, in practice the concern has to be for the individual. Many programmes fail because the mix of extremes of ability is too great. It is much more effective and caring to ensure that a person is not stressed by members who are either much more capable, or very much less able. A person with a severe impairment needs to gain confidence and awareness in the group session, without feeling he/she is much less able than the other members. Equally, a mildly impaired individual would lose confidence in a group where others did not, say, know their own names, and might, at worst, deteriorate, at best become bored. Three levels of groups may usefully be identified, with different emphases and slightly different methods but identical principles. There is always an overlap between them which allows flexibility in finding the right approach for individual needs.

The Basic Group consists of those whose confusional or deteriorated intellectual state is severe. They are those who take hardly any interest in events, in their surroundings or in themselves. They are severely disoriented and unresponsive; attention and concentration are very limited.

The Standard Group consists of those who are responsive and who can take a little interest in people and things. They are not as disoriented and confused.

The Advanced Group consists of those who are much more alert. This is a maintenance level for those who need to be kept stimulated, independent and involved. This group is for short-stay hospital patients, those about to be discharged, and for those who simply need a boost to encourage them to keep their interests and independence. It may be appropriate for elderly physically handicapped people, for many elderly chronic psychiatric patients, in clubs for stroke victims, and can be employed for some residents in old people's homes, attenders at clubs and at day-centres and in some long-stay units where 24 hour RO is successfully practised.

Helping the elderly person achieve success – and thereby greater self-esteem and confidence – is the aim of the social atmosphere and of the methods used at all three levels. RO also brings people into contact with reality, by helping them be aware of what is happening around them, and by re-awakening interest and involvement in the environment. The groups differ in the scope of awareness that is covered but all attempt to do this; all recognise that current reality makes sense only in relation to the past, so all use the person's store of past memories to some degree. Finally each level combats withdrawal – a process by which dementing elderly persons may appear much more impaired than in fact they are. At each level communication is encouraged, with the leaders and with other group members. Conditions are created where this can take place. These aims are summarised in Table 8.1

Table 8.1

All three levels aim to help the elderly person to:
1. Succeed
2. Know what is happening
3. Communicate

Basic group

This group should meet daily, for half an hour. In view of the severity of the problems there should be a maximum of two or three patients per therapist, so all can be kept occupied and their attention retained. During the first few days the therapist must break through resistance and withdrawal with gentleness and courtesy, whilst encouraging trust and response. A situation in which failure might occur must be avoided carefully, so the aims are simple. A routine is established during which basic information such as names, days, months and the weather are discussed. At this stage repetition is an essential aid to the relearning process. Repetition is more useful and interesting if a variety of methods are used. The session is commenced by a handshake and a personal greeting. 'Hello, my name is . . . .'. After the initial introductions it is appropriate to return to each individual with a further extended comment on names.

'Have I written your name properly? How would you like to be addressed – Mrs Jones, or would you prefer Mary?' 'Can you say my name?' If the therapist's name has been forgotten write it down and ask for it to be read. Simply writing the name, showing it and saying 'Look, this is how you spell my name' usually suffices. Large clear name badges can be useful in a small group, so that there is a visual reminder of group-members' names. If errors in reading occur further repetition is required. Names can be useful means of reaching out to the group. Discussing other people with similar names rein-forces the learning process and provides added interest.

The therapists in groups at this Basic level are extremely active in presenting information, directing the subject matter of the group and in sustaining the patients' attention. A board of some description is essential for the visual presentation of information. This can be fixed or portable, depending on the setting. If it is fixed it should be clearly in the view of group members; writing on it should be large enough to be seen by all. Boards are available with magnetic letters, or words on cards that slide into slots on the board or may be a simple blackboard, with information written up in chalk. One commercially available board is a 'Weather Board', which is approximately three feet by eighteen inches, and has infor-mation regarding day, date, month, year and weather on cards that are slotted in appropriately.

As part of the routine this board can be completed during the session. The participants are asked what day it is, usually individually. If the response is wrong the reply should be sufficiently gentle so there is no loss of face. 'Well, it is almost the weekend. It is Friday today', or 'Yesterday was Tuesday, so today it is Wednesday'. If the answer is correct praise is given. Reading the correct day from the board reinforces this process. Prompts and cues are useful here; if a blackboard

Fig. 8.2 Basic information in a RO session

is available the day can be written letter by letter until someone guesses the answer. If no one guesses the group can read the complete name, so whatever happens the correct response will be achieved. The clue of the first few letters could be given verbally of course. If the board is completed before the session then members can be encouraged to take their cue directly from the board, and so again be spared the risk of a wrong answer. A similar pattern is followed for the remaining information – month, year, date, whereabouts of the hospital or old peoples' home and weather are basics. In considering the month, help can be obtained from the view through the window. The introduction of seasonal flowers and fruit or calendar-like pictures can also be of assistance. The members are encouraged to look outside, to notice the sky and the state of growth of trees and plants. The look and smell of a spring or summer bouquet of flowers or a collection of fallen autumn leaves emphasises the season.

If answers to questions are vague, slow, unforthcoming or consistently incorrect the right answer is supplied gently and conversationally. Direct criticism or contradiction should be avoided as confidence could be destroyed. 'I just told you that' or 'No, that's wrong' are destructive remarks.

Once these areas of information have been covered the whole board is re-read by group members, with the therapist prompting those with reading or speech problems. Diaries are commonly used in RO for those without reading or writing difficulties. Some people enjoy keeping a diary and complete it in detail; generally only simple routine facts are recorded. This adds variety to the repetition, and members can read out their diary entries to the others. Large letter-cards can be used by patients who have lost the fine motor control required for writing; they can be given the letters needed to spell their name or a short word and asked to put them in the right order.

A further aspect of information to be given is time. Initially this may be in terms of morning, afternoon and evening, but where appropriate a large clock with adjustable hands can be used to show current time, time of meals and so on.

This level of group is quite demanding on the therapists, as they have to maintain the group members' attention throughout, because their concentration span is usually exceedingly short. Preferably there should be two therapists to support each other.

The group is made up of adults not children. To patronise, or talk down to the elderly is to guarantee that they will remain withdrawn or become agitated or resentful. Friendli-ness and courtesy create the right atmosphere for response. The session should always start and end with handshakes, hellos and farewells. Interruptions and 'observers' who do not participate are not helpful. In order to establish rapport with this level of group the subject matter may seem childish. As long as the therapist is gentle and unthreatening this initial period is necessary in order to establish a relationship of trust and expectation. As soon as the person is able to cope in a relaxed fashion with this level it is imperative that the simple aim be changed and the group member moved on to the next stage. Table 8.2 summarises the features of this level.

Table 8.2 *Features of the Basic group* (for the most severely disorientated and withdrawn patients)

2–3 patients per therapist. Daily. 30 minutes. Social setting.

Emphasis on basic information – presented and repeated. Repetition varied – reading from board, writing in diary etc. Many clues provided to guarantee successful response. Use of RO, or Weather Board. Also calendar, large letter cards (for those unable to write) and a teaching clock etc., also useful. Therapists extremely active in sustaining attention, directing group, presenting information. Patients moved into Standard group as soon as possible.

Standard group

This is the most flexible level of RO, and according to group members' needs can resemble the Basic group at one extreme or the Advanced group at the other. Rigidity in the programme will be demonstrated by complaints from individuals about being treated as though they were in school, or a refusal to attend because of boredom. It is better, though not always possible, to avoid such a situation by being prepared for improvement. The therapy must be adapted to the group not vice versa. As soon as there is some evidence of improved response – by assessment, observation or even as a result of some signs of restlessness – the aim, scope and methods are broadened.

Introductions, names and warm greetings remain the natural starting point for the session. Again the RO Board is used to present basic information, but this is achieved more quickly in this group. The information too may be in more depth and detail. Diaries are likely to be particularly useful here.

Following the basic information part of the session, a wide variety of activities is possible. The aim is to encourage one or more of the following:

1. The fostering of interpersonal relationships, social awareness and interest
2. The connection and comparison of past and present,

capitalising on the person's previous experiences to build up interest in the environment.

3. The stimulation of one or more of the person's senses.

The type of activities and equipment needed are described in Chapter 9.

Sessions are slightly less directed, and therapists will use the responses of group-members to develop a theme or to change tack entirely! Thus pictures of food may have been intended to start a discussion on shopping, prices etc., but may elicit more response on cooking and favourite foods. There is scope here to pursue topics flexibly, as long as the discussion remains reality oriented, with past and present being distinguished, as well as fact from fantasy!

It is important to have knowledge of individual histories, experiences and interests. More personal orientation is encouraged at this level. Age, date of birth, names and where-abouts of family members, previous occupations and inter-ests, places where the person has lived are among the items that might be covered over a number of sessions. Staff need to know this information themselves so they can reinforce the person appropriately. A separate index card with these details on it for each group member is of great value for this purpose.

Although the therapists are slightly less directive, their role is still demanding. Before sessions they need to plan topics and collect relevant materials. They need to guide discussion, encourage social interaction, gently praise appropriate responses, watch for patients who are bored through the level being either too basic or too advanced, and modify the methods used accordingly. Group sessions can last for up to an hour, where staff time permits.

In encouraging social relationships, common backgrounds, occupations, interests and experiences are important. Topics that are likely to establish such links include old and new pictures and maps of the area where patients used to live, common occupations and industries of the area, everyday items from the past.

For each topic a tangible focus is essential; a picture, an object, a newspaper, slides, a short film, materials, and even a collection of smells. Everyday objects such as fruit or even a cup and saucer, can lead to consideration of colour, shape, taste, smell, texture, preferences (in the case of fruit) or material (bone china or plastic!), design, texture, function, and memories of tea parties (in the case of a cup and saucer). The latter discussion would end of course with a cup of tea for the group!

The group does not have to be static in the RO room. If mobility and weather permits, why not make a collection of autumn leaves. If the topic is the hospital or home why not have a tour, with members pointing out 'landmarks' – the lounge, dining room, their own sleeping area etc.

At this level, as at the others, where gaps occur in members' memories, cues and prompts are given, so that the person does not fail. Rambling talk is dealt with as in 24 hour RO.

Humour is important; a group where laughter is frequent is likely to be much more useful and effective than an over-serious group. For example, one 93 year old man caused a stir by describing how he had made his wife *walk* several hundred miles to meet his family. Female group members castigated him for his irresponsible behaviour, and he with a broad grin responded by adding more outrageous detail, to the delight of all concerned.

In another group a series of everyday objects was being named; one was a woollen tea-pot cover which one group-member then put on as a hat and proceeded to dance a jig around the room, whilst everyone collapsed with laughter.

Reality is not of course constant happiness; the whole range of emotions may arise in the group. Topics should not be banned in order to 'protect' the elderly people. A moving group session was stimulated by a poppy, reminding partici-pants of the 1914–1918 war and the awful loss of young men there.

Rather than banning religion and politics the topics can be usefully employed to arouse active response and healthy emotion.

Sex, love and marriage should not be taboo either. Relationships between the sexes can do a great deal to combat withdrawal, and the group should be mixed for this reason. Their attitude towards sex is often humorous and teasing and they can turn the tables to tease the therapist when so inclined. Some useful and most amusing sessions can develop as a result of open discussion on their attitudes to sex and members of the opposite sex.

Death too is something that is too frequently a taboo subject. If one of the group should fall sick, or there should be a death on the ward or in the Home there is no reason to fear open discussion. Those in contact with the elderly often underestimate their ability to cope with natural emotion and become overprotective.

Table 8.3 lists the main features of this group and Chapter 9 should be referred to for detailed ideas for sessions.

Table 8.3 *Features of the Standard group* (for majority of moderately disorientated patients)

2–3 patients per therapist. Daily 30–60 minutes. Social setting.

Begin with basic information. Follow with wide variety of activities, topics for discussion etc. Stimulate all senses. Encourage social awareness and interest. Past is bridge to present. Prompts, clues used as necessary. Weather Board used initially. Then a variety of sensorial aids. Reminders of the past. Money, pictures, everyday objects, food, newspapers, fresh fruit etc. Therapist needs to plan, collect relevant materials, watch for boredom, guide discussion. Patients move on to Advanced level if possible, but may remain in the group for some time.

Advanced group

If an elderly person – or a whole group – makes a great deal of progress with the Standard RO group, then he/she can be moved on to this third and final level. Realistically, this 'graduation' will not occur for every patient, in view of the nature of the disabilities involved, but some patients are able to advance in this way.

The Advanced group is usually a maintenance level used for less deteriorated short-stay patients, people who have recovered from an illness and need stimulation in order to be sufficiently motivated to return home, and those who have physical problems that make total independence impossible. Those in the community who are beginning to show signs of impairment or confusion will also benefit. 'Stroke' clubs and day-centres may find these methods relevant for some of their members. The aims at this level are those of independence and self-determination. The number of participants can be increased up to 10. The therapist acts as an adviser and guide, encouraging activities and achievements and monitoring progress. A watch is kept for signs of regression or deterioration so that early preventive steps can be taken. Self-help and self-care are included in the aims. Leadership can be from the members themselves. They can decide what activities are needed, and direct the sessions themselves. Relatives and friends should be included where appropriate, to help them use this approach at home.

Meetings can be less frequent – perhaps once, twice or three times a week depending on practicability. Basic information is still mentioned and an information board is present, but the scope is directed towards awareness of the wider world. Introductions, names, social relationships, past and present comparisons and sensory stimulation continue to be emphasised.

Outings and visits start during the Standard group but should be extended and become more ambitious. The therapist can make suggestions and advise, but final decisions come from the group. General needs are the responsibility of the therapist, who also watches for the more submissive and retiring people so that their needs are not overlooked. Responsibilities can be shared. Group living plans could be introduced where appropriate in residential settings. Active participation in hobbies and pastimes including gardening, painting, handicrafts etc. are to be encouraged. Places of interest can be visited, parties, picnics and competitions organised. Events for sessions require planning: a committee

Table 8.4 *Features of the Advanced group* (for mildly disorientated people – useful in community settings)

Larger groups feasible
Less frequent
Social setting

Group self-determination of activities where possible. Mention of basic information but extended towards awareness of the world and community. RO Board present. Other material dependent on group needs and choice. Cooking, shopping outings, music, active involvement. Therapist acts as guide, encourages, assists and advises. Patients in group for some time. Maintenance procedure.

of the elderly themselves would be ideal. Film shows and the use of audio-visual equipment have a place here. Extensive use of reminiscences about the past and comparisons with the present would also be appropriate.

Major features of the Advanced group are summarised briefly in Table 8.4.

FINAL POINTS

The atmosphere for RO sessions must be relaxed and non-threatening. Therapists must approach the situation with an awareness of the individual and of the dangers of rigidity. Withdrawal can result from boredom, too fast a pace, or by setting aims too high; these factors are under the influence of the therapists. Too many questions can prove very threatening and unnatural in a social situation. Conversations are not one-sided or composed of questions and answers. Retraining needs to be subtle and hidden in conversation. An interrogation where questions are asked as quickly as the patient fails to answer them is not RO! Failure must be avoided as it could prove disastrous to the patient's progress.

If the aims are low initially success becomes more probable. As each step forward is achieved praise is given and another simple aim set. Praise can be freely given for minor successes. Many elderly people with dementia have received very little praise, because of their difficult behaviour. Aggressive, domineering people need to be encouraged to help the less forceful so that they do not receive more than their fair share of attention. Praise can prove too fulsome for the more independent and may sound patronising. In this situation reinforcement can be satisfactorily achieved by a gentle, matter-of-fact comment of approval. Generally the enjoyment of social interactions and achievement is reinforcing in itself.

Therapists need feedback as well as patients. The coordinator can ensure that results and progress are made available to the staff. The expectations of staff must be realistic. Changes may be very slow or only minimal in certain cases. RO is hard work and demanding. Initially the elderly patient may be too confused or unable to respond without considerable effort on the part of the therapist. It requires good planning, realistic aims, energy and imagination to obtain worthwhile reactions and progress.

SUMMARY

1. Create atmosphere. A special room modified for use as a pub, living room or clubhouse is ideal. A social setting helps remotivation and resocialisation.

2. Routine consists of the basic information concerning day, month, year, place and weather in Basic and Standard groups. Different ways of repeating them need planning.

3. Elderly people with dementia have a short attention and memory span. Constant stimulation is required to maintain interest and cooperation.

4. Constant repetition is necessary; this must be varied.

5. Praise and approval can reinforce re-learning

6. Informal RO is necessary to reinforce the achievements of the structured session.

7. Patients may be confused and withdrawn, but are not children. Their knowledge and experience are buried and need restoring.

8. Friendliness, courtesy and knowledge about the individual are vital aids in re-establishing confidence.

9. Therapists and clients should know and use each other's names – the formal title or the intimate first-name basis must be decided among them.

10. Signs of authority do not help relationships. Uniforms can be changed or disguised.

11. Rigidity is retarding. A relearning programme once assimilated indicates the need to progress.

12. As soon as possible, individuals should be involved in group activities as social interaction is important to rehabilitation processes. Interpersonal relationships can be encouraged even in the early stages of therapy.

13. Sensorial stimulation should be used – interesting smells tastes and the feel of things are as valuable as visual material.

14. Clients must be placed in appropriate groups so that suitable levels can be provided and realistic aims set.

15. Therapist needs to be friendly, involved and capable of using imagination and initiative.

16. Relatives can be included but need guidance and monitoring as family attitudes can cause reversal.

17. Basic to the therapy is the capitalisation on the client's long-term memory stores. Their prime of life – roughly 1920–50 – is the period they remember the best. They are secure in discussing this era. This makes it possible to direct their attention to the present and bring them up to date by comparisons between then and now.

18. Patients can be helped to succeed by the use of clues and prompts, and by avoidance of exposure of disabilities.

'The greatest source of pleasure is variety.' Dr Johnson

9

101 ideas for formal RO sessions

Making a programme
Basic group
Standard group
Advanced group
Record-keeping

MAKING A PROGRAMME

Frequently it becomes difficult to think of a topic or to plan a day-to-day programme for group sessions. As a result the session deteriorates into a time when the staff and patients/residents just sit about and talk vaguely and without purpose. This can also arise when the therapists are tired or have been too busy to have time to prepare topics. The following suggestions are intended to help in such situations. They are not exhaustive, but illustrate the range of possibilities.

The small pocket book 'R.O. Reminders' (Holden 1984d) together with many of the items listed in Appendix 3 as aids to RO and Reminiscence, is an additional source of ideas for stimulating, purposeful activities and for extending the range of possible programmes. Leaders should select and adapt topics and ideas carefully to be appropriate for the abilities and interests of the particular group. From the ideas here, and others that can be added, a set of 20 or 30 different programmes for RO sessions, suitable for a particular setting, clientele and group level, can be constructed. A card is then chosen at random and can be used to give structure for the session; also any equipment needed can be assembled just prior to the session. Example cards are shown in Table 9.1; these were used with a Standard group in an old people's home where most residents suffered from some form of dementia. Use of such a system ensures variety in the sessions and helps when the therapist's creativity runs dry. They should be quickly ignored when a group leader has a new or better idea or if something emerges from the group. They are to fall back on rather than to be used rigidly.

A cupboard for accumulated items of interest is essential, preferably in the room where the group session takes place. An alternative approach to planning a topic is to start with a piece of equipment. A small box of cards in two sizes can be used as an index. Each piece of available equipment can be given a separate large card, e.g. MAPS, HERBS AND SPICES, CLOTH, etc. Under each of these headings an appropriate letter or letters will indicate which of the smaller cards to consult. Placed in alphabetical order the small cards supply suggested topics that may be relevant to the use of the equipment. For instance under T suggestions for topics could

Table 9.1 Examples of possible Programme cards

A	B
1. Introductions – greet each other by name.	1. Introductions – greet each other by name.
2. Enter day, date, name of home on RO board; change calendar; copy into personal diaries.	2. Enter day, date, name of home on RO board; change calendar; copy into personal diaries.
3. Use spelling boards to rearrange mixed-up words. Start with shorter words and use longer words only when residents gain confidence.	3. Enter age and date of birth and place of birth in diary. Discuss who is oldest, youngest etc.
4. Bring in common objects: cup, saucer, plate, spoon, comb, hat, pencil, key, umbrella etc. Name the object and its colour; what shape is it? What does it feel like? Cold, warm, rough, smooth, hard, soft? Draw round the object.	4. Discuss weather using weather board. Is it as expected for time of year? Is it changeable? What weather is forecast? What clothes would be needed outside today? Find appropriate weather picture.
5. Prepare a menu of residents' favourite foods. Compare with actual menu!	5. Play picture dominoes; small prize for winner.
Equipment: Diaries Spelling boards and letters Common objects Pencils and paper	Equipment: Diaries and pens Weatherboard and pictures Picture dominoes Small prize

include Travel, Taste, Touch, Transport, Tailoring etc. So in order to find suggestions for the use of a bag of cloth the therapist would look up the card headed CLOTH and find, for instance, the letters TCOH. On consulting the smaller card 'C' appropriate topics would be Clothing, Cost, Colour; under T, Tailoring, Touch; under O, Occupations; and under H, Household jobs, Homecrafts, and so forth. Each provides a useful starting point for discussion and stimulation. The topics included depend entirely on the experience and imagination of the therapist which can by this means be used collectively. Cues are needed by staff as well as by the group members!

Ideas for sessions are best described by breaking them up into those suitable for each group level. The following ideas are not intended to inspire rigidity, they are simply suggestions. A group may have interests which require other avenues not included. There are differences in every group, and in people from every area and cultural background. After only a few meetings these differences are noticeable and should be recognised.

BASIC GROUP

Essentially the ideas here are limited as this stage is merely to get people started.

1. Introductions – always a good (and necessary) starting point. Shake hands – use large name labels.

2. Large Weather Board, comprising main board and a collection of smaller pieces which slot into or adhere magnetically onto the board. On these are written the Days, Months, comments and pictures about the Weather. Can be made or purchased (see Appendix 3). Used to present relevant information and stimulate some discussion.

3. Personal diaries – those who retain writing skills can copy basic information into their diaries, providing further repetition. Also scope for personal entries about past, current and future events. Gives person ongoing record to refer to. All members can have their own 'This is your life' book, including details of important events and people in the person's life. Wherever possible this should be illustrated. Such a book helps the person show others more of what they have experienced and achieved in their life than they may now be able to communicate readily. If put together carefully with the help of relatives and friends it also aids the group leader in reinforcing accurate information about the person's circumstances. A suitable booklet is available (The Memory Diary, see Appendix 3), or it can be made from scrap-books and photographs.

4. Large letters: on wooden squares, or on cards (as in 'Lexicon'), or plastic letters with magnets attached for use with metal spelling boards. All can be used to spell out simple items of basic information, particularly where group members have difficulty writing. For instance, they could be used to spell out the day of the week, letter by letter, until someone guesses the correct answer.

5. Flowers – fresh and seasonal to emphasise the time of

year and stimulate sight, touch and smell. Also fallen leaves in autumn.

6. Fruit – again fresh to emphasise seasons and stimulate senses – including taste!

7. Food – other items of food can be brought in where appropriate – cakes, sweets. Raw ingredients – flour, salt, raisins etc., vegetables, sandwiches etc., to stimulate senses and discussion, once they have been identified.

8. Drink – provide various beverages – tea, coffee, fruit drinks, sherry, wine, beer etc. for taste, identification, smell and enjoyment!

9. Maps – plastic or wood shapes of Great Britain, America, Australia and Europe etc. Large, clear map of local city or town. Maps help in orientation, discussion of 'where we are' and 'where we come from'. Several members may be from the same area, so the maps help to identify possible neighbours or common knowledge. In later stages, 'where we have been' is another topic arising from maps.

10. Large Clock Face with movable hands (as realistic as possible). The clock can be used to indicate present time, breakfast, dinner, and bed time.

11. Chalkboard and chalk – has many uses in repeating and reinforcing whatever is discussed. More able patients should be encouraged to write on the board for others.

12. Collages – these can be made in the group; members search through magazines looking for pictures that illustrate the particular theme, cut these out and stick them on a large piece of paper.

13. Collages of seasons – to aid discussion of time of year.

14. Collages of food – can emphasise time, by depicting different meals for different times of day. Also discussion about preferences, ingredients, prices etc.

15. Collages of children – to emphasise sense of life-span, memories of their own childhood and their own children, grandchildren etc.

16. Collages of places – local pictures or further afield, can be used in conjunction with maps. Reminders of the group's previous 'haunts' – the main street, shops, local landmarks and so on – assist in recreating a temporarily forgotten daily existence.

17. Picture cards illustrating occupations e.g. – postman,

window cleaner, miner etc. Occupation cards can be useful in reminding people about everyday jobs which provide day-to-day contact in the environment. The postman, the butcher and the bus conductor are part of everyday reality.

STANDARD GROUP

By using visual and other stimulation and by encouraging reminiscences through related materials elderly people can be persuaded to respond well. Learning more about them as individuals with specific interests can assist in the search for suitable equipment and relevant approaches, all of which can be exploited in building up good relationships.

18. 'Then' and 'Now': Most towns have produced a book full of photographs of places and familiar landmarks of Then and Now. These are invaluable for discussion, showing how the town has changed since group members were children. If such a book is not available then libraries etc. often have collections of old photographs, copies or slides of which could be obtained, together with up to date comparisons. If there is an area where most of the group live, it is possible that they also had schools in common. They have memories of the buildings, streets and activities of the district, and may well have mutual friends and acquaintances. They may have shopped in the same shopping centre, been married in the same church etc. Finding such things in common can greatly help a group interact.

19. Old newspapers, national and local, again provide a stimulus to reminiscence that can aid grasp of current reality as it is brought up-to-date into the present. Libraries often have collections of old newspapers.

20. Gardening – pictures and books may elicit memories and knowledge of plants, flowers, vegetables etc. Advanced groups could try indoor gardening – bulbs, plants, cress and so on – as a continuing activity.

21. Cookery – pictures and recipe books are useful (as well as real food). Discuss favourite recipes, particularly for traditional foods. More advanced groups could carry out simple cookery – all can help mix ingredients for cakes and sweets as a group exercise, and enjoy the smell of cooking, as well as sampling the finished product!

22. Clothes – books and pictures of fashions over the years, may prompt fascinating reminiscences; current fashions always produce interesting comments! If costumes from the patient's young days can be obtained these can be 'modelled'.

23. Occupations – in any given region or area there are many employed in particular local industries or occupations and knowledge of these is valuable too. Any relevant material from such industries inspires discussion and reminiscences. It also provides therapists with opportunities to introduce present-day comparisons. Pictures of coalmines and miners in the 1920s and 1930s can bind a group together, in a mining area, for instance. Many members of groups may have spent some time in domestic service. Local or national firms may prove helpful. Films can be hired, there may be a library or museum on the subject, and most homes have objects or materials which would prove invaluable – old typewriters, miner's lamps, models of ships, old tools, looms etc. Things lying around the home for years unnoticed suddenly assume importance as they could provoke memories and

Fig. 9.1 Aids to reminiscence, like these 'Nostalgia packs' are now widely available.

experiences. It is equally important to have a supply of modern material to show how things have changed.

24. Royalty – in the UK books and pictures of the Royal Family past and present often stimulate interest; tracing the Royal family tree through the use of pictures gives the elderly person a sense of their own ageing and development.

25. Cars – group members will have lived through massive changes in the motor car (and other forms of transportation). Old and new pictures and models are useful here. Members may recall their first car, or their first journey.

26. Homecrafts – members may have had previously interests in sewing, embroidery, knitting, crochet and so on. Discussion of these crafts, together with finished articles and pictures, may produce a number of memories, and may encourage members to attempt some tasks themselves.

27. Travel – a number of topics arise from this theme; members can describe their furthest travels, the method of travel, speed of journeys and so on. Pictures of places near and far will aid such a discussion.

28. Animals – pictures would be the stimulus here; have you ever seen a lion? ever ridden a horse? milked a cow? The questions draw on well-learned knowledge, and may evoke memories e.g. one old seaman vividly described his experiences with whales.

29. Pets – the real thing can be provided here, as well as pictures. It can start a discussion of pets people have had and the sometimes harsh reality of not having them in the Hospital or Home. Different breeds of dogs and cats may also be a discussion topic, using relevant photographs.

30. Birds – this topic could be developed as above, with pet birds and wild birds being observed 'live' or in photographs. A bird table just outside the ward or home would facilitate this, and provide a daily routine of feeding the birds.

31. Art – interest in paintings, drawings and sculpture could be explored with the help of large colourful reproductions. Some popular paintings will be identified; others can be appreciated or in some cases can be the cause of group bewilderment! According to ability, a group art session of painting, drawing, modelling in clay, simple printing, sticking on of coloured shapes or whatever can be a good activity.

32. Stamps – even if members have not been avid collec-

tors, interest can be aroused by colourful stamps from around the world (use with a map) or using a range of stamps from the person's life-time, the historical changes (and changes in price of sending a letter) can be a cause for comment.

33. Coins – different value coins (and notes) can be identified, and used to carry out simple arithmetic. The dates and heads on the coins are also worthy of discussion. Coins and notes from around the world could also be used; in the UK pre-decimal coins could evoke memories and comparisons.

34. Holidays – a rich source of discussion – prompted by picture postcards, brochures etc. What sort of holiday – seaside, country; hotel, camping, boarding house; home or abroad. Where did members go on holiday? What did they do whilst on holiday? Where would they like to have gone?

35. Famous houses, castles, palaces and so on – particularly if local. Pictures will help recall visits to such places.

36. Countryside – pictures of local country areas may remind members of country walks, the rural life, the country year and so on.

37. Mountains – pictures of grand mountain scenery provide another topic, with mountain sports and dangers being possibilities for discussion.

38. Racing – pictures of famous horses and jockeys of the past, together with comparisons with the present scene will interest former racing followers.

39. Small antiques – pieces of furniture or bric-a-brac brought into the group can promote discussion of the purpose of the items and whether group members had anything similar; what would be used now?

40. Old toys – again a comparison can be made e.g. between lead and plastic soldiers, clockwork and electric trains, china dolls and dolls whose hair grow! Computer games defy comparison!

41. Traditional cards – greetings cards and postcards were collected by many families, and make a fascinating contrast in materials and design with their modern counterparts.

42. Souvenirs – the small ornaments people brought back from holiday – often china miniatures – will again evoke memories of the time and places.

43. Jewelry – compare old and new pieces; many group members will have some jewelry – a ring or brooch; does it

have special significance. Naming precious stones, trying on necklaces, bracelets and so on.

44. Old kitchen equipment – bring in the oldest kitchen utensils that can be found or borrowed – discuss all the gadgets and labour-saving devices of today – compare pictures of automatic washing machines with the 'dolly-tub' and so on.

45. War memories – pictures of life during the world wars; memories of air raids, women at work, fire-watching, friends who were lost in action, and so on. The Flanders poppy is an evocative visual aid around Remembrance Day.

46. Medals – what were they awarded for? Action in World War 1, and in the Second World War; where were they stationed? What did they do? What was it really like? Some will have pictures of themselves in uniform to show the group.

47. Ration books – and other reminders of the effects of war on life at home; how did members stretch the rations allowed – special recipes or menus? Comparison with present-day standards of food and clothing.

48. Mementoes of war-time leaders – pictures, other mementoes of Churchill; the 'V' sign; a brief tape of his voice.

49. The depression – pictures of life in the 1930s; mass unemployment, huge marches and so on; how were group members affected? Comparison with present-day levels of poverty and state benefits.

50. Emigration – did members consider emigrating, or have they actually emigrated? Any family abroad? Pictures and maps are useful here.

51. Prices – pictures of food and other items; discuss current prices, prices in pevious years; also rise in wages. Make up a typical shopping basket for £1, £5 then and now.

52. Religion – what beliefs do members have? Did they go to church because they had to or because they wanted to? Do they attend church now? What other beliefs are there?

53. Marriage – were they (or are they) married? Where did they get married? What sort of wedding? (photograph albums here are a great help). What do they think of marriage now? What do they think of people living together – without being married?. . . . .

54. Education – where did they go to school? What age were they when they left? What was it like? What did they learn? Were there opportunities for further education? Were they trained for a particular job as an apprenticeship etc? Did they go to college? Would they have liked to?

55. Local festivities – many towns have long-established traditions of annual fairs, festivals and celebrations. Pictorial comparisons of past and present will jog memories in the group about them.

56. Families – using family photograph albums, each group member's family history can be pieced together pictorially: pictures of the person when young can be compared with ones taken as they are now; the development of their own children into adults and (possibly elderly people themselves) can be seen.

57. The role of women – a brief illustrated article on 'women's lib' can stimulate a useful discussion about changing roles – particularly in a mixed group.

58. Sports – old newspapers, magazines and illustrated books provide the material for a discussion of sporting interests; sporting heroes of the past – and what has become of them; teams supported by group members, changes in sports clothing, athletic ability, styles of play.

59. Local public transport – use old pictures of trams, horse and motor drawn, trolley-buses, early buses and charabancs, together with modern counterparts. Fare prices might also be discussed.

60. Film-stars, singers and other celebrities – a scrap-book might be made of favourites from the group members' younger days, with pictures showing the stars in their prime, and also as they aged. Reminders of particular films, songs and catch-phrases would be relevant here.

61. Old-fashioned shop goods – old tin boxes (which preceded packets) might be unearthed; old adverts from newspapers and magazines; 'then' and 'now' comparison.

62. Special events on TV – it is not always necessary to oversee viewing particularly when the observers are deeply involved, but frequently the proceedings are meaningless to people with severe memory problems unless someone directs their attention to certain aspects of the programme. If a video machine is available, this could be used to repeat such

events. In one day centre a group regularly watches and discusses the lunch time news bulletin on TV.

63. Music – unlike other sounds used in isolation, music is extremely useful in RO. Music for enjoyment's sake is more part of 24 hour RO, where it should be remembered that tastes differ widely. One use of music in RO sessions is to play a tape made up of brief extracts of singers well known in the group members' younger days; these can be combined with pictures of the singers as in 60 above.

64. Music to reinforce RO – a second use is in aiding the repetition of basic information; appropriate songs and rhymes are sung to back up the current information; e.g. 'April Showers', 'White Christmas', 'Easter Bonnet', 'Here we go gathering nuts in May' etc.

65. Music-making – a third use is as a coordinated group activity; simple rhythm instruments can be made in the group – shakers, blocks of wood to hit together, kazoos and so on.

66. Movement to music – simple, gentle group physical exercises are carried out to music; this can be done with group members seated.

67. Touch – Hot and Cold. The weather or the temperature can be stressed by a pair of cold hands just in from the snow or frost. The temperature of the room can be shown by the warm hands of the residents. Use a thermometer to show the temperature. Food and drink is hot or cold; bring in some ice! Parts of the world have different temperatures (use maps and pictures).

68. Touch – Soft and Hard, Rough and Smooth. Many things can be used to discuss these concepts. Skin, fabrics, animal fur, surfaces, pumice stone, rock collections, scouring pads and powders, wallpapers, clothing, sand and tissue paper. Fruit – apples, bananas, oranges etc. Food can be examined to tell, by feel, if it is fresh, ripe or rotten.

69. Touch – Dry and Wet. Spills of liquid can be used. Travel cloths, sponges, mop heads, towels, washing.

70. Cloth – provide a bag of pieces of material for the group to feel; they will reminisce about old fabrics such as chenille, flannel, tulle and cretonne. They will dismiss a piece of denim as something which is too 'rough' and be surprised by the cost of trousers made from it! Drip-dry fabrics will

produce stories of difficult ironing problems. What would different types of material be used for? What colours and patterns go together?

71. Heating – old and new – pictures of old-fashioned stoves and fires; discussion of work they involved; pictures of modern heating systems – advantages and disadvantages.

72. Smell – some elderly people, particularly men, appear to have lost their sense of smell, but generally this is a very rewarding sense to use as a tool for RO. A box of smells made up with the help of a kindly pharmacist is needed. Little bottles containing for example: attar of roses, lemon, peppermint, almonds, cinnamon, cloves, lavender, orange, menthol, cherries, Sloan's liniment. The bottled smell can be used as in a game, with clues and quick identification so as not to lose interest. The purpose is to arouse memories and excite discussion of use. For example the smell of almond essence provokes thoughts of Easter and Simnel cake, Christmas and Christmas cake.

73. Smell – herbs and spices. Discuss the smells and uses of collections of herbs and spices from the kitchen shelf, potpourri and collections of fresh herbs from the garden: Thyme, Sage, Rosemary, Mint, Lavender, Chives, Marjoram. Uses in cooking, as air-fresheners and for keeping clothes fresh.

74. Smell – fruit and flowers: Fresh Flowers: Roses, Carnations, Sweet peas, Lilac, Daffodils as available. Fresh Fruit: Tangerines, Oranges, Lemons, Apples, Bananas, Strawberries etc. Also discuss colours, likes, dislikes, of flowers and fruit.

75. Smells in the kitchen – kitchen smells, coffee, soaps, moth balls, ammonia, cooking, polishes etc. Compare carbolic and perfumed soap. Cooking smells can be introduced in an actual session by providing half-cooked bread from the supermarket. Old herbal remedies and medicines provoke memories that are often amusing and provide easy comparisons with today.

76. Smells – perfume; compare various perfumes, lavender water, eau de cologne etc. Current toiletries – deodorants, aftershave, talc etc.

77. Taste – this is closely associated with sense of smell. A game can be made of identifying foods and drinks from their

taste, with eyes closed. Tea, coffee, beer, fruit, bread, cake etc. can be used in this way.

78. Taste – sweet and sour; contrast sweet and sour food, leading into discussion of preferences etc. Lemon juice, vinegar, unsweetened cooking apples, rhubarb etc. compared with sugar, jam, syrup, treacle, sweets, cakes and so on.

79. Tastes – unpleasant and disputed; medicine, cod liver oil, taste of cigarettes, cold tea, stale food, disliked food, bitter aloes, alcohol, real v. instant coffee, tea bags v. tea leaves; all to stimulate discussion and response on food memories, preferences, current opportunities.

80. Tastes – hot; peppers, spices, curry powder, radishes, raw onion, salad dressing, sauces, chillies and so on.

81. Menus – popular and unpopular food. Modern tastes. Wartime food – dehydrated eggs, milk etc. Potatoes for flour in cakes. Funny recipes for icing sugar and almond paste. Wartime recipe books. Foods and tastes once enjoyed, now unobtainable. Food from other countries. Prepare typical menus from different times of members' lives, including the present. Discuss choices available – or lack of them.

82. Newspapers and journals on the table provide day-to-day current information that can be incorporated into discussions about current events. The TV pages stimulate discussions about favourite programmes and personalities; the horoscope encourages members to recall their birth-date; some groups have been seen to attempt a simple crossword.

83. Magazines – are similarly a potentially rich source of discussion starters; a short paragraph from an article or a letter can be read out (perhaps from the problem page!); pictures accompanying articles and advertisements can also be used in this way – in addition to their use in collages mentioned above.

84. Current events – local, national and world events can provide a continuing topic. An election for example could be the subject of a large poster with names and pictures of those involved, and the polling date clearly indicated. Reminiscences about previous elections, political argument and interest in the outcome could be stimulated. Posters of other continuing news stories could be made – e.g. royal tours, strikes, wars etc.

85. Current events – politicians; pictures of current leaders

could be mounted on a poster or in a scrap book with their names, parties and office. A montage of former Prime Ministers or Presidents going back to the early years of this century, will allow comparisons and a historical perspective.

86. Current events – sports; major sporting events, Olympic Games, Soccer's World Cup or FA Cup Final, Cricket Test Matches, Tennis Championships and so on can be discussed in advance, the outcome predicted and watched. Major horse races could form the basis for a sweepstake, depending on the interests of the group.

87. Everyday objects – any common articles can be brought into the group, identified, and their use demonstrated; discussions of shape, colour and so on can be stimulated. Cups and saucers, knife, fork and spoon, shoes, hat, ball, light-bulb, umbrella, saucepan, key and padlock, purse and radio are among the sort of objects that could be used in this way.

88. Anagrams – large letter cards or blocks can be used; a word is given in mixed-up order for the group member to rearrange into the correct order. The difficulty can be adjusted according to ability from two letters upward!

89. Word games can be played with letter cards – turning up say the letter E and then naming a word beginning with E. If the next card is T, thinking what word could be made from ET . . . .

90. Number games – use a simple version of Bingo, with only the numbers 1–20 to bring the game within the person's reduced memory and attention span. Each person would have four numbers on a card to cover when they are called out; dominoes can also be used – with different colour spots for each number and large size dominoes. Small prizes for winners are essential.

91. Picture Games – the picture equivalent of the above. In picture Bingo each person has a card with four or five easily identifiable pictures on it; there could be 20 or so pictures altogether, taken one at a time from a bag – the winner being the first to match all his pictures. Picture dominoes is another possibility, with pictures of common objects replacing the usual numbers. Again prizes should be given.

92. Shape puzzles – these are games where a number of plastic or wooden shapes are fitted into corresponding holes

in a board. These can spark off discussion on shapes – squares, triangles, circles etc. – what else is a triangle? point to the two squares and so on; and also colours, if the pieces have different colours; find another the same colour as this; what else is green? Has anyone any clothes the same colour as this? Use matching where naming is difficult for group members.

93. Jig-saw puzzles – these can be a useful activity if the number of pieces is small, the size of the pieces is large, and the finished picture is not childish. The completed picture can then be a topic for discussion.

94. Outings – these assist memory, reminiscence and socialisation. Relevant visits can be made to the home area, shopping area, churches where people were married; parks; picnic and beauty spots well remembered. Where physically possible visits to shops and new supermarkets and shopping precincts are valuable. Local pub outings are always welcome.

ADVANCED GROUP

Much of the material and techniques used for Standard groups would be relevant suitably adapted to the ability level and interests of the group members. The aims for this group are Independence, Self-esteem and Self-help. The group should be encouraged to initiate their own programmes and make their own decisions as far as possible, so the items listed here are more in the form of headings.

95. Events – a number of special events can be arranged; a fashion show, a brief film show, a school band or choir and so on can arouse interest.

96. Demonstration – by gardeners, beauticians, cookery experts, artists, local theatre, dance groups, handicraft experts and so on may be within the attention span of this group.

97. Cooking – a complete group meal could be possible, with stronger members of the group helping and encouraging the more infirm.

98. Games – more complex card games and so on will be feasible; perhaps competitions can be organized.

99. Parties – with a special or relevant theme; Halloween, Christmas, Easter bonnet competitions etc. The right food, the right decor, suitable entertainments can all be organised between the therapist and the group.

100. Making decorations – for parties at Christmas and for members' birthdays.

101. Reminiscence theatre – a local group putting on a show with music hall items and memories of life in previous years could be appreciated by this group. Making a reminiscence display, illustrating local history or group members life experiences can be attempted. Volunteers, relatives, school children and local societies may help to track down appropriate items for display; local radio may help with an appeal for specific pictures or objects. The local library and museum may also be of assistance.

Each group can indicate where their interests and abilities lie, and with suitable support and imagination on the part of the therapist can succeed in their aims and so increase their own self-esteem.

RECORD-KEEPING

Each day immediately at the end of the session a written record should be made of the group. A large book can be used with a page for each day.

Record: Group members present
Group leaders and other staff present.
Times group began and ended
Topics discussed, equipment used
A brief note about each group member's reaction
Anything discovered in the group about likes, dislikes, interests, abilities – things that should be developed, things that should be avoided!
General appraisal of the session.

10

Practical issues

In this chapter are discussed some of the key practical points that may arise when care staff seek to introduce positive approaches such as RO into their work with elderly people.

Intensity

How often must RO be 'done' to be useful? Is a weekend break harmful? Can it be omitted when there is a staff shortage? Would sessions twice a day be more beneficial than sessions once a day?

At first sight it seems that these are important questions in the operation of RO which have implications for the amount of staff involvement required. In fact they reflect a total misconception of the basic principles by assuming that RO is like a pill to be taken so many times a day after meals! They ignore the importance of the basic approach, of the use of every interaction between staff member and elderly person to increase awareness and orientation. If RO is seen as a positive approach, a way of working which is in operation for 24 hours a day, most of these questions become spurious. In some settings staff-resident interactions are few and far between; such situations can hardly be regarded as positive. Sometimes RO sessions, particular individual or group programmes, are perceived as an alternative to a satisfactory level of interaction throughout the day. There is no substitute, however, for such consistent support. Sessions supplement 24 hour RO, and help staff and residents to get to know each other better, in a friendly, relaxed atmosphere; this then facilitates the continuous daily contact.

The following points can be made regarding intensity:

1. The amount of staff-resident contact needs to be increased as far as is possible, and encouragement given to use RO in each of these contacts. In some settings talking with the residents is seen as avoiding real work; though in many senses, if it is done properly it is perhaps more demanding than other more physical forms of work. Many of the routine physical tasks of the Home or ward can be carried out whilst talking with a resident quite easily.

2. Generally speaking the more intensive RO can be, the more the resident will benefit from it. However, the elderly person must be allowed to respond to information supplied

so that it can be absorbed gradually. Bombarding the person with information which cannot be assimilated, or pressurising the person to respond are *not* part of an intensive approach! A supportive, respectful approach that recognises the person's individual psychological needs at all times is the aim.

3. The more confused and disorientated a person is the more intensive the RO needs to be in order to stimulate learning. This may be reflected in the slower pace of learning and the much lower level of information required. Two and a half hours a week is hardly adequate to promote change. Even in a group it is vital to provide individual attention, but the social atmosphere always proves a valuable aid. Very disturbed and restless deteriorated patients may particularly benefit from individual contacts, if their concentration is too limited for a group session. The activity and atmosphere provided by the 24 hour approach will prove helpful, as stimulation and aids to self-help will be readily available.

4. There is relatively little benefit in having more than one RO group session per day, and the additional time could be utilized with briefer individual sessions. There are suggestions that not having group sessions at weekends may tend to detract from some of the gains previously made, and if at all feasible group activities should be offered at weekends also.

Consistency

It is important that all staff work closely together to increase a patient's level of awareness. It is possible for inconsistencies to occur as the staff are made up of individuals. Each of them can perceive ward or home policies, and the way to implement those policies, in their own way. Furthermore if team spirit is weak, understanding of such policies is limited. For example, in a situation where most staff members are employing RO principles with a particular patient their efforts to help her to realise where she is could be destroyed by the faulty approach of a single staff member. Without appreciating the consequence this nurse could seek to reassure the patient by telling her she is in a hotel at the coast! The effects of RO would be weakened if messages received by patients were inconsistent. In effect they would reinforce confusion.

When team feeling exists and is encouraged such problems

will be minimised. This relates particularly to how any positive approach is implemented (see below). The necessity for staff to feel involved in the programme must be emphasised – rather than it being presented as another chore. Other staff who might not normally be included in a staff training programme e.g. cleaners, domestics, orderlies, porters etc., have in fact often a great deal of contact and interaction with patients. It may well be important, if a consistent approach is to be maintained, that they are at least informed of what is happening and the rationale behind it. Similarly visitors to the ward, volunteers and most importantly relatives need guidance on how best to communicate with patients on the ward. A brief printed sheet may be helpful, giving details of the approach, but perhaps the best way of getting the approach across is by the care-staff being seen to put it into practice at all times themselves. In many ways RO could be a uniting force among staff, helping all to feel there is something useful that they can do, that they are important and valuable members of the care-team, whether or not they have degrees, qualifications or certificates. If these feelings can be nurtured – and they stand in marked contrast to the feelings of helplessness and uselessness so often experienced by staff working with elderly people with dementia – then the all-important consistency of approach is more likely to be achieved. It should be borne in mind of course that it is consistency of approach that is needed, and not necessarily consistency of method. Thus in RO to help sessions be more enjoyable for all concerned variety is important. There is here a great deal of scope for individual personalities, flair and imagination.

Limited goals

However encouraging the results of studies of RO might be, we have attempted to emphasise that the gains have often been quite small, and often not as clear in the person's general functioning as in their mental state. RO is not a cure for dementia; severely demented people will almost certainly not be discharged in their hundreds from long-stay hospitals if RO is introduced!

The potential of RO and similar approaches lies in the

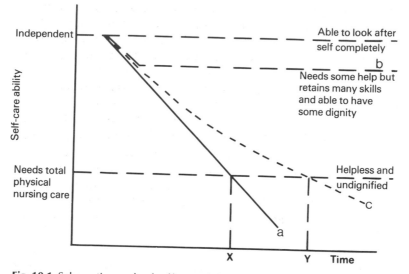

Fig. 10.1 Schematic graph of self-care ability in dementia, illustrating that halting or even slowing down deterioration can be useful aims.

  a represents 'usual' deterioration in dementia

  b represents stabilisation of self-care ability at an intermediate level

  c represents a slowing down of deterioration resulting in a higher quality of life for (c) as compared with (a) for the period of time X–Y.

nature of dementia. Figure 10.1 is a notional graph of self-care ability in dementia. Line (a) illustrates what generally seems to happen in dementia. Initially the person is independent but gradually needs more and more assistance as skills decline, until there is a need for almost total physical nursing care. At this point, when the person is virtually being dressed, toiletted and washed etc., it is difficult to see how any semblance of dignity can be retained, however caring and sympathetic the care-staff may be. Line (b) represents a stabilisation of self-care ability at a level where there is considerable independence; if a therapeutic approach could achieve this, then clearly this would be an acceptable aim as the stage of total nursing care is not reached. Line (c) represents a slowing down of the deterioration, with the person taking somewhat longer to reach the area of greatest indignity. Thus by comparison with line (a) we could say this person has overall a better quality of life as more skill has been retained and there has been more independence.

Slowing down of deterioration can then also be an acceptable goal. In addition, total physical nursing care is costly in time and in the extra stress and burden for staff. However there is a problem here; if slowing down deterioration is the aim then the care-staff will continue to see their patients deteriorate despite their best endeavours to carry out RO, and cannot know for certain that they are achieving anything. Untreated comparison groups are probably the best way to ascertain possible changes as a result of intervention. It is not always possible to use these so it is often difficult to show that deterioration is being slowed down. Those using RO need to be aware of the variability of deterioration in individuals and of the importance of close communication with patients in order to note even the smallest of changes in their behaviour, or in our interaction with them.

Aspiration levels should not be set so high that only dramatic changes are expected. Such expectations are courting disappointment and will lead to lack of confidence in the approach. While some patients can show impressive changes the improvements of those with degenerative disorders may only be minimal. To miss small changes could prove disastrous to the programme as there would be no appreciation that a step forward had been achieved. A number of little steps can combine into a substantial one. Realistic attitudes can help to analyse the progress and so permit staff to set or reset appropriate goals by lowering or raising them as is necessary.

RO is not a therapy in the sense that it can be applied for a few months and then withdrawn with improvements being then maintained. At the present time it does seem that if RO is withdrawn the effects are likely to wear off fairly quickly. RO is perhaps better viewed as a continuing part of the person's environment. Hopefully the person will make progress in some areas but it is unlikely that they will cease to need support. It may be that the effects of RO diminish when a programme ceases because the situation becomes a negative one. If an active programme is followed by an atmosphere where there is no stimulation, no activity and no encouragement the result will be institutionalisation: the very thing RO and other interventions are attempting to combat!

In summary then, RO with all its associated programmes and the 24 hour philosophy and approach needs to be seen as a continuing process.

Staff attitudes

Attitudes underly and colour so much of what we do or say, so no apology will be made for dealing with this topic at greater length, in this and succeeding sections, in view of its importance in programmes like RO (see Woods & Britton 1977). If we have a negative approach to a task we will probably do it badly; if we have a negative attitude to a person then we may say pleasant polite words to them, but our real attitude will probably be communicated in the way they are said. Conversely positive attitudes are more likely to lead to enthusiasm and to convey warmth.

What are our attitudes, firstly to elderly people in general, and secondly to those with memory difficulties who are the focus of this book? If this question were asked of the general population a wide variety of replies would be received. These could range from those who believe in advocating euthanasia for all elderly people to those who would find it difficult to see elderly people as a group and would talk about attitudes to individuals who happen, by conventional arbitrary criteria, to be labelled 'elderly'. How do our attitudes to elderly people develop? One powerful learning experience may have been the way in which elderly people in our own family were treated when we were young. Were they revered and respected, or were they despised? Were they frail – or were they strong and powerful? These types of considerations may lead to our first ideas about elderly people. The attitude of society itself is another strong influence, as are the attitudes of those sub-groups of society to which we belong. Society often seems to emphasise youthful qualities like speed and productivity, and to devalue the mature contributions of experience, perspective and emotional stability. A third major influence may well be our fantasies of what being elderly would be like, our projection of our own old age, which must have associated with it some of our feelings about death and dying. Given the various influences and learning experiences that each of us have undergone it is hardly surprising that in any group of care-staff there will be a multiplicity of attitudes. There are even a number of different reasons for being involved in work with the elderly at all, from genuine interest to purely economic ones.

It is important for all staff members to think about their own attitudes and to consider what experiences have led them to their current position; it is useful for staff to discuss their attitudes together, noting both agreements and differences. Attitudes cannot be changed overnight; what is necessary is a willingness to try alternative strategies of working with elderly people, and not to reject them out of hand. When elderly people previously considered to be confused and totally dependent actually respond in an RO session, then attitudes begin to be modified. When the face of the elderly lady – who previously seemed rather ugly and unapproachable – lights up as an item from the past acts as an entry into communication with her and as we begin to see the person behind the 'geriatric patient' stereotype, once again we begin to change our ideas.

Not all staff are so willing to try new ideas, of course, and it is important that change proceeds at a rate that does not leave some staff feeling railroaded and coerced by others. It is important that staff at all levels really do communicate with each other, about their aims in their work and what they see as the means of achieving them. This may happen informally but is perhaps more likely to occur if there are regular, frequent meetings of the staff-group. The introduction of the Nursing Process has helped to structure meetings and is assisting nurses to look in more depth at these aspects (see Stockwell 1985). The recording and identification of target areas for each individual patient has greatly increased discussion and understanding.

Again the importance of all staff being involved must be emphasised. This is not only for reasons of consistency, but also because if a small group of staff is chosen to lead, say, RO sessions tensions may result. The staff omitted may see RO as a higher level activity than the general chores and feel resentful. At the other extreme RO may be seen as an officially recognised way of avoiding the 'real' (physical) work that needs to be done, so those leading the sessions will be regarded as idle when they laugh and chat with the elderly people! To allocate the work of therapist to certain staff members may seem satisfactory in delegation of responsibility, but in practice it is not to be recommended. The result can isolate the staff, be the cause of jealousy and feelings of strain, and furthermore will make consistency of approach from all staff impossible to obtain. The programme would be jeopardised by sick and holiday leave, not to mention staff changes. In 1980 at Leeds seven people representing different disciplines acted as therapists in a two month study. Video tapes of the sessions suggested that it was not necessary to involve the same staff. The group related well to all the therapists and it is in our view the consistency of approach that is important.

The basic approach to RO involves an awareness of the elderly person's psychological, as well as physical needs. Attitudes need to allow the elderly person individuality, dignity, self-respect and choice. There is a need to avoid the sort of caring that stifles the person's attempts at independence: 'Let me help you with that, it takes you such a long time on your own'; that treats the person as a child rather than as the adult they have been for 50-odd years: 'What you want is. . . .' or 'Come along now, eat it up'; that treats the person as an object: staff member to visitor in front of resident, 'Now this man here is very confused and incontinent'; that misunderstands positive approaches: 'Why interfere, leave them alone, it is our turn to do things for them'. The person needs to be nurtured; allowing as much independence of us as possible. As with the parent-teenager relationship this can be a painful process. We must hold back, suppressing the desire to take over and dress the person who is having difficulties, because we know she will manage eventually on her own. It means sometimes taking risks because to be wrapped up in cotton wool is to be deprived of freedom.

Finally, we need to be positive; if we are not our negative feelings will show and may simply add to the helplessness of the situation. We need to challenge expectations and myths, realising that these can colour events, responses and outcome. Those who use positive approaches, new ideas and have the determination to succeed can create their own special 'miracles'. A realistic optimism and expectation that some change is possible may help to increase elderly persons' self-confidence, and so in fact make change more likely to actually occur.

Selection of clients for groups

If RO is seen not simply as a daily 'therapy' group for a proportion of our patients or residents but as a 24 hour approach, as part of the elderly person's environment, then the issue of which patients are selected for the group is transformed into the question of which aspects of RO are best suited to different types of person. That it is suitable for a range of elderly people is seen in its successful application in psychiatric and geriatric hospitals, nursing and residential homes, day hospitals and day centres etc. The following principles may be useful:

a. People with a severe level of dementia have been reported in some studies as receiving least benefit from RO sessions in isolation from the basic approach (while others have found them to respond as well as less demented patients). With this type of patient it is especially important to continue the re-orientation process throughout the day.

b. Moderately impaired patients benefit from both sessional RO and the 24 hour approach. Particular care needs to be given to finding the appropriate level of activities so that they do not find the sessions boring or insulting to their intelligence.

c. The same consideration applies when patients without dementia receive RO. These may be patients who have had a stroke or in some instances patients who have been in a psychiatric hospital for a number of years. Where disorientation is not evident then the basic approach should aim to draw out from the patient what is happening in their surroundings – both in the immediate vicinity and more generally in the world. Consideration should be given to activity sessions at a higher level than conventional RO groups.

d. Severely deaf patients, where the hearing loss cannot be corrected, often do not fit well in any sort of group because of their hearing impairment and may require more individual orientation work. It is worth remembering that hearing aid systems are continually being improved, and some models specially designed for use in groups, using a microphone and earphones, are becoming available.

e. Patients with very poor eyesight may have difficulty with a number of tasks often included in a RO session. Again individual work is indicated, or a group specifically aimed at utilizing the other senses.

f. Patients who are extremely restless and cannot sit in a chair for a few minutes are not suited to a group approach in view of the disruption they cause. RO here may have to be done literally on the move – around the lounge, down the corridor. . . ! If they can concentrate for a few minutes it is better to use those minutes intensively with that person, prehaps several times a day, aiming to gradually increase their span till they are settled enough to remain in a group session.

g. Patients with speech problems need careful help. Those whose major difficulty is in expressing themselves may not find the group situation too stressful, whereas those who have particular difficulty in understanding the meaning of what is said may well find the group session a threatening experience; they are then best helped on an individual basis.

Group membership should not be constantly changing. If in the early stages a member appears to be unsuitable a closer investigation is advisable. Problems may concern behaviour or specific disability, but the person may just be slow to respond. If essential, exclusion should be made, but individual aid should be considered.

In summary then, the basic RO approach is flexible enough for it to be used with a wide range of elderly patients. If only a proportion of patients can be accommodated in RO sessions a good rule of thumb is to work with the most restless and disturbed patients on an individual basis, to encourage the least impaired to initiate their own activities (providing materials and interest) and to work with the other patients in RO groups, i.e. those who are moderately severely impaired. Often these are a comparatively neglected group, needing less physical care than the severely disturbed group and being less able than the mildly impaired group to interact with the care-staff.

Application to community residents

Most of the aspects outlined so far – and indeed virtually all the research that has been carried out on RO – has been primarily concerned with patients in hospital or residents in old people's homes. Yet only 4 or 5% of all elderly people reside in such institutions (Craig 1983), and even when considering those suffering from some form of dementing condition, a large majority live in the community, alone or with supporting relatives. The reasons for the primary development of RO within institutional settings are clear and include the greater impact of people with dementia grouped together in a ward or home as compared with those scattered in the community, the greater ease of carrying out and evaluating intensive treatment programmes consistently and the availability there of more experienced, less emotionally involved care-staff.

Current thinking, rightly in our view, stresses the importance of maintaining elderly persons in their own surroundings, if this is their wish, providing the necessary support, and, especially important, support and relief for those such as relatives involved in their care. What part has RO to play in this endeavour?

a. Work by Greene and his colleagues in Glasgow (Greene et al 1979; 1983) has shown that some impact can be made on the person's orientation and awareness by RO sessions two or three days a week in a psychogeriatric day unit. In the latter study improvements in the supporting relative's mood were noted during the RO phase of the study. This is encouraging in suggesting that work carried out at a day-hospital or day-centre may have some carry-over to the person's situation at home. A number of day-centres and clubs catering for some elderly people with dementia on a long-term basis are now being established. Applying positive approaches in these settings is a feasible and valuable endeavour. Close links between the day-centre and relatives and other community supports are essential, in order to work towards a consistent approach to the individual person.

RO and reminiscence sessions can certainly be set up in such centres. Mildly impaired people will show benefit even from a fairly infrequent attendance; ideally more impaired people would need to attend 3 or more times a week for gains to be maintained. Volunteer helpers could well lead sessions in day-centres and clubs, with suitable training and support.

b. For the elderly person living alone there are major difficulties in carrying over work done at a day centre into the person's home. Obviously regular visitors to the person's home – home help, neighbours, meals on wheels attendant, volunteer visitor, etc., can be given some guidance as to the RO approach, but some memory aid is needed for the times when the person is alone. It may be that in the future micro-processor technology will allow the use of electronic memory aids in the person's home – giving reminders and acting as a source of current information (Jones & Adam 1979). For the present however, less sophisticated measures have to suffice. Many elderly people have a newspaper delivered regularly and keep the current one available as a reminder of the date, others leave notes in strategic places. Some have a large diary to refer to; in one case the home-help assisted in keeping this up-to-date and the elderly person learned to consult it, when-ever something arose about which she was uncertain. A large electric clock, perhaps with an automatic calendar, might also prove useful. Basically of course these are memory aids that most people use at one time or another. When people have memory deficits the problem is how to teach them to make use of these aids, and it is here that much useful work can be done in the person's own home. They might for instance usefully make a list for shopping but need to learn where to keep it so it can be easily consulted in the shops. The person may well continually 'lose' a purse or handbag and needs to be taught to keep these sort of items in particular places. A brightly coloured tag on a key-ring, or a reflective strip on a purse may assist in finding frequently lost items. Thus an RO session can actually be carried out in the person's home, with the emphasis being on developing and using memory aids and reminders.

Lodge & McReynolds (1983) describe a scheme in Leices-tershire where volunteers are recruited specifically to work with elderly people with dementia. They provide two forms of help; firstly, practical help to compensate for the person's loss of skill, and secondly, providing memory cues and monitoring people with dementia throughout the day. These volunteers are trained and supported in their work, which helps to structure the elderly person's day and ensures that important appointments are kept, day-centre attendance is kept up and meals and drinks and medications are taken regularly.

This is one of a number of community care schemes that are being developed throughout the UK. It is rare for its explicit focus on the particular problems associated with dementing conditions. Probably the most thoroughly evaluated of all these schemes is the Kent Community Care Scheme (Challis & Davies 1985), which aimed to support older people at home, whatever their disability. In the final report of the evaluation project Challis & Davies (1985) made it clear that a number of people with dementia were included in the research project, and highlighted four particular issues which were encountered in supporting people with dementia at home.

In the first place, gaining access was often difficult. Some elderly people might well believe that they have no need of help. So it was vital to establish good relationships initially. This meant offering to meet the needs that *they* perceived rather than the more obvious ones they did not see. Support could be built up once this pattern had been accepted.

Secondly, 'process risks' were identified. This refers to areas of increasing decline relating to self-neglect and loss of coping skills, leading to a gradual increase of danger to the person, rather than an immediate crisis. Care was organised (often using local people, neighbours and friends as paid helpers) to provide supervision of food, medicines etc. and regular stimulation, using RO techniques.

'Event risks', the danger of a gas explosion, wandering off and getting lost etc. etc., were dealt with by practical solutions (turning off the gas supply!) and by establishing routines with close supervision.

Fourthly, a clear and regular pattern of care was established, based upon the person's positive, retained abilities. A structured timetable was built around the person's own daily routine, to be meaningful and relevant to the person. Again, RO techniques were emphasised to enhance communication and reinforce the structure being created.

c. The community care schemes also, successfully, offer

support to carers looking after dementing people at home. Indeed, one of the groups for whom the Kent scheme proved most cost-effective consisted of extremely dependent elderly people with both dementia and physical problems being cared for at home by a relative. There is some scope for giving relatives guidance about the techniques of RO and related approaches. Indeed a number of booklets are now readily available (see Appendix 3) which provide this sort of guidance alongside information about dementia, coping with the emotions that accompany caring and so on. A note of caution must however be sounded. Living with a person with dementia is often very difficult for a relative and in many cases, however caring the relative is, and however good the relationship has been, there may well be some tension, anger and resentment in the relationship. Occasionally, particularly when the relative receives no relief or support, rejection of the elderly person occurs. We would reiterate the importance of the basic attitudes on which RO is dependent: dignity, individuality, self-respect, choice, the person being treated as an adult. Where there are difficulties in the relationship between relatives and the elderly person some opportunity is necessary to allow the relative to air these negative feelings and the possible resultant guilt. It may then be possible for the relative – with continued support – to allow the elderly person dignity, adulthood etc., where previously the difficulties in the relationship precluded these attitudes. If it is not possible for this change to occur – perhaps the tensions and resentment and bitterness being too entrenched – then we would not recommend teaching the relative to use RO.

Be this as it may be there is no doubt that any procedure of this kind is more difficult for a relative to carry out than for a nurse because of the long-standing emotional attachments and expectations that have built up over the years. However the relatives do have certain advantages in using RO, reminiscence etc. They are much more aware of the person's previous interests; they see the elderly person in familiar surroundings; there is ready access to family photographs, souvenirs etc. from the past right up to the present time; they can work with one individual only; and they can involve the elderly person in tasks around the home.

There has been little study of the use of these approaches

by relatives. Davies (1981) reports a wife who was able to improve her communication with her severely disabled husband using reminiscence. Generally, an effective way of working with relatives is to work through relatives' support groups, preferably made up of people living close by each other. In this setting relatives may well be able to help each other through such a group by sharing experiences, difficulties, problems and solutions, and might be able to help each other in practical ways e.g. providing relief for an afternoon or evening on a reciprocal basis.

A number of descriptions of relatives' groups have been published (e.g. Fuller et al 1979; Hausman 1979), and Woods & Britton (1985) provide a full review of the issues involved. Church & Linge (1982) report that their group was particularly appreciative of information about the condition and the practical and financial help available. Relatives were surprised to find they were not alone in their task, and found meeting others with similar problems helpful. Collins (1983) emphasises that individual support may also be necessary, particularly if the carer's own behaviour in relation to the elderly person needs to be adapted. Some relatives are actively seeking information as to how best to communicate with the person with dementia; at present they often feel helpless in the face of the seemingly inevitable deterioration. Procedures like RO may help these carers find some purpose in their interaction with the elderly person and to draw from them their maximal level of functioning.

Some relatives are able to participate regularly in a self-help group (such as those organised by the Alzheimer's Disease Society), and grow in confidence and knowledge together. Often such groups begin to act as a pressure-group, calling for better facilities and more resources for older people with dementing conditions. Such groups are valuable in raising awareness of the needs of carers, and of their vital role in supporting the majority of elderly people with dementia. In time their pressure will lead hopefully to major improvements in the quality and quantity of support services available.

Initiating change and setting up programmes

It is well known that the more things change the more they

stay the same! The difficulties of promoting and maintaining change have a long history. New laws or policies have been introduced and even torture and execution have not led to the acceptance of some of them! The new broom works hard and causes a stir for a while; new governments make new policies, only to have them turned around by a succeeding one; committees organise all sorts of new schemes and when their time is up their notes get lost!

We often make more progress when we make changes in our life-style and only have ourselves to consider. The influence of family, friends and loved ones complicate decision-making. When it comes to implementing a new system in an institutional setting the problems divide and multiply.

All the evidence that has accumulated over the years in various fields – with the mentally handicapped, children, chronic psychiatric patients etc., indicates that it can be extremely difficult to establish any positive psychological programme in an institution and that once established these endeavours are liable to encounter difficulties of various kinds. Often such difficulties lead to the programme being discontinued or simply drifting into disuse. This process, it should be emphasised, may occur independently of the demonstrated effectiveness of the therapeutic intervention. It seems to be related to the well-documented difficulties in caring for people in institutions of any kind, where the needs of the institution are given greater importance than those of the patients they are intended to serve, and where change seems to be resisted and blocked.

Accounts have been written of failure due to apparently trivial matters. The problem is consistently raised at meetings and seminars. 'I agree, I want to do this, but how can *I* influence change?' Senior officers are too set in their ways, junior staff are resentful, there is no money, no time, no staff – the excuses and concerns are legion. We canot offer the perfect answer, but it must be noted that the past decade has shown remarkable changes in interest in programmes such as RO in hospital and residential settings. The wind of change has already blown far afield.

Where there is a climate for change there is a chance of success. It is impossible to provide a blue-print to guarantee success, but we can provide some suggestions and describe some general issues which can be adapted to meet the differing needs experienced in practice.

The wrong way

The first question to be raised is where does the intiative and impetus for the establishment of RO come from? Does it emanate from an 'outsider' e.g. a psychologist wanting to set up RO in a residential home, or from someone in a position of authority in the hierarchy of the institution e.g. a senior nursing officer or a consultant, or from someone in a position of authority within the ward or residential home unit e.g. a sister on a ward or a superintendent of an old people's home, or from 'shop-floor' level e.g. a care attendant or ward nurse.

Clearly there may be different reactions to each of these initiators. However, no matter who initiates change, no matter how inspired that person might be, no matter how interesting or well proven an intervention might be, it is fatal to start today, or even tomorrow!

Unquestionably the first stumbling block will be provided by other people. Saboteurs are many in number and are often the least expected antagonists.

Junior staff – may feel that they are being imposed upon, asked to do more than they are able or need to do, or that this is yet another of Sister's or Matron's crack-pot ideas.

Staff at the same level – may feel that the innovator is above him or himself as the initiator, is attempting to become ingratiated with senior staff, and is too 'pushy' and ambitious.

Senior staff – could resent ideas from lower levels, seeing them as personal criticism or as examples of junior staff interfering and overstepping their responsibility.

Administrative staff – could resent not being consulted, believing other programmes have priority. They may feel concerned about implications for financial resources, about job descriptions possibly being changed without consultation, about paying wages for one sort of job and being supplied with another, and they may well worry about 'What the trade unions would say'.

All staff – may feel threatened if the initiator comes from 'ouside' the institution, e.g. a community psychiatric nurse in a residential home, a psychologist in a day-centre. They may feel the very suggestion of change in the pattern of care must constitute a criticism of current standards and procedures. There may be a feeling that the 'outsider' cannot really know the clients in the way the staff do.

Any of these reactions could stifle an idea at birth. Even if the instigator persists and continues to work in the chosen way, responses could be so antagonistic that the person could be forced to leave and the new system, with so much promise, would die unceremoniously with his or her departure.

To start immediately indicates that planning has been overlooked. Many aspects must be considered. For example, where is this going to take place, is there enough room? What about equipment – if needed it takes time to gather together. What about timing? To run a group session on a ward at the same time as a ward round will hardly win friends! Policies of the institution require consideration in planning, or the whole project will fail.

Preparation is vital. To commence a new scheme without first reading the relevant literature and gathering as much information as possible is to guarantee that mistakes will occur. Clients are not going to happily sit and wait while a therapist races off to read notes before proceeding! Measures of change also need consideration. No one starts a diet without first checking his or her weight so that any loss can be measured!

The methods to be used must be clearly stated from the beginning so that the programme is not changing constantly with ideas being introduced too late in the day to be useful. Staff resources must be evaluated. Illness, time off, new or different staff must all be catered for or else there will be no back-up system or continuity. If the instigator is the sole leader or therapist an absence or departure will guarantee that the programme will stop abruptly.

There are some people who do naturally plan well, can 'sell' ideas to other staff and possess the charisma to inspire and convince, but they are very few in number. The 'hero-innovator' who rushes in without preparation and careful thought will indeed, as Georgiades & Phillimore (1975) suggest, be eaten for breakfast by the institutional dragon!

Far from saving anyone, or improving anything, this individual creates havoc. A little patience and a great deal of work and thought might prove more effective and indicate possible strategies for a would-be innovator.

Strategies for change

1. Find some allies.
2. Clearly identify what you want to do.
3. Employ salesmanship; consider how to promote change painlessly.
4. Lay the foundations for the new programme.
5. Provide relevant training.
6. Consider the problem of time (and lack of it!).
7. Ensure the assessment and monitoring system is prepared.
8. Consider how to maintain the programme.

1. Find some allies

Identify a group of people with similar ideas to your own, with a shared vision of what might be achieved in the future. The process of change can be stressful and demanding – without the support of like-minded people the going could get very tough. Include in the group people with particular influence or flexibility in their role who could be a particular asset in the process. They too will need continued encouragement and support in facing the obstacles that inevitably other people will place in their paths. Meet regularly to re-inforce each other's efforts, to plan a joint strategy and to co-ordinate a concerted attack on the forces of resistance in the institution.

2. What you want to do

What form is the change to be in? Read, discuss, visit relevant centres and people and attend relevant courses. Be sure the subject is fully understood. Begin to plan the programme. What will happen during it, what will it contain, what are the essential aims, how long will it run and how will it end, or what will replace it? What equipment, space or adaptations will be required? Present policies must be studied. In order to accommodate the programme do any need to be changed or modified? Who will this affect and how can their co-operation be obtained? All the difficulties that might arise should be covered – illness, staff changes, support systems and people, holidays, rotas and regular meetings or ward rounds.

Involve the administrative staff. Find out how your scheme can be included if there are other priorities in the institution. Ask for help: they may have access to equipment, space and other resources of which you were unaware.

Are you going to assess any changes occurring in the clients (or in the staff)? What measures would be appropriate? Does the programme involve selecting particular clients? How will this be carried out? What steps will be taken to consult with the clients before introducing any changes affecting them? Check carefully that any goals set for the programme are appropriate, relevant and realistic.

Is the change being carried out in the form of a research programme? In some instances, approval from the appropriate Ethical Committee will be needed. If groups of clients are to be compared, ensure they are matched on all the relevant attributes (age, sex, level of impairment, etc.).

3. Salesmanship

This word has been frowned upon in the NHS and Social Services in the UK – although even this is changing! Another heading for this section might be Machinations, Manipulations and Manoeuvering!

It is not so much a massive public relations drive that is required as a willingness to listen to the needs, fears, reservations, hopes and anxieties of those whose support and permission are required for the changes to happen. Then it will be possible in many instances to answer or find a way around their particular problems and worries concerning the programme.

In Table 10.1 we present some common situations and possible response strategies that might be adapted according to the specific circumstances. The aim should be to make people think for themselves, identify areas that could

Table 10.1 Overcoming obstacles to change

Possible situation/problem	Possible strategy in response
1. Medical or senior staff opposed to the proposed approach or change	1. Do not persist with that particular unit. Try to set up the change programme in an adjoining unit where staff initially invited to give support can observe successful changes there. This could encourage them to take a second look
2. The person 'in charge' is unconvinced or disinterested.	2. Make influential friends – particularly more senior staff. Explain and try to convince them. Enlist enthusiastic support from junior staff. Present a united front
3. A common response to a new idea is: 'It's not my/their job to do this'	3. Again, enlist the help of others. Talk freely at meetings, encourage open discussion. If in a position to do so, offer training, or even demonstrate approach/change in some way. It is important that *all* staff should know that employing authorities include working *with* the elderly as part of the job
4. Other comments include: a. 'The elderly need total care' b. 'I've been running the unit this way for years' c. 'The elderly are used to their routine'	4. a & b. As above, Example and training with open discussion help. Listing advantages of change, solving staff's problems and meeting *their* needs often opens doors. c. Offering a choice is more acceptable than enforcing a routine which may be boring and meaningless
5. Excuses include: 'I'd love to, but – no time' 'I'd love to but – no staff'	5. If staff are convinced that *they* want change, then change will happen. Tempt interest by the use of videos, courses, visiting speakers, arranging visits to active units. Ask staff what *they* need. Examine time – ask staff to look at their way of working: are there ways or things which would improve matters? Use their suggestions. Encourage open discussion. Work to involve staff in planning and expressing ideas and feelings

(Cont'd)

Table 10.1 (*Cont'd*)

Possible situation/problem	Possible strategy in response
6. 'I don't know what to do, or where to start'	6. Confidence is increased by knowledge and practice. All the information from lectures, seminars, articles, etc., plus training and action research projects, can lead to more confidence and certainty in ability to cope with change

change, either convince them that the proposed idea is a good one, or accept another positive approach that they feel is important. *Thinking It Through* (Holden 1984c) could be useful here, as a basis for discussing some of the important issues involved in care for older people.

It is important to identify sources of power and money. Those who control policies and finances will not support new ideas unless they see a call for them. To initiate change their support is needed. With a good plan backing *can* be found. It is useful to locate someone in authority who will advise and help to overcome obstacles. Most authorities are, in fact, anxious to promote good practice. Junior staff are often unaware of this drive to gain prestige or that often the ideas envisaged are the very ones the authority concerned wishes to see in operation. At any level, constant and public 'nagging' can prove very effective – providing the argument is logical and well thought out. It might take time to identify supportive people or areas, but it is time well spent. Immovable objects can be circumnavigated and outdated methods can be challenged by more efficient and satisfying ones.

'Authority' can be convinced by demonstrations, good planning and knowledge, considerations of cost and the use of time. Equally valuable is a plea of 'Have you seen what *they* are doing, surely we're just as capable?' Competitiveness is a useful tool!

4. Laying foundations

Appropriate training is the best foundation of all. However, before specific training is started other enticements to think again might be required.

Good speakers at interesting seminars can help. Relevant films, TV programmes and interesting literature or aids all play their part. Competitiveness is found at all levels, so visits or awareness of exciting things happening elsewhere can prove inspiring. Organise regular meetings so that everyone becomes accustomed to open discussion and the exchange of ideas, opinions and concerns. This also provides the opportunity for feedback and encouragement. Always include the night staff – even if it means working overnight to meet them and explain.

A search for the hidden leaders in the unit, and an awareness of those less popular can indicate where further work is needed. Identify potential leaders or therapists. They will need training, confidence and support. A small pilot study of, for instance, formal RO or reminiscence might prove an inducement. Many staff are afraid of making mistakes, of encountering unexpected problems. Training helps, but the experience of seeing a change in a client as a result of a simple project, with support, has the greatest impact on confidence and will convince staff better than any outside encouragement.

Make sure that your plan includes early and regular submission of reports to whoever might require one. It is much more satisfactory and establishes better confidence if such reports are sent without first being requested. It is preferable to report in your own words rather than to be forced to answer questions which prove to be totally irrelevant or for which answers are not yet available.

5. Providing relevant training

Crucial to the success of any programme is adequate training, so that the staff feel confident in what they are doing and so that their uncertainty is minimised. It must be on-going so that new staff can be familiar with the way others are working, and continuity is protected. Refresher courses are valuable to everyone, so this must be considered in order to avoid boredom and staff becoming stale and running out of ideas.

Who is to lead the training? This implies imparting knowledge and skills so the training should be led either by people who already have some knowledge or skills or by people who are prepared to do some background reading, some visiting of other centres etc. The work may fall on a few people with prior knowledge or experience or on a larger group of staff prepared to learn together. If only a few staff are to lead the training obviously those with the ability to communicate – from whatever profession – will be most useful.

What form should the training take? This depends very much on the individual situation, but we have found the following components of training particularly valuable.

a. Lectures. These should be informal and provide plenty of opportunity for discussion throughout, thus helping the 'lecturer' to ensure real understanding. Some discussion of general attitudes and an understanding of important factors, for instance the basic psychology of ageing, is worth including. It can help staff to consider the behaviour, needs and external influences affecting old people. Specific training will depend on the programme being implemented. A programme such as RO should highlight:

The rationale underlying RO
The general principles of the basic 24 hour approach
Examples of the use of 24 hour approach
Environmental factors
Dealing with rambling and confused talk
General guidelines for RO sessions
Specific examples of methods for use in RO sessions
Goals and limitations of RO
How RO is to be applied in the particular setting.

b. Audio-visual aids. However interesting the lecture, there is no doubt that carefully chosen audio-visual aids are extremely useful in bringing the subject matter to life – particularly when the subject matter is as practical as is RO.

Slides are particularly useful in illustrating what happens in an RO session or in setting the scene for 24 hour RO. They can be used in conjunction with snippets of audio-tape recorded in RO sessions to show what staff can do to draw the patients out and how they can respond appropriately.

A tape-slide programme providing a recorded talk on RO illustrated by a set of slides can be extremely useful. It enables the same talk to be repeated on several occasions – which is helpful in view of shift work. When new staff join the ward they can work through the tape-slide programme and so receive some training without another course needing to be established. Staff can work through the programme at their own pace. A set of questions to accompany the tape-slide programme is useful to direct the staff-member's attention to key points.

Another useful form of audio-visual aid is a video tape, showing parts of RO sessions and illustrating the communication that the leader attempts to establish. Careful editing is needed to ensure that salient points are made – it can be difficult to watch a video tape of a whole RO session as the pace is somewhat slower than TV programmes to which staff are accustomed! A commentary directing attention to particular principles and methods is also advisable.

c. *Hand-outs* – for staff to keep, peruse at their leisure and refer to when necessary are very important to reinforce the lectures and talks given. They should cover briefly the main points made in the lecture, giving examples as well as guidelines.

d. *Demonstration* – of the application of RO techniques again clarifies and helps to make tangible what is covered in any lectures given. This may be provided by a visit to a centre where RO is already taking place. A person with prior experience could lead a small group with other staff members observing, or someone could lead a session with some other staff role-playing the parts of the patients and others observing. It is in this demonstration that staff observe how the principles are actually put into practice, how the staff member can be encouraging rather than patronizing, how even the most deteriorated person can be helped to succeed rather than having their failure reinforced yet again. After each demonstration plenty of time should be allowed for comments and discussion of what took place. This should then be followed by:

e. *Role play and involvement.* Training group members enjoy remembering their first impressions of age, listing their expectations of ageing and attempting definitions and explanations. The aim should be to help understanding of older folk by referring to everyone's own, personal experience. Staff in training take the role of group leader whilst other staff play the confused elderly patients once more, and other staff observe. This is valuable not only in giving the leaders a gradual exposure to running an actual RO session, but also for those role-playing the part of a confused elderly person and seeing RO from the recipient's angle. The role-played group sessions should be interrupted frequently for observers to make suggestions to leaders or patients and for leaders to ask for help if uncertain how to respond to a patient or how to involve them in the group. This then leads on to:

f. *Feedback.* Where other staff (including those who played the patients) tell the group leaders in the role-play what they thought helpful about what they did and said and about their attitude that came across, and of course what seemed to be less helpful. Giving feedback is never easy, particularly if it is negative. It is important that these training sessions are relaxed and open and that it is remembered that RO involves certain skills which can only be learned properly if we are able to have our performance monitored – just as when we are, for example, learning to drive a car. If access to video tape equipment is available this provides a way in which staff members can see their performance for themselves and, in a sense, provide their own feedback in addition to that of others.

From feedback the training session may lead on to further demonstrations, more role-play and more feedback. For example in one training session, in a role-play one staff member tended to 'interrogate' the 'patients', pressurising them with questions they were unable to answer, leaving an uncomfortable pause in which the 'patient' seemed likely to become acutely aware of having failed. Feedback was given on this point and a further demonstration showed how the same areas of information could be covered without making the 'patient' feel threatened. The staff member then repeated the role-play and was able to be much less interrogative, helping the 'patients' to find the answers for themselves. Feedback was then given by the other staff on how much better this second role-play now was and on the noticeable change there had been, and how the 'patients' responded much better to this more gentle approach.

Feedback should not be confined to training sessions, and it can be helpful in preventing staff from slipping into bad habits once they have been involved in RO for a while (again the analogy with driving a car applies!), and in encouraging them as they find innovative ways to deal with the variety of situations that arise in RO sessions and elsewhere. Feedback should be mutual, not just given by senior staff! What is needed is a continued willingness to learn and to improve the skills in RO, not to become over-confident and above all to continue to be sensitive to the elderly, their needs and what *they* can teach us.

g. *Action research.* It is valuable when running courses to encourage staff to use some of the skills that they have encountered during the training session. The best way to do this is to encourage them to form groups and agree on a mini-project that they can attempt on their own unit. When the 'Action Research' (Towell & Harries 1979) has been decided upon, the groups are invited to report back to a follow-up session, in, say, 8 weeks. Support and contact is offered for those who might run into difficulties or need advice. Many ideas, new policies and new problems can be highlighted by this method. Staff learn from it and confidence grows. The skills learned in the training session are then much more likely to actually be applied!

Appendix 3 lists a number of training materials that will be useful for organising training on RO and related approaches, and provide a number of ideas for particular activities that can be used within this framework.

6. Time

There are 24 hours in the day, not all should be spent at work! No one can extend the day, nor lengthen a minute. If time is the problem then only the individual can reorganise his or her priorities to fit something else in. To say 'It *must* be done' is to no purpose – only the person concerned can effectively reorganise things to meet the demand. The desire to change must be present in order to achieve anything. When staff are determined to find a way they will voluntarily examine their routines, consider the merits of methods, look for more useful relevant equipment, policies and systems. Given support for their good ideas they will identify time-savers for themselves. One home's care staff discovered that if beds required changing they had to walk all the way downstairs to the linen store (and on the way were delayed by other events and meeting people); every evening they turned back bed clothes as in an hotel; every time something was soiled it was taken to the cleaners by one of the staff; they realised that their need to be seen to be 'working' was such that at mealtimes all staff were on hand, removing each plate as it was finished with. Accordingly, they arranged for linen to be on each floor, for a van to pay a weekly visit for dry cleaning items, left the bed turning to the residents and found a keen-to-help resident to sit at each of the dining tables to collect together the dirty dishes. Suddenly they had enough time to run a group each day! Furthermore, at mealtimes all their planned reorganisation became redundant as even the presence of one staff member became barely necessary as the residents took over clearing up without being asked!

If staff can communicate, feel that their ideas are respected and used and if regular meetings occur, many outdated routines will be replaced by more streamlined ones and time will be made available to encourage a more satisfying and stimulating atmosphere for all concerned. It is not always easy to find time for new approaches, but it is always worth trying!

7. Baseline assessments and monitoring

Much of this has been covered in detail in Chapter 6. A written record should be kept of all progress, programmes or sessions. It should list, as appropriate, all present, the subjects discussed, how each elderly person responded, any particular successes made and difficulties encountered. This is of great use when different staff lead sessions each day, so they can ensure variety and can build on previous successes and avoid previously discovered pitfalls. Senior staff can also use the record to monitor progress made by the elderly person in the sessions, and to help staff over any difficult issues that arise. If programmes, including RO, do not appear to be progressing according to the relevant measures in use, then it is advisable to discuss and examine the situation in order to find the problem.

At some stage ideas may need to be revised or a fresh approach might be indicated. Staff could be proceeding too fast or too slowly, illness may have affected the clients' response, new staff may not be conversant with the methods.

Boredom and lack of inspiration in the methods in use may make the staff regard it all as yet another routine. Our section below on the misuse of RO indicates some of the unwelcome developments that can occur if monitoring and supervision of the programme are inadequate. Whatever the problem it should be isolated and efforts made to overcome it.

8. Maintenance

The cautions mentioned above are equally applicable here. Everything possible should be done to ease the staff's taxing task of seeking to communicate with the elderly person. To help the staff member who comes to the RO session having had a busy morning with no time spare for planning an RO session a number of cards should be made available each with a different suggested programme for an RO session on it. Equipment should be readily available for the appropriate activities; the physical setting should be as attractive and comfortable as possible; cards giving details of the elderly person's background – age, number and name of children, occupation, interests etc. – should be available so the staff member can respond appropriately in conversation.

Other aids should be readily available for whatever activity programme is being used. A variety of aids are already available (see Appendix 3). Staff, relatives and volunteers can use imagination and ingenuity in making and finding their own. Quite often active residents or patients can contribute further ideas. Advanced RO groups encourage this self-help aim.

If a programme is to be continued once implemented, it needs to become part of the routine of the ward not an optional extra to be carried out when all other chores are completed. It may be necessary to establish a rota of staff to carry out RO sessions or other programmes, to avoid every staff member leaving it to everyone else to lead a group on any particular day. This also ensures that as many staff as possible are involved in the programme which helps to give the staff intensive practice in the basic approach. Perhaps the testing time for a new programme is when the first staff shortage occurs – what priority will it be awarded then? There will of course be times when it is extremely difficult to carry out the programme – an example of this is a Home where there was an outbreak of gastro-enteritis among residents and staff – and other situations which are difficult to legislate for! However it is important to plan what will happen during the more predictable staff shortage periods – at weekends, in winter when staff sickness reaches its peak, in summer when many staff will be enjoying a well-earned holiday, in March when perhaps many staff are on leave to complete their holiday entitlement for the year. If it grinds to a halt at times like these then only a small portion of the year will remain when it will be fully operational.

What is needed is of course an emphasis on a 24 hour approach which takes relatively little additional staff time together perhaps with a manageable number of patients involved in daily sessions. It is better to restrict sessions to a small number of patients rather than include a large number involving more staff resources than can always be available.

It may be tempting to include more patients by having a larger group in a session at any one time. Our view is that the group size should be no larger than the staff leading the group can keep fully occupied whilst maintaining attention. Depending on severity of deterioration this usually precludes a group size larger than 4–6. If it is desired to include eight patients it might be advantageous to split the time available between two groups of four rather than struggle to maintain the concentration of eight confused patients together.

Consideration should be given to the use of volunteers to help lead sessions, given suitable training and support of course. Having a structure like RO or reminiscence to work within can help a volunteer worker a great deal to contribute something useful to the care of the elderly person with dementia, and can help reduce the uncertainty and feelings of uselessness that lead to many a voluntary worker only coming to the ward or Home once or twice and not returning.

Other resources may also be explored, and it should be emphasised that the task of leading an RO session does not have to always fall on the care-staff – occupational therapy staff, or speech therapists, psychologists etc. may also be willing to be involved in this way. However when several groups of workers are involved exactly how the duties are to be shared should be made explicit. It is often said that if RO is stopped the clients will deteriorate quite quickly. As stated earlier, the regression could be due to replacing a positive, active environment with a negative or unnatural one. If a 24 hour approach or philosophy is operating, then simply to end formal RO will not lead to a definite deterioration. If there is no obvious reason for a deterioration after a regular involvement in a programme, then the environment should be carefully examined for negative, dehumanising factors.

Even when a programme is in full swing, certain events can have a damaging effect – illnesses, staff changes, absences, or the loss of a popular member of the group, staff or other well-known person. Other possibilities are boredom and staleness. Updating will help – another training session or course, an outsider who provides feedback in being impressed by the work being done, or even new equipment or books. Our daily lives are full of ups and downs, we try to find a fresh amusement or interest; so it should be with a ward or Home. A short rest from doing things in a particular way, thoughts on other ideas and alternative ways can put new life into a sagging system. Flexibility is desirable. Searching for another way can prove to be a challenge which in itself livens up proceedings!

Negative effects of RO

Can RO change patients for the worse and perhaps be harmful to them? Woods & Britton (1977) reviewed reports of negative trends occurring generally in psychological programmes with the elderly. They concluded that some reports (none involving RO at that time) indicated a change in the patient from being non-complaining, uncritical and acquiescent to becoming more critical, demanding and challenging due to improvement in general functioning and a better awareness of reality.

The change, perhaps, is from being an 'ideal' patient, presenting no nursing problems, to a person becoming aware of a reality which is often by any standards unsatisfactory, who seeks to bring about change by being more complaining and critical. This type of 'negative' change can be seen as in fact healthy and adaptive.

Some negative effects specifically related to RO have been identified. Zepelin et al (1981) report deterioration on a

number of behavioural measures, particularly social responsiveness, compared with residents in a home where RO was
not applied. These results may have emerged in part from
difficulties in matching residents adequately and from differences between raters in the two settings in the use of the
rating scales. Baines et al (1987) report lower levels of life
satisfaction following RO sessions, compared with reminiscence sessions. They suggest this related to RO helping
residents appraise more realistically the limitations of their
existence. In RO groups both negative and positive feelings
were expressed. The ability of residents to express anger and
sadness initially alarmed staff, before they realised these
issues deserved careful discussion with the residents.

Possible harmful effects of RO incorrectly carried out will
be considered in the next section. It must be emphasised
here however that even if properly executed RO does not
always make patients happy, because reality itself is never all
roses. However tactfully we discuss the death – even some
years ago – of a patient's spouse or discuss events during the
World Wars these cannot be dismissed with a joke. Reality
covers the whole range of emotions, however tempting it is
to only look at one side of life. Respect for the patient's
dignity may sometimes mean staff facing up to issues that
they find painful to talk about also, and so would rather
avoid. We do need to be aware of negative reactions,
however, and instead of blaming RO for them, be prepared
to work through them with the elderly person, providing
warmth in our support of them as they come to terms with
what is happening to them, helping them where possible to
express their feelings – which their mental state may make it
extremely difficult for them to do unaided.

A further word of warning when beginning work with a new
patient; it is important to take note of their previous environment. If they have been sitting quietly, withdrawn and non-
responsive on a psychogeriatric back-ward for some years it
is not sensible to rush in and stimulate them too quickly, and
a gradual approach is more likely to succeed. Change
presents difficulties for most people, and in a ward generally
gradual changes will be must less anxiety-provoking – for staff
as well as patients!

Misuse of RO

We have become increasingly concerned that a 'little knowledge' of RO can lead to it being misapplied, often inadvertently through lack of adequate training or from misunderstanding of the complexities of RO which, on the surface, seems so simple. The important article by Gubrium & Ksander (1975), mentioned in Chapter 5, is relevant here.

They described an inflexible, unthinking, mechanical approach to RO. We feel Gubrium & Ksander are right to ask what is the 'reality' of RO in these circumstances. The staff member has learned to go through the RO board, helping the patients to recite the information there. What he has not learned to do is to try to understand the elderly person's viewpoint, to look for what he is seeking to say, and go beyond the rigidly structured session to a situation where real communication can take place. This mechanical type of RO can occur when it is applied without warmth. We would emphasise the importance of staff approval in RO in rewarding appropriate behaviour but this means more than an automatic 'very good' or 'well done' if it is indeed to be rewarding.

Buckholt & Gubrium (1983) provide further examples of how RO can become an unhelpful approach. They show how in one Home's RO training programme staff are taught to label certain behaviours as 'confused', rather than to seek explanations for the problems, or to gain an understanding of what is happening to the person. In care-planning meetings they observed the use of this label 'confused' or 'disorientated' as an 'explanation' of problems (leading inevitably to RO being prescribed!), again without a search for alternative ways of looking at the person and his or her behaviour in a more individualised fashion. Finally, they show how the RO board's 'correct answer' dominated RO sessions at the Home to the detriment of real communication and interaction. When staff fail to try to understand the individual person as a whole person – despite the difficulties in communication – then this sort of abuse of RO and other approaches can arise.

The dangers of being too interrogative have already been mentioned in previous sections, but this does seem to be a common pitfall, often with the question being emphasised to the detriment of the answers which are glossed over as the next question is put to the beleaguered patient! An emphasis of putting the person right at all costs can lead to difficulties e.g. staff feeling they have to keep telling a patient his wife is dead when other strategies such as distraction might be usefully employed, especially as it is difficult to be continually tactful!

It is mistaken, in our view, to see RO as a replacement of other approaches to encouraging independence, and we would see it as part of a total programme, rather than standing in glorious isolation. Social, recreational and domestic activities are all necessary and the basic RO approach can be used in conjunction with them, rather than in place of them.

Finally the level of RO needs to be adjusted depending on the particular patient. The range of abilities in dementing patients is vast, and when RO is applied to elderly people with other difficulties the range becomes even larger. Some studies of RO (e.g. Voelkel 1978, MacDonald & Settin 1978) seem to have applied relatively low-level RO to patients with more ability, who have accordingly felt insulted by the topics covered. Similarly the converse would be unlikely to produce benefits to say a severely deteriorated, incoherent patient faced with a discussion of current political leaders. Again flexibility is the key-note, a readiness to adjust the activities to the particular group. For example, if a group is thought to be relatively undeteriorated, day and date could be covered by each person keeping a diary, beginning with the day and date entry, before moving on to higher-level topics, rather than feeling obliged to spend 10 minutes on repeating the day and date etc. simply because that is how the book says RO is to be done. A group of widely different levels can result in boredom and stress for patients and staff, as it makes this flexibility difficult to achieve.

To summarise the various misuses of RO perhaps it is fair to say that the application of the attitudes underlying RO is necessary rather than rigid adherence to the methods, and to examine our use of the methods in the light of these attitudes. It does not come amiss for any group leader to ask 'Did I in that session allow Mrs X dignity and respect? Did I help her have self-respect; did I see her as an individual adult person rather than as just another old demented patient?'

By keeping these issues alive in our minds we then have more chance of avoiding some of the pitfalls described here.

11

Concluding remarks

In previous chapters we have concluded that positive approaches can have measurable effects on people with dementia and those who care for them. We have emphasised that changes tend to occur in areas that are the specific focus of intervention. In Chapter 5 we have shown how those areas most significant and relevant for each person can be selected and targetted. We do not, however, underestimate the difficulties of working with people with dementia. Where progressive deterioration forms the normal pattern, goals must reflect the fact that a relatively small change is a major achievement. The responsiveness of people with dementia to the environment in which they live makes it possible for realistic, relevant and potentially valuable goals to be set and often achieved.

However, do these methods represent any change to the existing situation? For instance, we have come across many workers who have quite honestly been able to say that they were already carrying out RO, but had never given it a name! The value of these approaches is that they provide a structure in which staff can be helped to follow the practices of those who have been using them – perhaps less formally – for years. New staff can quickly receive guidance in the approach, and there is more chance of consistency of method and of all staff being involved.

We have focussed in this book on people with dementia, the disorders which surely pose the largest and most pressing problems to Health and Social Services. We have tried to indicate simple treatment methods for those with specific neurological dysfunctions. We are aware of programmes like RO being applied to patients who have been hospitalised for 40 years or more (usually with a diagnosis of chronic schizophrenia) with some success – indeed some of the American studies have been concerned mainly with this type of chronic population. Elderly people with depression as a component of their problems have also been suggested as benefiting from RO. In these cases it is important to consider other treatment approaches outside the scope of this book, e.g. token economies, which have proved helpful for elderly chronic psychiatric patients, or cognitive therapy for elderly people with depression (see Woods & Britton 1985). There is interest in the application of RO principles in areas such as rehabilitation following head injury (Corrigan et al 1985) as well as with elderly people with life-long mental handicap. As with dementia, whilst the specific techniques of RO may be helpful to particular patients in certain circumstances, the emphasis needs to be on an individualised approach based on the person's strengths and needs.

With elderly people whose decision-making capacity is impaired for one reason or another it is important to make explicit the ethical issues involved as they form such a vulnerable group, perhaps unable to assert their rights and needs in a conventional manner. We are often asked if these approaches could be harmful (See Ch. 10). Does RO, for instance, treat patients like children, taking them back to 'school'? Should the person who is 'happily demented' be 'disturbed' by being brought back to reality? Would it not be kinder to leave such people in their twilight world and not expose them to the reality of old age, infirmity, an unsatisfactory environment and so forth.

These and similar questions raise the important issue of the ethics of RO and other psychological approaches to people with dementia. Often these issues arouse a great deal of emotion, perhaps as those working with the elderly imagine themselves in the position of the person with dementia, a fantasy that most people would find threatening and disturbing. Some people favour a passive approach, providing for physical needs until death occurs, keeping the person 'happy' by ensuring a 'no demand' situation. Others opt for a more positive, active approach encouraging awareness and independence. The ethical issues are complex. In some areas of behavioural intervention it is possible to arrive at an agreed treatment contract with the client, acceptable to both parties. This is extremely difficult – if not impossible – with the person with a severe degree of impairment arising from a dementia. Thus there is a need for those working with this group to be clear about their own ethical position as a dementing person may not be capable of making a fully informed decision about treatment.

We will try to make clear the assumptions that we make as we outline the reasons for our preference for the positive approach.

Firstly, it must be emphasised that whether we adopt a positive approach or not we are intervening in some way. Not doing anything with a patient still represents some kind of programme, ill defined as it may be. The advantage of these approaches is that they make explicit what is being attempted and makes it more difficult to shirk responsibility and avoid ethical problems. This is of added importance as those with dementia are a particularly vulnerable group who are less likely to be able to use conventional means of self-protection.

Secondly, we see patients with dementia as people, with basic human needs – both physical and emotional. In our view attempts to meet both sorts of needs are the responsibility of those in the caring role. Emotional needs are more difficult to meet, but should not be ignored on this account. Thus elderly people who are deteriorating need to feel cared for and permitted to have opportunities to express care for others. We recognise that these needs may find expression in more restricted ways than in the person without dementia, of course. In so far as these approaches aid communication and encourage self-respect, then we would see them as helping in the satisfaction of these emotional needs.

Thirdly, we would draw a parallel with other disabilities, where increasingly the principle of 'normalisation' is being applied. This approach seeks to help a person lead as normal and as valued a life as possible, given the disability that is present (see Ch. 7). We would argue that these positive approaches can be used to help people with dementia experience and achieve much more that is valued than approaches which deny the full range of needs of the person with dementia.

To return to the original question of the 'happily' dementing person, it is difficult to judge to what extent this state *does* represent a high quality of life; this could be yet another assumption on the part of the onlooker as the people concerned are not capable of expressing their feelings and attitudes coherently. Indeed the situation may be a means of coping with the failures and difficulties of the dementing process. There may even be a sense in which, by withdrawing in this fashion, the person is missing out to some degree. What we would advocate is to provide opportunities to return to reality, and also to provide a choice. To force the issue is not acceptable, but to nurture and encourage still leaves the options open. In the final analysis elderly people will shut off the stimulation or will respond to it. Unfortunately they are not given the choice often enough and it is assumed that they would rather remain lost in fantasy. We have tried to make it clear that our approach is tactful, flexible and warm rather than pressurised and aggressive. There are dangers with RO and like approaches with the wrong attitudes; there is a need for discussion of ethical issues and monitoring of programmes by those outside the institution as well as those actively involved. Regrettably, advocates for the rights of people with dementia and their supporters are rare; discussion often centres on placement rather than on management and treatment.

Working with the supporter and the nurse, the care attendant or relative should also be considered. Here the ethical situation is simpler; staff members and relatives can make an informed decision about what they find helpful in caring for and communicating with the elderly person.

A large component of these programmes is in changing the environment rather than necessarily inducing change in the individual. Again some sort of environment has to be provided: the issue is what the nature of this should be. The environment described in Chapter 7, with its emphasis on basic humanitarian values of respect, dignity and interaction, is an improvement – psychologically – over many current settings. The techniques for facilitating communication also increase the person's quality of life by improving interaction with the staff.

Is it worth adopting a positive approach when the person is to be transferred to a setting where only basic care is given? Again a quality of life consideration applies; if this can be increased in the present then it can be seen as valuable, whatever might or might not happen in the future. There are now fewer and fewer places where some thought is not being given to these approaches. The example of one ward or Home can inspire many others. Contact over a particular patient who has benefitted from an individualised approach helps to spread the positive attitudes that are needed for real progress to be achieved. These attitudes ensure that there is an ethical, humanitarian basis to these approaches. Abuses are possible (see Ch. 10), but where the approaches are used explicitly and the Home or ward is open to external monitoring and scrutiny these can be guarded against.

Much work remains to be done. Environmental design needs to be researched further, so that appropriate prosthetic environments can be provided for people with dementia. There is interest in computer-aided memory re-training programmes (Skilbeck 1984), and software for computerised RO is available (see Appendix 3). Whilst we do not see the personal touch becoming redundant, these systems may enable some patients to receive the many repetitions of particular items they need for learning to take place, whilst maintaining their attention and interest.

Fundamental research on the nature of psychological functioning in dementia and related conditions is also required, to aid in the further rational development of programmes. Above all a positive approach combined with efforts to critically evaluate the effectiveness of these psychological programmes and their component parts is required if real progress is to be made in this field.

Approaches like RO may be exceedingly simple in concept; in practice there are many difficulties and obstacles to their successful implementation; there are many questions which remain to be fully answered. The last few years have seen tremendous progress in many centres, as a determination to work with people with dementia as *people* first and foremost has become widely held. To be a therapist demands no formal qualification; all who care for the elderly can be involved, but to do so they need support. These programmes are hard work, require considerable imagination, the ability to keep things going, to forget about oneself, to plan, to remember, and even a willingness to make a fool of oneself if it achieves the aim! Yet many staff who have used a positive approach find it extremely satisfying as at last they communicate and make personal contact with the elderly person who has appeared so confused, disorientated and inaccessible.

Appendix 1

Test of verbal orientation and personal and current information

Instructions – ask questions conversationally, varying the exact words used as appropriate to ensure the person understands what is being asked; scoring may be lenient, but no help in giving answers may be offered.

1 What is your name?		0	1
2 How old are you?		0	1
3 When were you born?	All correct	0	1
	Date correct	0	1
	Month correct	0	1
	Year correct	0	1
4 Where were you born?		0	1
5 What school did you attend?		0	1
6 What was your occupation (or spouse's)?		0	1
7 Where did you (or spouse) work – which town?		0	1
8 Name of employers for whom you worked?		0	1
9 Name of spouse or sibling?		0	1
10 What is the name of this place?		0	1
11 What type of place is it? i.e. hospital, old people's home etc.		0	1

12 What is the address of this place?
i.e. approximate location.   0 1

  13 What is the name of this town/city? 0 1

  14 What time of day is it now –
morning, afternoon, evening etc.?   0 1

  15 What time is it now? (accept answer
if within 30 minutes of actual time.) 0 1

  16 What day of the week is it today? 0 1

  17 What season is it now – spring,
summer, autumn, winter?   0 1

  18 What month is it now?   0 1

  19 What day of the month is it now? 0 1

  20 What year is it now?   0 1

  21 Recognition of persons (cleaner,
doctor, staff-member, resident, relative –
any two available) 1 point for each
person.   0 1 2

  22 Who is the prime minister at
present?   0 1

  23 Who was the prime minister
immediately before this one?   0 1

  24 Who is the president of the USA at
present?   0 1

25 Who is on the	1 point for	
throne at present?	name	0 1 2
26 Who was on the	1 point for	
throne immediately	number	
before them?		0 1 2

  27 What are the colours of the
Union Jack?   0 1

28 When did the	1 point for	
First World War	each	
begin, and end?	allow 2 years	0 1 2
	error	

  29 When did the
Second World War
begin, and end?   0 1 2

  30 Repeat this name and
address after me:
/Mr John/Brown/   0 1 2 3 4 5
42/West Street/Gateshead/

Ask for recall after five minutes; score 1
point for each segment recalled correctly.
Modify address to suit locality!

Total-score   (42 maximum)

As used in Woods' (1979) study.

Holden communication scale

Score:	0	1	2	3	4
Conversation					
1. Response:	Initiates conversation, deeply involved with anyone	Good for those familiar to him/her	Fair response to those close by. No initiation of conversation	Rather confused Poor comprehension	Rarely or never converses
2. Interest in past events:	Long full account of past events	Fairly good description	Short. Description a little confused	Confused or disinterested	No response
3. Pleasure:	Shows real pleasure in situation/ achievement	Smiles and shows interest	Variable response, slight smile, vague	Rarely shows even a smile	No response or just weeps
4. Humour:	Creates situation or tells funny story on own initiative	Enjoys comic situations or stories	Needs an explanation and encouragement to respond	Vague smile, simply copies others	No response or negativistic
Awareness and knowledge					
5. Names:	Knows most people's names on ward	Knows a few names	Needs a constant reminder	Knows own name only	Forgotten even own name
6. General orientation:	Knows day, month, weather, time and whereabouts	Can forget one or two items	Usually gets two right but tries	Vague, may guess one	Very confused

(Cont'd)

Score:	0	1	2	3	4
7. General knowledge:	Good on current events, generally able	Outstanding events only Fair on general knowledge	No current knowledge Poor general information	Confused about many things · Gets anxious and upset	Confused about everything Does not respond
8. Ability to join in Game etc:	Joins in games and activities with ease	Requires careful instructions but joins in	Can only join in simple activities	Becomes anxious and upset	Cannot or will not join in
Communication					
9. Speech:	No known difficulty	Slight hesitation or odd wording	Very few words, mainly automatic phrases	Inappropriate words, odd sounds. Nodding	Little or no verbalization
10. Attempts at communication	Communicates with ease	Tries hard to speak clearly	Tries to draw – gesticulates needs etc.	Euphoric laughter, weeping, aggressive	No attempt
11. Interest and response to objects:	Responds with interest and comment	Despite difficulties, shows interest	Shows some interest, but rather vague	Weeps, rejects objects, shows aggression	No response No comprehension
12. Success in communication:	Clearly understood	Uses gestures and sounds effectively	Understanding restricted to a few people	Becomes frustrated and angry	Makes no attempt

Appendix 3

Training aids, sources of materials, practical manuals, orientation aids

1. Video-tapes

a. Black & White tape showing group-work at basic and standard RO levels and showing a group over a six week period, including pre- and post-group assessments. Details of availability from Una Holden.

b. Colour tape (30 minutes) showing RO sessions, available for rent from:
   Orientation Aids,
   Dalebank, Glencaple,
   Dumfries, Scotland DG1 4RD
   Telephone: Glencaple 241

c. Colour tape (30 minutes) 'Reminiscence and Recall' showing reminiscence sessions, illustrating use of 'Recall' materials (see below) available from:
   Help the Aged Education Department,
   PO Box 460, 16 & 18 St James's Walk,
   London EC1
   Telephone: 01 253 0253

2. Tape-slide programmes

a. Covers basic attitudes and 24 hour RO (reference number 81–61) 30 minutes

b. Covers RO sessions (reference number 81–62) 30 minutes. Both prepared by Bob Woods, and are based on Chapters 7 & 8 of this book, respectively. Available for sale or hire from:
> Graves Medical Audio-visual Library,
> Holly House, 220 New London Road,
> Chelmsford, Essex CM2 9BJ
> Telephone: 0245 83351

3. Training manuals

a. *Reality orientation – principles & practice*, by Lorna Rimmer. Available from:
> Winslow Press,
> Telford Road,
> Bicester, Oxfordshire OX6 OTS
> Telephone: 0869 244644

b. *A manual for the modification of confused behaviour*, by Ian Hanley. Available from Orientation Aids (address above).

c. *RO reminders*, by Una Holden. A pocket reference of RO ideas. Winslow Press (address above).

d. *Thinking it through*, by Una Holden. A handbook for those working with the elderly. Winslow Press.

e. *Goal planning with elderly people; making plans to meet individual needs: a manual of instruction*, by Christine Barrowclough & Ian Fleming, 1986. Manchester University Press, Manchester. ISBN: 0 7190 1802 1

f. *Reminiscence*, by Andrew Norris. Winslow Press.

g. *An introduction to group work with the elderly*, by Mike Bender & Andrew Norris. Winslow Press.

h. *Wandering*, by Graham Stokes. Winslow Press.

i. *Shouting & Screaming*, by Graham Stokes. Winslow Press.

j. *Aggression*, by Graham Stokes. Winslow Press.

k. *Incontinence and Inappropriate Urinating*, by Graham Stokes. Winslow Press.

4. Orientation aids

a. Memory boards, calendars and signposts available from Orientation Aids (address above) or from Nottingham

Rehab Ltd, 17 Ludlow Hill Road, West Bridgford, Nottingham NG2 1BR.
b. Computer programme for 'reality orientation' training included in Norris D E, Skilbeck C E, Hayward A E & Torpy D M 1985 Microcomputers in clinical practice. J. Wiley & Sons, Chichester.

5. Reminiscence aids

a. Recall – a set of six tape-slide sequences which illustrate the last 80 years for older people. Handbook about the use of Recall also available.
From: Help the Aged Education Department (address above).
b. Memory diary; autobiographical scrap book, for writing and recording life events. Winslow Press.
c. Nostalgia: photographic reminiscence aids from Winslow Press. Sets include:
    Banner Headlines (front pages of newspapers from 1910–1950)
    Royalty – Royal faces and events
    Famous Faces (from sports, politics and entertainment)
    Then & Now Objects (modern photograph contrasted with one from earlier in the century)
    Then & Now Vehicles
d. Bygone Decades: Remembering – two sets of photographs covering the 1920s and 1930s respectively. Also available as slides. From Winslow Press.

6. Training packages

a. *Over the hill and far away* . . . .
A video-assisted training package for staff and volunteers working with 'elderly mentally infirm' people. Available from:
    ESCATA, Social Services, P Block,
    Brighton Polytechnic, Falmer, Brighton, East Sussex.
b. Age Concern England also produce relevant training materials.
    Age Concern England, Training Department,
    Bernard Sunley House, Pitcairn Road, Mitcham, Surrey CR4 3LL.

7. Booklets for relatives

a. *24 Hour approach to the problem of confusion in elderly people*, by Una Holden, Carol Martin & Margaret White. Winslow Press.

b. *Caring for the person with dementia – a guide for families and other carers*, by Chris Lay & Bob Woods. From:
   Alzheimer's Disease Society,
   Bank Buildings, Fulham Broadway,
   London SW6 1EP
   Telephone: 01 381 3177

c. *Who cares? Information & support for the carers of confused people*. Health Education Council 1986. Available from local Health Education Units.

d. *The 36-Hour Day*, by Nancy Mace and Peter Rabins. British edition available from Age Concern, England.

8. Notes

a. Many of the organisations referred to produce brochures or lists of their publications.

b. Most suppliers will forward their publications outside the UK, but please check availability, conditions and charges.

c. Some of the materials, e.g. some of the reminiscence aids, are not relevant outside the UK.

References

Adams J, Davies J E, Northwood J 1979 Ridge Hill – a home, not a ward. Nursing Times 75: 1659–1661, 1725–1726, 1769–1770

Adelson R, Nasti A, Sprafkin J N, Marinelli R, Primavera L H, Gorman B S 1982 Behavioral ratings of health professionals' interactions with the geriatric patient. Gerontologist 22: 277–281

Albert M L, Sparks R W, Helm N 1973 Melodic intonation therapy for aphasia. Archives of Neurology 29: 130–131

Albyn-Davis A 1983 A survey of adult aphasia. Prentice Hall, London

Ankus M, Quarrington B 1972 Operant behaviour in the memory disordered. Journal of Gerontology 27: 500–510

Bailey E A, Brown S, Goble R E A, Holden U P 1986 24 hour reality orientation: changes for staff and patients. Journal of Advanced Nursing 11: 141–151

Baines S, Saxby P, Ehlert K 1987 Reality orientation and reminiscence therapy: a controlled cross-over study of elderly confused people. British Journal of Psychiatry (in press)

Baltes M M, Barton C M 1977 New approaches toward aging: a case for the operant model. Educational Gerontology 2: 383–405

Baltes M M, Burgess R L, Stewart R B 1980 Independence and dependence in self-care behaviours in nursing home residents: an operant-observational study. International Journal of Behavioural Development 3: 489–500

Baltes M M, Lascomb S L 1975 Creating a healthy institutional environment: the nurse as a change agent. International Journal of Nursing Studies 12: 5–12

Baltes M M, Zerbe M B 1976a Re-establishing self-feeding in a nursing home resident. Nursing Research 25: 24–26

Baltes M M, Zerbe M B 1976b Independence training in nursing-home residents. Gerontologist 16: 428–432

Barnes J A 1974 Effects of reality orientation classroom on memory loss,

confusion and disorientation in geriatric patients. Gerontologist
14: 138–142

Barns E K, Sack A, Shore H 1973 Guidelines to treatment approaches:
modalities and methods for use with the aged. Gerontologist 13: 513–527

Barrowclough C, Fleming I 1986 Goal planning with elderly people.
Manchester University Press, Manchester

Bassey E J 1985 Benefits of exercise in the elderly. In: Isaacs B (ed) Recent
advances in geriatric medicine – 3. Churchill Livingstone, Edinburgh

Bender M, Norris A 1987 An introduction to group work with the elderly.
Winslow Press, London

Berger R M, Rose S D 1977 Interpersonal skill training with institutionalized
elderly patients. Journal of Gerontology 32: 346–353

Bergert L, Jacobsson E 1976 Training of reality orientation with a group of
patients with senile dementia. Scandinavian Journal of Behaviour Therapy
5: 191–200

Bergmann K, Foster E M, Justice A W, Matthews V 1978 Management of the
demented elderly patient in the community. British Journal of Psychiatry
132: 441–449

Birchmore T, Clague S 1983 A behavioural approach to reduce shouting.
Nursing Times 79(16): 37–39

Birren J E, Schaie K W (eds) 1985 Handbook of the psychology of aging,
2nd edn. Van Nostrand Reinhold, New York

Blackman D K, Howe M, Pinkston E M 1976 Increasing participation in
social interaction of the institutionalized elderly. Gerontologist 16: 69–76

Blessed G, Tomlinson B E, Roth M 1968 The association between
quantitative measures of dementia and of senile change in the cerebral
grey matter of elderly subjects. British Journal of Psychiatry 114: 797–811

Blundell J 1975 Physiological psychology. Essential psychology series.
Methuen, London

Booth T, Phillips D 1987 Group living in homes for the elderly: a
comparative study of the outcomes of care. British Journal of Social
Work 17: 1–20

Botwinick J 1977 Intellectual abilities. In: Birren J E, Schaie K W (eds)
Handbook of the psychology of aging. Van Nostrand Reinhold, New
York

Botwinick J, Storandt M 1980 Recall and recognition of old information in
relation to age and sex. Journal of Gerontology 35: 70–76

Bowen D M, Davison A N 1978 Biochemical changes in normal ageing and
dementia. In: Isaacs B (ed) Recent advances in geriatric medicine.
Churchill Livingstone, Edinburgh

Bowen D M, Davison A N 1980 Biochemical changes in the cholinergic
system of the ageing brain and in senile dementia. Psychological
Medicine 10: 315–319

Bower H M 1967 Sensory stimulation and the treatment of senile dementia.
Medical Journal of Australia 1: 1113–1119

Brody E M, Cole C, Moss M 1973 Individualizing therapy for the mentally
impaired aged. Social Casework (October): 453–461

Brody E M, Kleban M H, Lawton M P, Silverman H A 1971 Excess disabilities
of mentally impaired aged: impact of individualized treatment.
Gerontologist 11: 124–133

Brody E M, Kleban M H, Lawton M P, Moss M 1974 A longitudinal look at
excess disabilities in the mentally impaired aged. Journal of Gerontology
29: 79–84

Bromley D B 1978 Approaches to the study of personality changes in adult life and old age. In: Isaacs A D, Post F (eds) Studies in geriatric psychiatry. J Wiley, Chichester

Brook P, Degun G, Mather M 1975 Reality orientation, a therapy for psychogeriatric patients: a controlled study. British Journal of Psychiatry 127: 42–45

Brotchie J, Brennan J, Wyke M 1985 Temporal orientation in the presenium and old age. British Journal of Psychiatry 147: 692–695

Buckholdt D R, Gubrium J F 1983 Therapeutic pretence in reality orientation. International Journal of Aging and Human Development 16: 167–181

Buell S J, Coleman P D 1981 Quantitative evidence for selective dendritic growth in normal human ageing brains, but not in senile dementia. Brain Research 214: 23–41

Burgio L D, Burgio K L, Engel B T, Tice L M 1986 Increasing distance and independence of ambulation in elderly nursing home residents. Journal of Applied Behavior Analysis 19: 357–366

Burton M 1980 Evaluation and change in a psychogeriatric ward through direct observation and feedback. British Journal of Psychiatry 137: 566–571

Burton M 1982 Reality orientation for the elderly: a critique. Journal of Advanced Nursing 7: 427–433

Burton M, Spall R 1981 Contributions of the behavioural approach to nursing the elderly. Nursing Times 77 (6): 247–248

Cameron D E 1941 Studies in senile nocturnal delirium. Psychiatric Quarterly 15: 47–53

Carroll K, Gray K 1981 Memory development: an approach to the mentally impaired elderly in the long-term care setting. International Journal of Ageing and Human Development 13: 15–35

Carstensen L L, Erickson R J 1986 Enhancing the social environments of elderly nursing home residents: are high rates of interaction enough? Journal of Applied Behavior Analysis 19: 349–355

Cautela J R 1966 Behaviour therapy and geriatrics. Journal of Genetic Psychology 108: 9–17

Cautela J R 1969 A classical conditioning approach to the development and modification of behaviour in the aged. Gerontologist 9: 109–113

Challis D, Davies B 1985 Long-term care for the elderly: the community care scheme. British Journal of Social Work 15: 563–580

Challis D, Davies B 1986 Case management in community care. Gower, Aldershot

Christensen A L 1975 Luria's neuropsychological investigation. Munksgaard, Copenhagen

Church M, Linge K 1982 Dealing with dementia in the community. Community Care (Nov. 25): 20–21

Citrin R S, Dixon D N 1977 Reality orientation: a milieu therapy used in an institution for the aged. Gerontologist 17: 39–43

Cluff P J, Campbell W H 1975 The social corridor: an environmental and behavioural evaluation. Gerontologist 15: 516–523

Cohen D, Kennedy G, Eisdorfer C 1984 Phases of change in the patient with Alzheimer's dementia. Journal of American Geriatrics Society 32: 11–15

Coleman P 1986 Issues in the therapeutic use of reminiscence with elderly people. In: Hanley I, Gilhooly M (eds) Psychological therapies for the elderly. Croom Helm, London

Collins P 1983 Caring for the confused elderly: an experimental support service. Department of Geriatric Medicine, University of Birmingham

Collins R W, Plaska T 1975 Mowrer's conditioning treatment for enuresis applied to geriatric residents of a nursing home. Behaviour Therapy 6: 632–638

Copeland J R M, Gurland B J 1985 International comparative studies. In: Arie T (ed) Recent advances in psychogeriatrics – 1. Churchill Livingstone, Edinburgh

Cornbleth T 1977 Effects of a protected hospital ward area on wandering and non-wandering geriatric patients. Journal of Gerontology 32: 573–577

Cornbleth T, Cornbleth C 1977 Reality orientation for the elderly. Journal supplement abstract service of the American Psychological Association MS 1539

Cornbleth T, Cornbleth C 1979 Evaluation of the effectiveness of reality orientation classes in a nursing home unit. Journal of American Geriatrics Society 27: 522–524

Corrigan J D, Arnett J A, Houck J A, Jackson R D 1985 Reality orientation for brain injured patients: group treatment and monitoring of recovery. Archives of Physical Medicine & Rehabilitation 66: 626–630

Corso J F 1967 The experimental psychology of sensory behaviour. Holt, Rinehart and Winston, New York

Cosin L Z, Mort M, Post F, Westropp C, Williams M 1958 Experimental treatment of persistent senile confusion. International Journal of Social Psychiatry 4: 24–42

Craig J 1983 The growth of the elderly population. Population Trends 32: 28–33

Craik F I M 1977 Age differences in human memory. In: Birren J E, Schaie K W (eds) Handbook of the psychology of aging. Van Nostrand Reinhold, New York

Cumming E, Henry W E 1961 Growing old, process of disengagement. Basic Books, New York

Cummings J L 1984 Treatable dementias. In: Mayeux R, Rosen W G (eds) Advances in Neurology – 38: The dementias. Raven Press, New York

Darley F L 1982 Aphasia. WB Saunders, Philadelphia

Davies A D M 1981 Neither wife nor widow: an intervention with the wife of a chronically handicapped man during hospital visits. Behaviour Research & Therapy 19: 449–451

Davies A D M 1982 Research with elderly people in long-term care: some social and organisational factors affecting psychological interventions. Ageing & Society 2: 285–298

Davies A D M & Snaith P 1980 The social behaviour of geriatric patients at meal-times: an observational and an intervention study. Age & Ageing 9: 93–99

Degun G 1976 Reality orientation: a multidisciplinary therapeutic approach. Nursing Times 72: 117–120

Diesfeldt H F A, Diesfeldt–Groenendijk H 1977 Improving cognitive performance in psychogeriatric patients: the influence of physical exercise. Age and Ageing 6: 58–64

Dimond S 1972 The double brain. Williams and Wilkins, Baltimore

Downes J J 1987 Classroom RO and the enhancement of orientation – a critical note. British Journal of Clinical Psychology 26: 147–148

Drummond L, Kirchoff L, Scarbrough D R 1978 A practical guide to reality orientation: a treatment approach for confusion and disorientation. Gerontologist 18: 568–573

Eisdorfer C, Wilkie F 1977 Stress, disease, aging and behaviour. In: Birren

J E, Schaie K W (eds) Handbook of the psychology of aging. Van Nostrand Reinhold, New York

Feil N 1982 Validation: the Feil method. Edward Feil Productions, Cleveland, Ohio

Fine W 1972 Geriatric ergonomics. Gerontologia Clinica 14: 322–332

Finger S, Walbran B, Stein D G 1973 Brain damage and behavioural recovery: serial lesion phenomena. Brain Research 63: 1–18

Folsom J C 1967 Intensive hospital therapy of geriatric patients. Current Psychiatric Iherapies 7: 209–215

Folsom J C 1968 Reality orientation for the elderly mental patient. Journal of Geriatric Psychiatry 1: 291–307

Folstein M F, Folstein S E, McHugh P R 1975 'Mini-Mental State': a practical method for grading the cognitive state of patients for the clinician. Journal of Psychiatric Research 12: 189–198

Foxx R M, Azrin N H 1973 Toilet training the retarded. Research Press, Champaign, Illinois

Fuller J, Ward E, Evans A, Massam K, Gardner A 1979 Dementia: supportive groups for relatives. British Medical Journal 1: 1684–1685

Garland J 1985 A model for the understanding and behavioural management of excess noise making by old people in residential care. Paper presented at XIIIth International Congress of Gerontology, New York

Gazzaniga M S 1970 The bisected brain. Appleton–Century–Crofts, New York

Gazzaniga M S 1974 Determinants of cerebral recovery. In: Stein D G (ed) Plasticity and recovery of function in the CNS. Academic Press, New York

Gazzaniga M S, Glass A V, Premack D 1972 Artificial language training in aphasics. Neuropsychologia 11: 95–103

Gazzaniga M S, Velletri A S, Premack D 1971 Language training in brain-damaged humans. Fed. Proc. Abstract 30 (2): 265

Geiger O G, Johnson L A 1974 Positive education for elderly persons – correct eating through reinforcement. Gerontologist 14: 432–436

Georgiades N J, Phillimore L 1975 The myth of the hero-innovator and alternative strategies for organisational change. In: Kiernan C C, Woodford F P (eds) Behaviour modification with the severely retarded. Associated Scientific Publishers, New York, pp 313–319

Gilhooly M 1984 The social dimensions of senile dementia. In: Hanley I, Hodge J (eds) Psychological approaches to the care of the elderly. Croom Helm, London, pp 88–135

Gilleard C J 1984a Assessment of cognitive impairment in the elderly. In: Hanley I, Hodge J (eds) Psychological approaches to the care of the elderly. Croom Helm, London

Gilleard C J 1984b Assessment of behavioural impairment in the elderly: a review. In: Hanley I, Hodge J (eds) Psychological approaches to the care of the elderly. Croom Helm, London

Gilleard C J 1984c Living with dementia. Croom Helm, London

Gilleard C J, Mitchell R G, Riordan J 1981 Ward orientation training with psychogeriatric patients. Journal of Advanced Nursing 6: 95–98

Godlove C, Dunn G, Wright H 1980 Caring for old people in New York and London: the 'nurses' aide' interviews. Journal of the Royal Society of Medicine 73: 713–723

Goldstein A 1973 Structured learning therapy. Academic Press, New York

Goldstein G, Turner S M, Holzman A, Kanagy M, Elmore S, Barry K 1982

An evaluation of reality orientation therapy. Journal of Behavioural Assessment 4: 165–178

Gray P, Stevenson J S 1980 Changes in verbal interaction among members of resocialisation groups. Journal of Gerontological Nursing 6: 86–90

Greene J G, Nicol R, Jamieson H 1979 Reality orientation with psychogeriatric patients. Behaviour Research and Therapy 17: 615–617

Greene J G, Smith R, Gardiner M, Timbury G C 1982 Measuring behavioural disturbance of elderly demented patients in the community and its effects on relatives: a factor-analytic study. Age & Ageing 11: 121–126

Greene J G, Timbury G C, Smith R, Gardiner M 1983 Reality Orientation with elderly patients in the community: an empirical evaluation. Age & Ageing 12: 38–43

Green G R, Linsk N L, Pinkston E M 1986 Modification of verbal behaviour of the mentally impaired elderly by their spouses. Journal of Applied Behavior Analysis 19: 329–336

Grosicki J P 1968 Effects of operant conditioning of modification of incontinence in neuropsychiatric geriatric patients. Nursing Research 17: 304–311

Gubrium J F, Ksander M 1975 On multiple realities and reality orientation. Gerontologist 15: 142–145

Gupta H 1979 Group living in residential homes for elderly people in Northamptonshire. In: Positive approaches to mental infirmity in elderly people. MIND Annual Conference, London

Gustafsson R 1976 Milieu therapy in a ward for patients with senile dementia. Scandinavian Journal of Behaviour Therapy 5: 27–39

Hahn K 1980 Using 24 hour reality orientation. Journal of Gerontological Nursing 6 (3): 130–135

Halberstam J L, Zaretsky H H 1969 Learning capacities of elderly and brain-damaged. Archives of Physical Medicine 50: 133–139

Halberstam J L, Zaretsky H H, Brucker B S, Guttman A R 1971 Avoidance conditioning of motor responses in elderly brain damaged patients. Archives of Physical Medicine and Rehabilitation 52: 318–336

Hall J N 1980 Ward rating scales for long-stay patients: a review. Psychological Medicine 10: 277–288

Hanley I G 1981 The use of signposts and active training to modify ward disorientation in elderly patients. Journal of Behaviour Therapy & Experimental Psychiatry 12: 241–247

Hanley I G 1982 A manual for the modification of confused behaviour. Lothian Regional Council Department of Social Work, Edinburgh

Hanley I G 1984 Theoretical and practical considerations in reality orientation therapy with the elderly. In: Hanley I, Hodge J (eds) Psychological approaches to the care of the elderly. Croom Helm, London

Hanley I G 1986 Reality orientation in the care of the elderly person with dementia – three case studies. In: Hanley I, Gilhooly M (eds) Psychological therapies for the elderly. Croom Helm, London

Hanley I G, Cleary E, Oates A, Walker M 1981 In touch with reality. Social Work Today 12 (42): 8–10

Hanley I G, Lusty K 1984 Memory aids in reality orientation: a single-case study. Behaviour Research & Therapy 22: 709–712

Hanley I G, McGuire R J, Boyd W D 1981 Reality orientation and dementia: a controlled trial of two approaches. British Journal of Psychiatry 138: 10–14

Harris C S, Ivory P B C B 1976 An outcome evaluation of reality orientation therapy with geriatric patients in a state mental hospital. Gerontologist 16: 496–503

Harris H, Lipman A, Slater R 1977 Architectural design: the spatial location and interactions of old people. Gerontology 23: 390–400

Harris S L, Snyder B D, Snyder R L, McGraw B 1977 Behaviour modification therapy with elderly demented patients: implementation and ethical considerations. Journal of Chronic Diseases 30: 129–134

Hart J, Fleming R 1985 An experimental evaluation of a modified reality orientation therapy. Clinical Gerontologist 3(4): 35–44

Haugen P K 1985 Dementia in old age – treatment approaches. Report 5/85, Norsk Gerontologisk Institutt, Oslo

Hausman C P 1979 Short-term counselling groups for people with elderly parents. Gerontologist 19: 102–107

Havighurst R, Neugarten B L, Tobin S S 1968 Disengagement and patterns of aging. In: Neugarten B L (ed) Middle age and aging: a reader in psychology. University of Chicago Press, Chicago

Hécaen H, Albert M L 1978 Human neuropsychology. John Wiley & Sons, New York

Hécaen H, Assal G 1970 A comparison of construction deficits following right and left hemisphere lesions. Neuropsychologia 8: 289 304

Help the Aged 1981 Recall – a handbook. Help the Aged Education Department, London

Hodge J 1984 Towards a behavioural analysis of dementia. In: Hanley I, Hodge J (eds) Psychological approaches to the care of the elderly. Croom Helm, London

Hoedt-Rasmussen R, Skinhoj E 1964 Transneuronal depression of the cerebral hemispheric metabolism in man. Acta neurologica scandinavica 40: 41–46

Hogstel M O 1979 Use of reality orientation with ageing confused patients. Nursing Research 28: 161–165

Holden U P 1979a Return to reality. Nursing Mirror 149(21): 26–30

Holden U P 1979b A flexible technique for rehabilitating the confused. Geriatric Medicine 9(7): 49–50

Holden U P 1984a Assessment of dementia: the case against standard test batteries. Clinical Gerontologist 3(2): 48–52

Holden U P (ed) 1984b Nostalgia series. Winslow Press, London

Holden U P 1984c Thinking it through. Winslow Press, London

Holden U P 1984d Reality orientation reminders. Winslow Press, London

Holden U P, Sinebruchow A 1978 Reality orientation therapy: a study investigating the value of this therapy in the rehabilitation of elderly people. Age and Ageing 7: 83–90

Holden U P, Sinebruchow A 1979 Validation of reality orientation therapy for use with the elderly. Unpublished manuscript

Hoyer W J, Lopez M A, Goldstein A P 1980 Correlates of social skills acquisition and transfer by elderly inpatients. Unpublished manuscript

Hoyer W J, Mishara B L, Riebel R G 1975 Problem behaviours as operants: applications with elderly individuals. Gerontologist 15: 452–456

Hussian R A 1981 Geriatric psychology: a behavioural perspective. Van Nostrand Reinhold, New York

Hussian R A 1984 Behavioral geriatrics. Progress in Behaviour Modification 16: 159–183

Hutt S J, Hutt C 1970 Direct observation and measurement of behaviour. Thomas, Springfield, Illinois

Inglis J 1962 Psychological practices in geriatric problems. Journal of Mental Science 108: 669–674

Jacoby R I, Levy R 1980 Computed tomography in the elderly. 2. Senile dementia: diagnosis and functional impairment. British Journal of Psychiatry 136: 256–259

Jacoby R J, Levy R, Bird J M 1981 Computed tomography and the outcome of affective disorder: a follow-up study of elderly patients. British Journal of Psychiatry 139: 288–292

Jenkins J, Felce D, Lunt B, Powell E 1977 Increasing engagement in activity of residents in old people's homes by providing recreational materials. Behaviour Research and Therapy 15: 429–434

Johnson C M, McLaren S M, McPherson F M 1981 The comparative effectiveness of three versions of 'classroom' reality orientation. Age & Ageing 10: 33–35

Jones G H, Adam J H 1979 Towards a prosthetic memory. Bulletin of the British Psychological Society 32: 165–167

Jones G M, Clark P 1984 The use of memory 'recall' on a psychogeriatric ward. British Journal of Occupational Therapy 47: 315–316

Kay D W K, Beamish P, Roth M 1964 Old age mental disorder in Newcastle–upon–Tyne. Part 1 – a study of prevalence. British Journal of Psychiatry 110: 146–158

Kear Colwell J J 1973 The structure of the Wechsler Memory Scale and its relationship to 'brain damage'. British Journal of Social and Clinical Psychology 12: 384–392

Kempinsky W H 1958 Experimental study of distant effects of acute focal brain injury. Archives of Neurology and Psychiatry 79: 376–389

Kendrick D C, Gibson A J, Moyes I C A 1979 The revised Kendrick Battery: clinical studies. British Journal of Social and Clinical Psychology 18: 329–340

Kiernat J M 1979 The use of life review activity with confused nursing home residents. American Journal of Occupational Therapy 33: 306–310

King M R 1980 Treatment of incontinence. Nursing Times 76 (June 5): 1006–1010

King's Fund 1986 Living well into old age: applying principles of good practice to services for elderly people with severe mental disabilities. King's Fund, London

Kochansky G E 1979 Psychiatric rating scales for assessing psychopathology in the elderly: a critical review. In: Raskin A, Jarvik L (eds) Psychiatric symptoms and cognitive loss in the elderly. Hemisphere Publishing Corporation, Washington

Kuriansky J, Gurland B 1976 The performance test of activities of daily living. International Journal of Aging and Human Development 7: 343–352

Kuriansky J, Gurland B, Cowan D 1976 The usefulness of a psychological test battery. International Journal of Aging and Human Development 7: 331–342

Lam D H, Woods R T 1986 Ward orientation training in dementia: a single-case study. International Journal of Geriatric Psychiatry 1: 145–147

Langer E J, Rodin J 1976 The effects of choice and enhanced personal responsibility for the aged: a field experiment in an institutional setting. Journal of Personality and Social Psychology 34: 191–198

Langley G E, Corder J M 1978 Workshop on the contribution of reminiscence theatre to reminiscence therapy with the elderly. Report on conference at Exe Vale Hospital, Exeter

Lawton M P 1971 The functional assessment of elderly people. Journal of American Geriatrics Society 19: 465–481

Lemke S, Moos R H 1980 Assessing the institutional policies of sheltered care settings. Journal of Gerontology 35: 96–107

Lemke S, Moos R 1986 Quality of residential settings for elderly adults. Journal of Gerontology 41: 268–276

Leng N 1982 Behavioural treatment of the elderly. Age & Ageing 11: 235–243

Lesser J, Lazarus L W, Frankel R, Havasy S 1981 Reminiscence group therapy with psychotic geriatric inpatients. Gerontologist 21: 291–296

LeVere T F 1975 Neural stability, sparing and behavioural recovery following brain damage. Psychological Review 82 (5): 344–358

Libb J W, Clements C B 1969 Token reinforcement in an exercise program for hospitalized geriatric patients. Perceptual and Motor Skills 28: 957–958

Lindsley O R 1964 Geriatric behavioural prosthetics. In: Kastenbaum R (ed) New thoughts on old age. Springer, New York

Linsk N, Howe M W, Pinkston E M 1975 Behavioural group work in a home for the aged. Social Work 20: 454–463

Lipman A 1968 A socio-architectural view of life in 3 homes for old people. Gerontologia Clinica 10: 88–101

Lipman A, Slater R 1977 Homes for old people: toward a positive environment, Gerontologist 17: 146–156

Little A G, Levy R, Chuaqui-Kidd P, Hand D 1985 A double-blind, placebo controlled trial of high dose lecithin in Alzheimer's Disease. Journal of Neurology, Neurosurgery and Psychiatry 48: 736–742

Little A G, Volans P J, Hemsley D R, Levy R 1986 The retention of new information in senile dementia. British Journal of Clinical Psychology 25: 71–72

Lodge B, McReynolds S 1983 Quadruple support for dementia. Age Concern Leicestershire, Leicester

Loew C A, Silverstone B M 1971 A program of intensified stimulation and response facilitation for the senile aged. Gerontologist 11: 341–347

Lopez M A, Hoyer W J, Goldstein A P, Gershaw N J, Spratkin R P 1980 Effects of overlearning and incentive on the acquisition and transfer of interpersonal skills with institutionalized elderly. Journal of Gerontology 35: 403–408

Luria A R 1963 Restoration of function after brain injury. Pergamon Press, Oxford

McClannahan L E, Risley T R 1974 Design of living environments for nursing home residents. Recruiting attendance at activities. Gerontologist 14: 236–240

McClannahan L E, Risley T R 1975 Design of living environments for nursing-home residents: increasing participation in recreation activities. Journal of Applied Behaviour Analysis 8: 261–268

McCormack D, Whitehead A 1981 The effect of providing recreational activities on the engagement level of long-stay geriatric patients. Age & Ageing 10: 287–291

MacDonald M L, Butler A K 1974 Reversal of helplessness: producing walking behaviour in nursing-home wheelchair residents using behaviour modification procedures. Journal of Gerontology 29: 97–101

MacDonald M L, Settin J M 1978 Reality orientation vs sheltered workshops as treatment for the institutionalized aging. Journal of Gerontology 33: 416–421

McFadyen M 1984 The measurement of engagement in the institutionalised elderly. In: Hanley I, Hodge J (eds) Psychological approaches to the care of the elderly. Croom Helm, London

McFadyen M, Prior T, Kindness K 1980 Engagement: an important variable in institutional care of the elderly. Paper presented at British Psychological Society Annual Conference, Aberdeen

Marsden C D 1978 The diagnosis of dementia. In: Isaacs A D, Post F (eds) Studies in geriatric psychiatry. J Wiley, Chichester

Marston N, Gupta H 1977 Interesting the old. Community Care (Nov. 16): 26–28

Matthews R, Kemp M 1979 Rooms of the past strike a chord in the mentally infirm. Geriatric Medicine 9 (June): 37–41

Mayes A, Meudell P 1981 How similar is the effect of cueing in amnesics and in normal subjects following forgetting? Cortex 17: 113–124

Melin L, Gotestam K G 1981 The effects of rearranging ward routines on communication and eating behaviours of psychogeriatric patients. Journal of Applied Behavioural Analysis 14: 47–51

Merchant M, Saxby P 1981 Reality orientation: a way forward. Nursing Times 77: No 33: 1442–1445

Merriam S 1980 The concept and function of reminiscence: a review of the research. Gerontologist 20: 604–608

Miller A 1985 A study of the dependency of elderly patients in wards using different methods of nursing care. Age & Ageing 14: 132–138

Miller E 1975 Impaired recall and the memory disturbance in pre-senile dementia. British Journal of Social and Clinical Psychology 14: 73–79

Miller E 1977a Abnormal ageing: the psychology of senile and pre-senile dementia. J Wiley, Chichester

Miller E 1977b The management of dementia: a review of some possibilities. British Journal of Social and Clinical Psychology 16: 77–83

Miller E 1980 Psychological intervention in the management and rehabilitation of neuropsychological impairments. Behaviour Research & Therapy 18: 527–535

Miller E 1984 Recovery and management of neuropsychological impairments. Wiley, Chichester

Milne D 1985 An observational evaluation of the effects of nurse training in behaviour therapy on unstructured ward activities and interactions. British Journal of Clinical Psychology 24: 149–158

von Monakow C 1914 Die lokalisation im grosshirn und der abbau der funktion durch cortikale. Herde, Wiesbaden

Moore V, Wyke M 1984 Drawing disability in patients with senile dementia. Psychological Medicine 14: 97–105

Moos R H, Lemke S 1980 Assessing the physical and architectural features of sheltered care settings. Journal of Gerontology 35: 571–583

Morris R, Wheatley J, Britton P G 1983 Retrieval from long term memory in senile dementia – cued recall revisited. British Journal of Clinical Psychology 22: 141–142

Nathanson B F, Reingold J 1969 A workshop for mentally impaired aged. Gerontologist 9: 293–295

Naylor G, Harwood E 1975 Old dogs, new tricks: age and ability. Psychology Today 1: 29–33

Nelson H E 1982 The National Adult Reading Test. NFER-Nelson, Windsor

Neugarten B L 1977 Personality and aging. In: Birren J E, Schaie K W (eds) Handbook of the psychology of aging. Van Nostrand Reinhold, New York

Norberg A, Melin E, Asplund K 1986 Reactions to music, touch and object presentation in the final stage of dementia: an exploratory study. International Journal of Nursing Studies 23: 315–323

Norris A 1986 Reminiscence. Winslow Press, London

Norris A, Abu el Eileh M 1982 Reminiscence groups. Nursing Times 78: 1368–1369

Oberleder M 1962 An attitude scale to determine adjustment in institutions for the aged Journal of Chronic Diseases 15: 915–923

Patterson R L 1982 Overcoming deficits of aging. a behavioural approach. Plenum Press, New York

Pattie A H, Gilleard C J 1979 Manual of the Clifton assessment procedures for the elderly (CAPE). Hodder and Stoughton Educational, Sevenoaks

Perry R, Perry E 1982 The ageing brain and its pathology. In: Levy R, Post F (eds) The psychiatry of late life. Blackwell, Oxford, pp 9–67

Peterson R F, Knapp T J, Rosen J C, Pither B F 1977 The effects of furniture arrangement on the behaviour of geriatric patients. Behaviour Therapy 8: 464–467

Pinkston E M, Linsk N L 1984 Care of the elderly: a family approach. Pergamon, New York

Pollock D P, Liberman R P 1974 Behaviour therapy of incontinence in demented in-patients. Gerontologist 14: 488–491

Post F 1965 The clinical psychiatry of late life. Pergamon Press, Oxford

Powell L, Felce D, Jenkins J, Lunt B 1979 Increasing engagement in a home for the elderly by providing an indoor gardening activity. Behaviour Research and Therapy 15: 127–136

Powell Proctor L, Miller E 1982 Reality orientation: a critical appraisal. British Journal of Psychiatry 140: 457–463

Powell R R 1974 Psychological effects of exercise therapy upon institutionalized geriatric mental patients. Gerontologist 14: 157–161

Praderas K, MacDonald M L 1986 Telephone conversational skills training with socially isolated, impaired nursing home residents. Journal of Applied Behavior Analysis 19: 337–348

Quattrochi-Tubin S, Jones J W, Breedlove V 1982 The burnout syndrome in geriatric counsellors and service workers. Activities, Adaptation and Aging 3: 65–76

Quilitch H R 1974 Purposeful activity increased on a geriatric ward through programmed recreation. Journal of the American Geriatrics Society 22: 226–229

Rebok G W, Hoyer W J 1977 The functional context of elderly behaviour. Gerontologist 17: 27–34

Reeve W, Ivison D 1985 Use of environmental manipulation and classroom and modified informal reality orientation with institutionalized, confused elderly patients. Age & Ageing 14: 119–121

Reisberg B 1981 Brain failure: an introduction to current concepts of senility. Free Press/Macmillan, New York

Riegler J 1980 Comparison of a reality orientation programme for geriatric patients with and without music. Journal of Music Therapy 17: 26–33

Rimmer L 1982 Reality orientation: principles and practice. Winslow Press, London

Rinke C L, Wiliams J J, Lloyd K E, Smith-Scott W 1978 The effects of prompting and reinforcement on self-bathing by elderly residents of a nursing home. Behavior Therapy 9: 873–881

Robinson B C 1983 Validation of a caregiver strain index. Journal of Gerontology 38: 344–348

Ron M A, Toone B K, Garralda M E, Lishman W A 1979 Diagnostic accuracy in pre-senile dementia. British Journal of Psychiatry 13: 161–168

Rona D, Bellwood S, Wylie B 1984 Assessment of a behavioural programme to treat incontinent patients in psychogeriatric wards. British Journal of Clinical Psychology 23: 273–280

Rona D, Wylie B, Bellwood S 1986 Behaviour treatment of daytime incontinence in elderly male and female patients. Behavioural Psychotherapy 14: 13–20

Rothi L J, Horner J 1983 Restitution and substitution: two theories of recovery with application to neurobehavioural treatment. Journal of Clinical Neuropsychology 5: 73–81

Rothwell N, Britton P G, Woods R T 1983 The effects of group living in a residential home for the elderly. British Journal of Social Work 13: 639–643

Royal College of Physicians 1981 Organic mental impairment in the elderly. Journal of the Royal College of Physicians, London 15: 141–147

Sachs D A 1975 Behavioural techniques in a residential nursing home facility. Journal of Behaviour Therapy and Experimental Psychiatry 6: 123–127

Sanavio E 1981 Toilet retraining psychogeriatric residents. Behavior Modification 5: 417–427

Savage R D 1973 Old age. In Eysenck H J (ed) Handbook of abnormal psychology. Pitman, London

Saxby P, Jeffery D 1983 In a strange land. Social Work Today 15 (Sept. 6): 16–17

Scarbrough D R, Drummond L, Kirchhoff L 1978 Letter to the editor. Journal of Gerontology 33:588

Schaie K W, Labouvie-Vief G 1974 Generational versus ontogenetic components of change in adult cognitive behaviour: a 14-year cross-sequential study. Developmental Psychology 10: 305–320

Schaie K W, Strother C R 1968 A cross-sequential study of age changes in cognitive behaviour. Psychological Bulletin 70: 671–680

Schnelle J F, Traughber B, Morgan D B, Embry J E, Binion A F, Coleman A 1983 Management of geriatric incontinence in nursing homes. Journal of Applied Behavior Analysis 16: 235–241

Schwenk M A 1981 Reality orientation for the institutionalized aged: does it help? Gerontologist 19: 373–377

Seidel H A, Hodgkinson P E 1979 Behaviour modification and long-term learning in Korsakoff's psychosis. Nursing Times 75: 1855–1857

Seligman M 1975 Helplessness: on depression, development and death. W H Freeman, San Francisco

Shaw J 1979 A literature review of treatment systems for mentally disabled old people. Journal of Gerontological Nursing 5 (5): 36–41

Shepherd G, Richardson A 1979 Organisation and interaction in psychiatric day-centres. Psychological Medicine 9: 573–579

Skilbeck C 1984 Computer assistance in the management of memory and cognitive impairment. In: Wilson B A, Moffat N (eds) Clinical management of memory problems. Croom Helm, London

Smith B J, Barker H R 1972 Influence of a reality orientation training programme on the attitudes of trainees towards the elderly. Gerontologist 12: 262–264

Smith P, Smith L 1986 Continence and incontinence: psychological approaches to development and treatment. Croom Helm, London

Snyder L H, Rupprecht P, Pyrek J, Brekhus S, Moss T 1978 Wandering. Gerontologist 18: 272–280

Sommer R, Ross H 1958 Social interaction on a geriatric ward. International Journal of Social Psychiatry 4: 128–133

Sparks R, Helm N, Albert M L 1974 Aphasia rehabilitation resulting from melodic intonation therapy. Cortex 10: 303–316

Stephens L P (ed) 1969 Reality orientation: a technique to rehabilitate elderly and brain-damaged patients with a moderate to severe degree of disorientation. American Psychiatric Association Hospital and Community Psychiatric Service, Washington DC

Stockwell F 1985 The nursing process in psychiatric nursing. Croom Helm, London

Stokes G 1986a Wandering. Winslow Press, London

Stokes G 1986b Screaming and shouting. Winslow Press, London

Tarrier N, Larner S 1983 The effects of manipulation of social reinforcement on toilet requests on a geriatric ward. Age & Ageing 12: 234–239

Taulbee L R, Folsom J C 1966 Reality orientation for geriatric patients. Hospital and Community Psychiatry 17: 133–135

Thornton S, Brotchie J 1987 Reminiscence: a critical review of the empirical literature. British Journal of Clinical Psychology 26: 93–111

Towell D, Harries C 1979 Innovations in patient care. Croom Helm, London

Turner R K 1980 A behavioural approach to the management of incontinence in the elderly. In: Mandelstam D (ed) Incontinence and its management. Croom Helm, London

Ulatowska H K (ed) 1985 The aging brain: communication in the elderly. Taylor & Francis, London

Voelkel D 1978 A study of reality orientation and resocialization groups with confused elderly. Journal of Gerotonological Nursing 4: 3–18

Wallis G G, Baldwin M, Higginbotham P 1983 Reality orientation therapy: a controlled trial. British Journal of Medical Psychology 56: 271–278

Walsh K W 1987 Neuropsychology: a clinical approach, 2nd edn. Churchill Livingstone, Edinburgh

Warrington E K, James M, Kinsbourne M 1966 Drawing disability in relation to laterality of lesion. Brain 89: 53–82

Warrington E K, Sanders H I 1971 The fate of old memories. Quarterly Journal of Experimental Psychology 23: 432–442

Wattis J P, Church M 1986 Practical psychiatry of old age. Croom Helm, London

Wilcock G 1984 Dementia. In: Dawson A M, Compston N, Besser G M (eds) Recent advances in medicine – 19. Churchill Livingstone, Edinburgh

Wilcock G, Esiri M M 1982 Plaques, tangles and dementia: a quantitative study. Journal of the Neurological Sciences 56: 343–356

Willmott M 1986 The effect of a vinyl floor surface and a carpeted floor surface upon walking in elderly hospital in-patients. Age & Ageing 15: 119–120

Wisocki P 1984 Behavioral approaches to gerontology. Progress in Behavior Modification 16: 121–157

Woods R T 1979 Reality orientation and staff attention: a controlled study. British Journal of Psychiatry 134: 502–507

Woods R T 1983 Specificity of learning in reality orientation sessions: a single-case study. Behaviour Research & Therapy 21: 173–175

Woods R T 1987 Psychological management of dementia. In: Pitt B (ed) Dementia. Churchill Livingstone, Edinburgh

Woods R T, Britton P G 1975 Psychological aspects of incontinence in a psychogeriatric population. Unpublished manuscript

Woods R T, Britton P G 1977 Psychological approaches to the treatment of the elderly. Age and Ageing 6: 104–112

Woods R T, Britton P G 1985 Clinical psychology with the elderly. Croom Helm, London

Woods R T, Piercy M 1974 A similarity between amnesic memory and normal forgetting. Neuropsychologia 12: 437–445

Woods R T, Simpson S, Nicol R 1980 Reality orientation: the relative effects of 24 hour RO and RO sessions. Unpublished manuscript

World Health Organisation 1986 Dementia in later life: research and action. WHO Technical report series no. 730, Geneva

Zepelin H, Wolfe C S, Kleinplatz F 1981 Evaluation of a year-long reality orientation program. Journal of Gerontology 36: 70–77

Author index

333

Subject index